D0947907

Good Sons Don't Just Happen

Also by
Catherine Musco Garcia-Prats and Joseph A. Garcia-Prats, M.D.

Good Families Don't Just Happen:
What we learned from raising our 10 sons and
how it can work for you

Good Marriages Don't Just Happen:
Keeping Our Relationship Alive While Raising Our Ten Sons

By
Joseph A. Garcia-Prats, M.D. and
Sharon Simmons Hornfischer, R.N., B.S.N.

What To Do When Your Baby Is Premature:
A Parent's Handbook for Coping with High-Risk Pregnancy
and Caring for the Preterm Infant

Special thanks to Maria Illich, Ann Boehm,
Cathy Brown, Veronica Cheung, and my literary
agent, Jim Hornfischer.

Good Sons
Don't
Just Happen

Insights on Raising Boys
from the Mother of 10 Sons

Catherine Musco Garcia-Prats

BOSCO
Publishing

Published by
Bosco Publishing
5502 Lymbar Drive
Houston, TX 77096-5022

ISBN: 978-0-9763294-1-1

Library of Congress Control Number: 2008935750

Printed in the United States of America

For information on quantity discounts for bulk purchases contact
Bosco Publishing
Web site: www.boscopublishing.com
Telephone: 713-721-1582
Fax: 713-721-9147

With love to Joseph,
my husband and the father of our sons:
Tony, David, Chris, Joe Pat,
Matthew, Mark, Tommy, Danny,
Jamie, and Timmy

Table of Contents

Introduction

Richard Nevle
Principal
Strake Jesuit College Preparatory
Houston, Texas

My first encounter with Cathy Garcia-Prats and her sons came one autumn afternoon when her first son was a freshman at Strake Jesuit College Preparatory. She had come by to pick him up, arriving early on what was to be the first of hundreds of trips to our campus. The students were still in class, so Cathy was standing on the edge of one of our practice fields watching the gaggle of small boys she had brought with her on her afternoon route. I was an assistant principal then, yet I had heard of the G-P's. Strake Jesuit is an all boys school and we knew about Cathy and Joe and the eight sons they had at the time. I remember telling her that day, "So those are all your sons." Somewhat shocked, she looked at me and exclaimed, "Oh no! That one in the goal is a neighbor's child."

The neighbor's child was, of course, welcome and probably delighted to be included in a family that eventually grew to ten boys. There are now two Garcia-Prats at Strake Jesuit. The youngest brother is a freshman; he practically grew up at Strake Jesuit. Before he was born his parents, though busy with a large family and committed to demanding careers, always found time to be there for their sons' games, banquets, and parent-teacher nights.

At one of the very first athletic banquets the Garcia-Prats family attended, I remember wondering how one mom and one dad were going to keep order with the table full of active, busy boys ranging in age from infancy to the early teens. I fully expected Joe and Cathy to divide and conquer somehow or another by placing themselves among the boys so as to quell any outbreaks of "boys being boys." But they did not; rather, the parents sat next to one another as adults—as a couple—while their sons were arranged by age, the older ones attending to their younger brothers. They had a good time cheering for their brother, and they did so with polite, sincere enthusiasm when he was recognized by his coaches.

Often we had as many as three Garcia-Prats enrolled at Strake Jesuit at one time. On such an occasion, three of them had all come to classes late—they were making a television appearance with their mom shortly after the publication of her first book. As they checked in at the Dean of Students' office, the Garcia-Prats principle was once again in operation. When the Dean's assistant started with the oldest of the three, he immediately stepped back and told her, "No, youngest first." To this day, now that there are grandchildren in the Garcia-Prats family, that same focus on taking care of the ones who need it most is still evident among the brothers as they pass their niece and nephews from one brother (one uncle) to the next with practiced care.

Even though they share a name, each Garcia-Prats is a unique individual. Nonetheless, each has a remarkably strong sense of care and responsibility. Despite being characteristically considerate, they are fierce competitors. Even before they were students at Strake Jesuit, they came to soccer games and cheered for their brothers. At half-time they would even take over the field for a game of their own. Once when Tommy was a freshman, his team had managed to get an invitation to a Junior Varsity tournament. Somehow they battled their way to the finals. That last game was played in nearly freezing weather. The small freshmen battled their way to a tie and then took the game into overtime. Tommy seemed to be all over the field. Though far smaller than his competitors, he more than held his own. The older team, embarrassed by its inability to put these freshmen away, resorted to using their larger size, playing more and more aggressively as they bounced their freshman opponents around the field. Finally, the older and bigger team scored, the game ended, and Tommy joined his teammates in congratulating the winners before falling to his knees on the field. There wasn't a soul in that stadium who didn't know who was the hero of that game.

Cathy and Joe did not raise, nor are they now, raising their sons in a vacuum. Their sons live in the same dangerous world that every young man and boy in this country faces—and the family faces those threats and dangers head on, not only with discipline, but also with love, care, and support. What is ironic is that now that their sons are growing older, it becomes very clear that one of the great sources of support in raising all of those boys was, and is, all of those boys. Their older sons are now young adults and leaders in their professions and communities. For example, Cathy and her son, David, shared a place on the founding advisory board of the Cristo Rey Jesuit College Preparatory School of Houston. Watching her son do well is no surprise for Cathy, but it is clearly a joy. Also, now that Tony has become a physician, it is easy to see that same joy (and no little pride) in hearing Joe, an outstanding physician in his own right, tell the story of his being known as Dr. Garcia-Prats's dad among the new generation of physicians with whom he now works.

There is a sense of responsibility and duty visible in the Garcia-Prats brothers to a man. Of course they make mistakes, but they face them, reflect on what they can learn from them, and then move on. Character is not something you so much teach as you build. It begins with developing a sense of self-worth. When parents and siblings let you know by their presence, their actions, and their support that they care about you, then you know not only that you are loved but that you have the power to love and care for other people as well—and that you should. Boys thrive on challenges, and leading a life in which other people depend on you to do your job—to know your duty and do it—is just the kind of challenge that gives a boy not only a sense of worth but also a sense of accomplishment. The Garcia-Prats are an accomplishment.

It's a Boy! Now What?

Whatever the times, one thing will never change:
Fathers and mothers, if you have children, they must come first.
Your success as a family, our success as a society, depends not on what
happens at the White House, but inside your house.
— *Barbara Bush*

If you bungle raising your children,
I don't think whatever else you do well matters very much.
—*Jacqueline Kennedy Onassis*

It's a boy! November 17, 1975, 4:02 P.M., Tony's birth—the first time I heard those exhilarating, life-changing words. But, in the back of my mind, I remember also thinking, "Now what?" Fast-forward to November 6, 1993, 10:12 P.M., Timmy's birth, when I heard "It's a boy!" for the tenth time. Ten sons—our surprise was no surprise! After Timmy's birth, though, my reaction was not "Now what?" but rather a simple "Thank you, God!" Raising sons after having been raised in a family of five girls was daunting at first. What did I know about raising a son? By the time Timmy was born, however, the learning curve had diminished and I felt confident, prepared, and eager to raise another son.

I was aware at the moment of Timmy's birth, in a way that I never could have imagined eighteen years earlier, of the awesome gift and responsibility that God had bestowed on me as the mother of a son. Becoming a mother, whether for the first time or the tenth time, evokes many emotions, differing with each of us and with each child born. For me each son's birth brought immeasurable joy mixed with a significant dose of humility and fear. Humility—God was entrusting me, Cathy, with the love, care, and upbringing of one of His children? Fear—was I up to the task of raising a son or another son as our family grew? How would I manage?

I have learned a lot in my years of parenting sons. I am reminded daily that parenting is challenging, demanding, and constant. I have learned how my day-to-day choices affect my sons. Mistakes are made and lessons are learned, whether raising a son or a daughter or both, whether raising one child or more than one, or whether raising a child with your husband, as a single parent, or in a blended family. No parent is perfect. No son is perfect. I am reassured, though, by the words of St. Francis de Sales: "Do not lose courage in considering your own imperfections but instantly start remedying them—in every day begin the task anew."

So each day I start anew. I begin each day with a simple prayer, before I even get out of bed in the morning. "Thank you, Lord, for the gift of Joe and the boys in my life. Help and guide me through the day with all the things I know I have to do and all those things that may creep into my day that I'm not expecting. May Joe and the boys feel my love from the minute they wake up this morning until they fall asleep tonight."

I knew from the beginning and I appreciate even more now that I cannot and do not raise my sons alone. I believe God gifted me with my sons. And I also believe He did not give them to me and then just wish me good luck. He is there to guide me through the challenges and choices I make each day. A woman once commented that she was glad prayer worked for me, but what she needed was case studies to make her a better mother. Without my faith all the studies in the world could not make me a better mom. Prayer is not just sitting around saying words for hours at a time and hoping whatever you "pray" for happens. That's a fairy tale approach. My concept entails an active role on my part: integrating my faith into my day-to-day choices—what I do or what I do not do for my sons, and making a conscious decision to do what I do with **LOVE**.

Also by my side is my husband, Joseph. We have been married for thirty-five wonderful years. Joe is a Professor of Pediatrics and Ethics at Baylor College of Medicine, and a practicing neonatologist, a pediatrician who specializes in the care of the critically ill newborn. We started our family while Joe was a fellow. His hours were horrendous in those early years. Although I sighed with relief when he walked in the door, I grew to appreciate even more the importance of the emotional support he provided me as we raised our sons.

When we started our family thirty-two years ago, I did not have all the answers, and I assure you that I still don't. But my experience has taught me that certain concepts are integral in raising strong, successful, and spirited sons. Many of the concepts apply to raising daughters as well. But boys are different from girls and not just physically. Acknowledging, appreciating, and understanding that boys are boys is essential in raising a son. Too often the "boys are boys" concept takes on a negative connotation. Society has stereotyped boys—and not usually in a positive light. Even many commercials on television depict boys and men as weak, ignorant, and less educated.

Boys are boys and they grow up to be the men we marry. As the mother of ten sons, I want those men to be strong—physically, emotionally, intellectually, and spiritually. I want them to be men who are loving, caring, compassionate, forgiving, responsible, respectful, well-educated, and faith-filled. I want them to appreciate that their self-worth and success will be measured in non-monetary terms, contrary to how society defines success. Rather, I want them to appreciate that their success will be measured by who they are, what they are doing with the gifts God has given them, and how they live their lives. That is what I looked for in my choice of a husband and what I found in my husband Joseph: a strong man who models love, compassion, respect, responsibility, and commitment; a strong man who is comfortable practicing and living his faith; a well-educated, strong man who chooses to be actively involved in the upbringing of his sons.

After each birth, the question "Now what?" challenged Joe and me to discern what we wanted for our sons, to consider what kind of parents we were going to be, to foster a home that would provide love and security for them, and to begin to make the choices that would enable our sons to be what I knew they could be in order to reach their full potential in the eyes of God. Easy? No. Possible? Yes! But it requires teamwork, faith, and love at all times which is why, "GOOD SONS DON'T JUST HAPPEN."

I never dreamed that one day I would be sharing my experiences as a mother in a public forum. I taught first grade before starting my family and then chose to stay home to raise them. After our tenth son, Timmy, was born, the daughter of one of the boys' teachers, a freelance writer, asked if we would consider interviewing for a story on family to appear in *The Houston Post*. The reporter went beyond the novelty of a family with ten sons. She focused on the fact that, after interviewing teachers and others who knew us, what impressed them most about our family was not that the boys excelled in academics and sports, but that they were courteous, responsible, and compassionate. The article mentioned how our family worked together and somehow kept an air of calm in the midst of chaos. The story related how we dealt with day-to-day activities, stayed organized, and through it all enjoyed our sons immensely. The article highlighted parenting tips we had provided the reporter. She told readers, "This is a positive story about good kids and a good family."

The article appeared in 1994. An article entitled "My Ten Sons" followed in *The Ladies' Home Journal*. I received requests to speak to various groups. I did not relish getting up in front of a group of people and speaking. But, after much cajoling by one mother, I offered to attend her moms' group and answer questions. Today I speak internationally on parenting, family, marriage, appreciating the women we are, and balancing our lives. People asked us to write a book. I laughed and jokingly told them that I would entitle it *In My Spare Time*. Eventually, Joe and I did write two books, *Good Families Don't Just Happen and Good Marriages Don't Just Happen*. Television appearances, locally and nationally, such as *The Oprah Winfrey Show, The Gayle King Show, American Journal* and *Positively Texas*, followed and more newspaper and magazine articles. People, especially moms, wanted to know how I did it.

At the time of *The Houston Post* article, the boys ranged in age from nineteen years old to one year old. Today the boys range in age from thirty-two years old to fourteen years old. The day-to-day demands are different, of course. I was changing diapers back then—lots of diapers. In fact, I changed diapers for 20 1/2 consecutive years. Three of the boys were in diapers simultaneously. Food consumption and grocery bills have normalized. When the boys were all home, they drank 5 to 6 gallons of milk a day. Dairy farmers loved us. At today's price for a gallon of milk, milk costs alone would have tallied close to $125 a week. The first five sons were born in six years, and those same five sons were all teenagers at the same time. Talk about challenging! Education expenses proved daunting when the boys reached the high school and college years. Yet, six of the boys have already graduated from college, one with a medical degree and three with masters. Educating the boys was a top priority and still is. The times are different: Danny, Jamie, and Timmy do not know a world without computers and cell phones. I worried about the influence of television time with the older boys. Today, though, the programming on television and the availability of violent and immoral video games and websites create additional challenges beyond just the time component.

As a mother of sons, I have an awesome responsibility to arm my sons with the emotional, physical, intellectual, and spiritual tools they need to be successful in a challenging and demanding society. My sons need me to embrace that responsibility as I guide them from infancy to young adulthood.

In my 32 years of parenting, I have learned that when raising a son is done well and with love, there is no greater reward for myself or for society. Families and society need strong, successful, spirited sons who become strong, successful, spirited men. As mothers, we have the ability to make the difference.

Raising sons is an adventure. Enjoy the adventure!

Peace,
Cathy

Chapter 1

The Adventure Begins
—And Then There Were Ten!

Behold, sons are a gift from the Lord.
Happy the man whose quiver is filled with them.
—Psalm 127: 3,5

There are different gifts but the same Spirit;
there are different ministries but the same Lord;
there are different works but the same God who accomplishes
all of them in everyone. To each person the
manifestation of the Spirit is given for the common good.
—1 Corinthians 12: 4-7

My husband, Joseph, and I did not plan on breaking any records or skewing statistics by having ten sons. Early in our marriage we decided we wanted a large family: Joe wanted five children and I wanted five children. Five and five is ten! Even with wanting a large family, never in a million years could I have dreamed that we would be the proud parents of ten sons. I did assume we would have a daughter along the way, especially since I have four sisters. We were not trying, though, to have a girl—the question I am most frequently asked. And, yes, we are Catholic—the second most frequently asked question. But our Catholic faith does not dictate that we have a specific number of children. Our faith does teach us to be open to children as well as to be responsible parents who meet the physical, emotional, intellectual, and spiritual needs of our children. A responsible parent being defined not by the number of children one has but, rather, by how one raises the children—one, two, or ten. And, the third most frequently asked question—Are you crazy? Answer to be determined!

The reactions and responses when people learn that I am the mother of ten boys range from amusing to tacky and rude. I remember the afternoon a friend and I drove to watch my third son, Chris, who played soccer for Trinity University in San Antonio, compete in a game against Southwestern University. While sitting in the stands, a mother a few rows behind us asked the mother sitting next to her who the player was who had just made the header. The second mom answered, "Chris Garcia-Prats." She then added, "I understand that he is one of ten." "No one has ten children any more," the first mom sarcastically responded. "Where did you hear that?" The second mom continued, "And I understand that they are **all** boys, **and** the mom has written a parenting book." The first mom laughs, "A woman has **ten** children, **all** boys **and** she has time to write a book? That is too funny!" Then there was the evening when the principal at the boys' high school, Richard Nevle, introduced me to a group of people. One woman, when she heard "the mother of ten boys," looked at me and pityingly said, "You poor thing!" Richard reached over, put his arm around me, looked this woman straight in the eye and stated, "No, ma'am! This is the richest woman I know."

While most people are amazed that I am the mother of ten sons, what amazes me the most is that each of our sons is an original—same mom, same dad, and yet not one carbon copy. In fact, they have been originals from the moment of conception. Each pregnancy, labor, and delivery was unique. **Tony**, our first son, was probably closest to the textbook labor and delivery, although with a touch of uncertainly when the nurse at the hospital was convinced that I was carrying twins. Not until I delivered *one* Tony (8 pounds, 1 ounce) was the nurse convinced there weren't twins. It would have been a joy, though, to have two Tonys. **David** (8 pounds, 2 ounces) arrived without a hitch, until the placenta wouldn't expel. So, after an anesthesia-free delivery, I was given Demerol to deliver the placenta. David is still full of the unpredictable and is wonderfully easygoing. **Christopher** was our first son delivered in a birthing room, to the sounds of Willie Nelson's *Stardust* album. I remember the words from the song "All of Me." And, like the song, I was beginning to want them to take all of me as I delivered a healthy 9 pound, 12 ounce boy. Twenty-eight years later at his wedding, Christopher and I danced to another Willie Nelson classic. **Joe Pat** (9 pounds, 10 ounces) decided to delay meeting his brothers by two weeks. I was induced, only to wait another eleven hours to hold Joe Pat. He was definitely worth the wait! **Matthew**, weighing a whopping 10 pounds, 9 ounces, was the talk of the hospital: this little petite mom had this HUGE baby. People assumed I was married to a linebacker, but anyone who knows Joe realizes I outweigh him when I'm pregnant. One friend commenting on Matthew's delivery said, "I prayed a decade of the rosary for a safe delivery. If I had known you were going to have a ten pounder, I would've prayed the whole rosary." My dad teased, "I know how you spelled relief: M-A-T-T-H-E-W." **Mark** (8 pounds, 6 ounces) emerged "sunny-side" up (facing up instead of down), looking like his brothers had already gotten to him—bruised and scratched from his difficulty delivery. My little raccoon healed quickly and is still doing things his way with a sunny disposition. On the night of **Tommy's** delivery, Joe and the three older boys had gone to a Houston Astros game. Joe called home (no cell phones back then) at the end of each inning to check on me, since I had felt contractions on and off all day. When he called after the sixth inning, I told him I had already called the obstetrician, Dr. Thomas Strama (a wonderfully caring man who delivered nine of the boys and still holds a special place in my heart). My mom, who was in town from Virginia, was relieved when Joe arrived home. She had no desire to deliver the baby. Tommy's delivery was quick and easy; he weighed 7 pounds, 14 ounces—little by our standards. Tommy was easy then and is still gentle and good-natured. **Danny's** delivery took an interesting turn when labor stalled at 9 centimeters. His brothers expected to hear the verdict, boy or girl, before they left for school. No such luck. Even the pediatrician, Dr. John Curtis, who was in the hospital making morning rounds, kept poking his head into our room joking, "Isn't that baby here yet?" Danny finally arrived, 9 pounds, 6 ounces, full of creative energy and life. On the day of **Jamie's** delivery, I had a one o'clock appointment with Dr. Strama. I had been emotional most of the morning, but attributed it to leaving Danny at his first day of preschool. When Dr. Strama examined me, he announced I was at 5 centimeters, in active labor with my bag of water ready to burst. He wanted to admit me to the hospital on the spot, but in typical fashion, I wanted to go home and get organized. I rationalized that I needed to get the car home so my mom, who was in town from Virginia again, could pick up the boys from school. I went home and made it back in plenty of time for Jamie's delivery at 8 pounds, 8 ounces—a joy to behold then and now. With **Timmy's** delivery (9 pounds, 8 ounces), I was at 8 centimeters, thank goodness, when I arrived at the hospital. Dr. Strama, who arrived from a gala wearing a tux, delivered Timmy shortly after. Talk about a first class delivery! There was so much electricity in the air that night as we waited to see whether we would have a "perfect 10"—ten boys, that is. (Although definitely curious, I never wanted to know the sex of the baby beforehand, even when I had an ultrasound. Not knowing beforehand gave me added incentive as I labored to learn the fruit of my labor. I used to tease, though, that "Our surprise was no surprise.") The laughter, shrieks, and amazement that followed Timmy's delivery will always be remembered, especially the phone call home to tell his nine brothers.

The uniqueness didn't stop there. Each of the boys had his own style of nursing, sleeping, and playing. Tony was a voracious eater, while David couldn't be bothered with food his first year of life, although he's made up for it since. Joe Pat needed absolute silence to sleep; Chris fell asleep easily and slept through anything. Some of the boys liked to be carried in a Snugli, while others preferred the swing or their crib. Two of the boys sucked their thumbs, two liked the pacifier, and the others preferred neither.

The uniqueness continues to this day. While all the boys attended St. Francis de Sales Catholic School and 8 of the boys have graduated to date from Strake Jesuit College Preparatory, the similarity stops there. After graduating from Strake Jesuit College Preparatory, the boys spread their wings. They have attended eight different undergraduate universities and majored in different disciplines. From business to medicine, from coaching to teaching, from international affairs to engineering, each of the boys has found his niche and is using his God-given gifts.

Tony, 32 years old, attended St. Louis University where he majored in chemistry and biology. During his years at St. Louis University, he swam on the university swim team, competing in the long distance events. He continued his education at Baylor College of Medicine in Houston. How wonderful to have him closer to home. And how I loved the afternoon phone call, "Hey, Mom, what's for dinner?" If he liked what was on the menu, he would join us; if not, he made other plans. After medical school, Tony completed a pediatric residency, also at Baylor College of Medicine, receiving the 2004-2005 Drs. Ralph and Judith Feigin Outstanding Pediatric Resident of the Year honors. He was also the recipient of the 2004 McNamara Award presented by the Pele Chandler Endowment for contributions to child health and safety. Tony now serves in the Pediatric AIDS Corps, a Baylor International Pediatric AIDS Initiative. He and his wife, Heather, a biostatistician, work at the Baylor Children's Clinical Center of Excellence in Maseru, Lesotho, Africa.

Tony was a bright, quiet, sensitive young man growing up. He found success in the classroom and in the pool. Not one to draw attention to himself, he led through his example of hard work and determination. As his mother, I saw him grow more and more confident in speaking out on issues that captured his heart. Speaking in front of a group of people or even on the phone was not his idea of fun. To have known Tony in the early years, you would never imagine him interviewing for NPR, ABC Nightly News, or newspaper and magazine stories. But he found his voice in fighting for the children of the world.

I attended a Children's Defense Fund luncheon a couple years ago. As I was leaving the luncheon, a member of the organization stopped me to show me some materials. She noticed my nametag and commented that there were probably not too many people with my last name. ("More than you'd think," quipped Shirley, who had invited me to the luncheon.) She had worked on an education project with a Tony Garcia-Prats and wondered if I knew him. When I shared that I was his mother, she went on to relate how helpful he had been working with children in the schools. She was amazed at how natural he was with them, bending down to talk to them at their level and making them feel comfortable. I wasn't surprised because I knew how he interacted with his brothers. When I asked her if she realized Tony had nine younger brothers, she stared in disbelief. His big brother love and experience had shone through.

David, 31 years old and only 360 days younger than Tony (Irish twins, people used to tease), attended Creighton University after high school. David possesses a real love of life. I could always count on David to add humor and light-heartedness to any situation. He's no different now. I once teased him that I should have named him Peter. He thought I meant after St. Peter. I quickly corrected him—Peter Pan!

David majored in English at Creighton University, a great fit with his love for the written language. During those years he wrote poetry, another love of his. Following graduation from Creighton University, unsure about what to do with his English degree and wanting to reconnect with Jamie and Timmy who were only one and three years old when he left for college, he returned to Houston where he taught 3 year olds at Epiphany Day School and worked in the after-school program at St. Francis de Sales Catholic School. The next year he continued at St. Francis de Sales School in the afternoons but taught in the program for 4 year olds at St. Laurence Catholic School. David realized teaching was his calling. Fortunately he learned of a unique education master's program at the University of Notre Dame, ACE (Alliance for Catholic Education). ACE is a two-year service program comprised of three components: teaching, community, and spirituality. During the two years of the program, David attended classes during the summers at the University of Notre Dame, taught second grade during the school year at St. Anthony Catholic School in Harlingen, Texas, lived with other ACE teachers, and shared in retreats and spiritually oriented activities organized through the university. On completion of his masters degree, David moved to Los Angeles and taught middle school English and literature at St. Malachy Catholic School and served as assistant principal. Since then David, and his wife, Rita, also a teacher, are living and teaching in Houston. David is the assistant principal at Our

Lady of Guadalupe Catholic School and teaches middle school English and literature, gifting his students with his love of literature and his love of life. Rita teaches fourth grade at St. Francis de Sales Catholic School where all the boys have attended. They have two children: Gabriela, our first granddaughter, and Matías.

David is reconnecting again with his younger brothers in new and exciting ways now that they are older. As for Jamie and Timmy, who didn't have the same experience of helping with little brothers that David had being the second oldest in the family, they are actively involved in the lives of Gabriela and Matías on an almost daily basis, a win-win situation from every point of view.

Christopher, 29 years old, chose to attend Trinity University in San Antonio after graduating from Strake Jesuit, where he knew he would obtain an excellent education but also where he would be able to continue playing competitive soccer, a great love of his. Chris started off his college years majoring in business but quickly recognized that business was not a good fit. He decided instead, motivated by his experiences working with children and his brothers, to pursue a degree in education, completing Trinity's five-year masters degree program in education. During the first four years, Chris played soccer for Trinity University, one of the most successful college soccer programs in the country, and in his fifth year while working on his masters degree, he accepted the role of assistant coach at Trinity University.

The year following graduate school, Chris taught fourth grade in the San Antonio schools. But again a switch in careers was on the horizon. I remember the morning he called with that tone in his voice that perks up a mother's ears. He shared with me that he enjoyed teaching but he realized his real love was coaching soccer and that that's what he wanted to do. I couldn't help but encourage him because I had witnessed his coaching skills when he coached the middle school team at St. Francis de Sales School during his high school years as well as his leadership skills while playing on the field. I knew he would touch lives whether in a classroom or on a field. And that's what he did.

While continuing his role as assistant coach at Trinity University, Chris also took on the head soccer coaching responsibilities at Central Catholic High School, an all boys high school in San Antonio. He faced a challenge at Central Catholic because the team had won only one game the year before. Chris trained and encouraged the team one game at a time. They won their first game, and their second, and then their third, beating a long time rival. An opposing coach confronted Chris with the question, "Are you trying to turn the team around in one year?" Chris just focused on one game at a time. Chris's focus and inspiration led the team from a one-win season to a one-loss season and a place in the state finals where they lost 1-0. Chris was named San Antonio High School Soccer Coach of the Year—another special phone call I received one morning. And Chris's success with the team was not just evident on the soccer field. Parents and faculty alike noticed a change in the boys' attitude and approach at home and in the classroom.

After playing and coaching at Trinity University for ten years, Chris accepted the position as head coach of men's soccer at Luther College in Decorah, Iowa. I will enjoy watching the Luther program develop under Chris's leadership. His love of the game, his ability to motivate and bring out the best in each player, and his big heart will serve him well. I saw these skills develop during his childhood. He was organized and focused and loved running the show even at a young age. So Chris and his wife, Stephanie, a social worker, make their home in Iowa.

Joe Pat, 27 years old, short for Joseph Patrick, or **Patty** as Timmy lovingly nicknamed him, headed to Regis University in Denver, Colorado, upon graduation from Strake Jesuit. Joe Pat leaned from the beginning towards a major in International Business and Spanish. Joe Pat is our son who was always uniquely gifted socially. He's the kind of person you meet and feel like you have known all your life. It seemed no matter where we went someone knew Joe Pat, even in his younger years. Being a former first grade teacher, I used to wonder at times, "Is this a good thing or a not so good thing?" But people, young and old, were drawn to and loved Joe Pat and his warm, down-to-earth personality. During his years at Strake Jesuit, Joe Pat was often asked to provide tours to prospective students and their parents. He enjoyed sharing his experiences while bringing the campus alive. (Being legitimately out of class was a plus as well.) He sold Strake Jesuit to many an eighth grader and his family.

Working with the public is still his strength. Upon graduation from Regis University, Joe Pat moved to Chicago to work in the cell phone industry. The reason for moving to Chicago was due to the fact that his wife, Megan, was from Chicago. (Joe Pat met Megan, a criminal justice major, during his first week at Regis University.) His strong social skills continue to be his strength as he successfully develops an excellent rapport with his clients and colleagues, a reflection of his ability to work and communicate with people.

Joe Pat and Megan have two sons, Logan and Lucas, our first two grandchildren. (My daughters-in-law began to wonder if we would ever see a Garcia-Prats girl.) I had so much fun watching Joe Pat and Megan parent. The first time I visited after Logan's birth, I commented to Joe Pat on his diapering expertise. His response: "I've changed a few of these in my life!" As the fourth in line, he spoke the truth. He and Megan enjoy the boys immensely and are quickly adapting to the different personalities of Logan and Lucas.

Matthew, 26 years old, chose to head west to the University of San Diego to attend college. I was always curious to see where God would lead Matthew. He is a young man with a strong sense of justice and a determination to make a difference, which led to some interesting discussions over dinner. He wants things to be right whether at home, school, the community, or the world. He ended up majoring in Sociology. His brother David encouraged him, on completion of his bachelors degree, to participate in a program at Loyola Marymount University called PLACE, Partners in Los Angeles Catholic Education. Similar in structure to the ACE program at the University of Notre Dame, Matthew taught middle school math and social studies at St. Raymond Catholic School for two years while taking graduate level education courses. He received a Master of Education and decided to remain at St. Raymond to teach while his fiancée, Mary, completed her masters degree through the same program. Fortunately, for us and Houston, Matty and his wife Mary are returning to Houston. Matty will teach middle school math and coach after school sports at Our Lady of Guadalupe Catholic School; Mary will teach first grade at St. Laurence Catholic School.

Mark, 23 years old, our free-spirited son, or the "smoothest" as his brothers named him, wanted to experience college in the Northwest. He chose Seattle University to continue his education. Mark majored in English, not a surprise since he loved books from an early age and has a strong command of the written word. (Mary Ellen, his godmother and a librarian, is proud.) In addition, he enjoys writing.

Mark, although quiet natured and unassuming, brought and continues to bring much humor and laughter to our home. When I went through photos for Joe to compile Joe Pat's rehearsal dinner slideshow, I was amazed at all the photos of Mark in get-up after get-up and comical expression after comical expression—true to his free spirit.

His free spirit, along with the need for a summer job, led him to work on a salmon fishing boat in the Alaskan waters one summer. Talk about an adventure and hard work—and a worried mom! The family reaped the rewards of his labor—Mark returned home with 75 pounds of fresh salmon.

Mark rejects, wisely I might add, the excesses in our society and the drive for "the more, the bigger, and the better." He lives simply and contently. As of this writing, he works for the National Park Service in Big Bend National Park in Texas. He finds time to enjoy the outdoors and, I understand from his brothers, that he is also finding time to write. With his love of literature and the written word, I am not surprised. Now whether I will understand what he writes, only time will tell.

Tommy, 21 years old, endearingly nicknamed Chop by his brothers, picked the opposite side of the country to attend school from Mark. Tommy attends Providence College in Rhode Island where he majors in Global Affairs with an emphasis on Latin America. Providence is where I am originally from so he is reconnecting with many of my aunts, uncles, and cousins and allowing me to do so too. His junior year he studied abroad: first semester he studied in Managua, Nicaragua, and second semester in Lima, Peru, living with a family in both countries. Taking advantage of this opportunity and the money he earned from summer jobs during high school and college, Tommy traveled throughout Central America and South America experiencing the many cultures and perfecting his Spanish. I'll be curious to see where these experiences and adventures ultimately lead him.

Tommy is a fun-loving, witty, confident young man. He captures your heart with his smile and sense of serenity. I see him as the peacemaker, always ready to help out, give, share, and work for what is right. His wittiness, inherited from his dad, brightens many a day. I remember the morning I needed two tens for a twenty dollar bill. I asked Joe if he had any. He responded that he only had one. I told him that I would take the ten for the twenty. Tommy didn't miss a beat: "Mom, I'll give you a ten for a twenty!" Or when Matty emailed to all the family a photo of my dad and Mary taken at the 82nd birthday party of my dad and his twin brother. Mary looked wonderful in the photo but my dad's eyes were closed so that he appeared asleep. Matty jokingly added the following comment to the photo: "I tried to take a nice picture with Mary and Papa. Unfortunately, he was unable to stay awake while I snapped the picture." The jokes and comments went back and forth for days. Finally, my dad, who was enjoying this parley as much as the boys, sent out an email that implied that if Tommy were around he would defend his Papa. Then from Nicaragua a response from Tommy, seemingly in defense of my dad: "Come on guys, stop making fun of Papa." Only to add, "After all, that's the best picture we've had of him in ages."

Danny, 19 years old, felt strongly during his high school years that he wanted to pursue a degree in engineering. He enjoyed and excelled in math, and he appreciated his gift of imagination and creativity. Santa Clara University lured Danny to their program when he observed during the campus visit students working in labs on various projects. I could picture Danny in the lab tinkering and creating. It brought back years of memories of Danny building for hours with our bins of Legos. I used to tease Danny that he would one day design the spacecraft that would take a man to Mars. He is one step closer as he pursues an engineering degree at Santa Clara University. Our Lego investment (and the years at St. Francis de Sales School and Strake Jesuit College Prep) was paying off.

Danny's creativity expressed itself at an early age. He drew with great perception and imagination. I remember his *Free Willy* picture drawn at 3 years of age. We went to the movie and then later that day I found him drawing a picture of the last scene where Willy sailed over the reef to his freedom. It was very detailed and true to life. When I questioned him about what he was using to draw the picture, since I didn't see a picture of the scene in front of him, he matter-of-factly responded, "Mommy, it's in my head." I might have the picture in my head but I would never be able to transfer the image to paper. Danny's mind also works in detail: the book report cover in third grade where he drew a produce department of the grocery store with the fruits and vegetables precisely displayed in their individual bins, or the minute-by-minute narrative of his day while I prepared dinner. I often tease, "If you don't have time to listen to his answer, don't ask Danny the question." His creativity and imagination have proven gifts to our entire family as we turn to him for his assistance on almost any project needing his skills. I am especially grateful for his patience in teaching me many of the computer skills I need to fulfill various responsibilities. His brothers, too, are convinced that one day he will design something spectacular.

Jamie, 16 years old, is a junior at Strake Jesuit College Preparatory. He is a young man with a sensitive heart—"a friend to all" as Sandra Mendez described him when she presented the St. Francis de Sales Principal Award to him at his eighth grade graduation. Quiet, bright, fun-loving, athletically gifted yet unassuming, Jamie adds a special touch to our family. He, like Tommy, has a sense of peace about him, in both his demeanor and his approach to people. A teacher once commented that Jamie lifted her spirits each day when he entered the classroom with his smile and good nature. He loves soccer, the Garcia-Prats sport of choice, and is gifted with both a natural left foot and eight older brothers who taught him how to successfully use that left foot. I feared early on that he wouldn't want to play any sport because when he was a baby he was shuffled from one of his brother's sport's events to another: swimming, water polo, basketball, and soccer—whistles and constant noise and commotion. And I didn't think he would ever learn to bounce or throw a ball since his brothers were constantly chanting, "No hands!" as soccer took precedence over other sports. My fears were unwarranted—he loves sports, especially soccer.

Where will Jamie attend college? I assume not one of the aforementioned universities attended by his brothers. I often wonder if the boys secretly formulated an unwritten rule that each of them attends a different university—eight universities to date plus three additional institutions for graduate school. Not that I'm complaining. Joe and I, due to their college choices, have had the chance to visit different parts of our country and expand our horizons as well. Jamie, no doubt, will have opportunities that will evolve over the next few years. His abilities and personality will strengthen his options.

Timmy, 14 years old and nicknamed Bor, is a freshman at Strake Jesuit College Preparatory. Not only is he, as the youngest of ten sons, at a disadvantage at home with parents who have "been there, done that, don't try it," he attends a high school where most of the faculty knew him before he was born. Strake Jesuit is like a second home. Both he and Jamie were born during the years Tony and David were in attendance at the school. When Timmy graduated from St. Francis de Sales Catholic School in May 2008, he completed a memorable chapter in our family's life story—all ten of the boys attended and graduated from the school. Timmy's graduation also means, on a different front, that I survived the challenging middle school years. And now, Timmy's start at Strake Jesuit is in some ways the beginning of the end of another chapter in our lives. I find with Timmy there are many "lasts" and final transitions—many bittersweet. I'm not sure who had the harder time, for example, when he went to first grade all day. And now he's embarking on high school.

Timmy is a young man full of life and love. While he adds sunshine to my days, his position in the family fosters unique relationships with his brothers. They, after all, had a hand in his upbringing, along with that of Jamie. Timmy is blessed with a quick mind, a joyful spirit, and an easygoing personality. If there's ever going to be a politician in the family, Timmy may be the one. He is a strong soccer player, thanks to all the years of playing with his brothers, who gave him little slack. He's already talking about colleges in the Chicago area, for no other reason than that Joe Pat lives north of Chicago.

Ten unique individuals from the beginning to the present. Their individuality provided me no room for boredom or complacency. As their mother, I faced the daunting challenge of determining how to meet each son's needs, recognizing that one size did not fit all. Each son provided new challenges and experiences that broadened my understanding of raising sons and reminded me often that parenting requires continuing education learned in the school of life. Although I have learned a lot over these last thirty-two years, dare I ever think that I have mastered the art of parenting?

Chapter 2

Creating a Home of Love

Keep alert, stand firm in your faith, be courageous, be strong.
Let all that you do be done in love.
— 1 Corinthians 16:13-14

Unless the Lord build the house,
They labor in vain who build it.
—Psalm 127:1

One of my most important responsibilities as a mother is to create a loving home. A home filled with love, laughter, respect, and faith. A home where each individual feels loved and secure. A home where each family member is encouraged, appreciated, and respected. A home where physical, emotional, intellectual, and spiritual needs are met.

A good home, though, doesn't just happen because I want it. Every day entails making a conscious choice to create that home of love, understanding that the atmosphere and environment that my sons experience and live at home every day strongly influences their evolution from good sons to good men. That atmosphere and environment is largely determined by the interactions of the people in the home. If a child witnesses healthy relationships at home, he is much more likely to develop a healthy self-image and healthy relationships himself. Leo Buscaglia once said, "Live what you want your children to be and watch them grow."

So before I can address the nitty-gritty details of raising a son, I find it imperative to address the importance of creating a day-to-day home of love. Although a home of love depends on the entire family, creating that home of love begins with me—with my attitude, with my approach to each day, with my self-image, and with my relationships with my husband, Joe, and the boys.

I learned over the years that my attitude and approach—whether cheerful, calm, and positive or surly, frazzled, and negative—affected everyone else in the family. It may seem unfair that I have that much influence on the flow of the day, but to me it is a reality and a challenge I still face each and every day. Starting my day off with the simple prayer of gratitude for Joe and the boys in my life and then asking God for his grace to see me through the day is my first step in setting my attitude and approach for the day.

In addition, in order to love, respect, accept and meet the needs of the people in my life, I need to love, respect and accept myself. I have to strive to meet my own physical, emotional, intellectual, and spiritual needs—not an easy task when you are a wife and mother of ten. In a world that too often emphasizes the "me," meeting my needs and having self-love and respect can be misconstrued as being self-centered and selfish. But there is a difference between self-love and selfish love. Self-love focuses on my belief that I am a child of God, created in His image and with the same dignity that He created Joe and the boys. And, if I am to follow Christ's command to "love your neighbor as yourself," I must love myself in order to love my neighbor—my "neighbor" first and foremost being Joe and the boys. They go hand in hand.

I must know and love myself, then, before I can attempt to develop healthy relationships with others. I must appreciate and understand self-respect and self-acceptance—my strengths and challenges, and those things about myself that I can change and those things that I can't. I must determine what my priorities are and where my commitments lie. And I must decide how and to what degree I will integrate my faith into my daily activities and choices.

Over the last thirty-five years of marriage and thirty-two years of parenting, **the principles of love, respect, commitment, and faith evolved into my mantra**. All four are intertwined and inseparable. They guide my choices, they direct my values, and they shape my goals. All four principles will weave through the pages of the book as I share my experiences raising sons. They are the foundation of how I raise my sons in a home of love.

The Principle of Love

Love: A Decision and a Promise

There are many facets to love and ways to love. The word "love" is used freely and in many contexts. But what is love? What does it mean to love another? To quote Eric Fromm: "To love somebody is not just a strong feeling—it is a decision, it is a judgment, it is a promise." If I believe that statement, then loving Joe and the boys is a decision and a promise that I need to make every day. It is not just a feeling—feelings come and go. Along the same lines, St. Thomas Aquinas tells us: "To love is to will the good of another." I must decide to make my spouse and children a priority in my life and to make choices that enable and encourage them to become the best that they can be. In the process, I have the opportunity to grow and become a better individual as well.

Love, thus, becomes a reflection of the choices I make and whether these choices are in the best interest of my sons as a whole. Mother Teresa told us: "It is simple but not easy." How right she was! The choices I made over the years and continue to make have not always been easy. I, too, live in a society that focuses on and sometimes pulls me away from the values and goals that I know are in the best interest of my family. At times, my self-interest and pride cloud and muddle my vision and goals. It's not always easy either to make decisions for the boys that I know are countercultural, such as restricting which television shows or movies they can watch when most other kids face little or no restrictions. I remember the night that Danny was invited to go to a movie for a friend's birthday. Unfortunately, the movie was rated PG-13 and Danny was eleven years old. The rule in our home is that unless you are thirteen years old, you do not see a PG-13 movie. And just because you are thirteen years old does not mean you can view any PG-13 movie. Danny was most unhappy with my "no" but I explained to him that God holds me accountable for what I do or don't do for him. The movie was inappropriate for an eleven year old, and I would accept his wrath rather than God's later down the line for giving into him and allowing him to see what I knew was inappropriate. Although the "no" was simple in theory, it was not easy in practice.

So each and every morning I am faced, like each of us, with the decision to love or not to love. When I wake up, I can throw up my hands and lament about all the responsibilities I have to fulfill that day: the unending wash, the bills to be paid, the meals to prepare, the groceries to buy, the house to clean, the homework to complete, the children to transport to school, doctor and orthodontist appointments, soccer or swim practices, school and church functions, and on and on. Or I can wake up each morning and thank God for the gift of Joe and the boys in my life and ask Him for guidance in taking care of them and the strength and patience to meet the demands and challenges of the day—both the planned activities and the unexpected surprises.

My accepting and cheerful attitude and approach to the day right from the start is an expression of my love for Joe and the boys. (Definitely a challenge when morning sickness or fatigue rears its head—a frequent occurrence for my first eighteen years as a mother.) My disposition shows Joe that I am glad to be his wife and shows the boys that I am glad to be their mother in spite of the demands, challenges, and constancy. I want my family to feel that they are an integral, meaningful part of my life—not a burden and another obligation to fulfill.

Unfortunately, we live in a society that too often implies that children are a burden in our lives instead of gifts from God. We are bombarded with news about the added expenses, the added responsibilities, the effect on a career, and a lack of time for personal pursuits. There is no denying that all that's true. But what is too often omitted are the rewards reaped from the investment of our time and money.

When I taught first grade, many of the children came to school full of life, eager to face the adventures of the day, while other children arrived with less zest and enthusiasm. As I observed the children and their families, I noticed a difference in the attitude and approach of the parents. The parents who displayed a true enjoyment of their children and appreciated the opportunities to be involved in their lives had children who were happy and excited about their day. On the other hand, the children who were less enthusiastic had parents who complained about every little thing they had to do for their children. Their parental responsibilities were obligations to fulfill, not acts of love to unconditionally provide. I noticed how similar responsibilities and challenges evoked different responses from different parents.

If I want my sons to feel loved and special, then I need to accept my parental responsibilities—the cooking, cleaning, laundry, homework, expenses, jostling of schedules—as part and parcel of raising children and demonstrate that life with children is worthwhile. If my sons constantly hear me complaining about how much time, money, and energy they require, they assume that they are an inconvenience and burden in my life—not gifts. I am convinced that children "know" the difference.

Through my faith, I garnered an understanding of the importance of striving for a positive, loving attitude. The words of St. Paul to the Corinthians reflect the significance of love being the essential ingredient in our everyday actions. "If I speak with human tongues and angelic as well, but do not have love, I am a noisy gong, a clanging cymbal. If I have the gift of prophecy and, with full knowledge comprehend all mysteries, if I have faith great enough to move mountains, but have not love, I am nothing. If I give everything I have to feed the poor and hand over my body to be burned, but have not love, I gain nothing" (1 Corinthians 13:1-3).

As a wife and mother I can easily relate to St. Paul's words. If I boast about the importance of my faith but do not lovingly integrate it into my actions, I am a noisy gong and a clanging cymbal. If I understand the importance of fulfilling responsibilities and sharing the gift of my time, talent, and treasures with my family and others but do not act with love, my actions mean nothing. If I prepare wonderful meals for my family every day, if I wash twenty-five loads of laundry a week and keep a spotless, picture-perfect home but do not do them with love in my heart, I gain nothing in the eyes of God. **Love must be the driving force behind my words and actions.** Otherwise, my words and actions are wasted and mean nothing. I might appear impressive to those around me, but if the things I do and the words I say are without love, I am probably an unhappy, unfulfilled individual. I believe the people closest to us feel and know when love is a part of the equation. When love is absent, those same people feel as if they are an inconvenience and a burden. The love behind the actions is what brings joy and peace to the lover and the loved. **Mother Teresa reminds us: "It's not how much we do, it's how much love we put into the doing."**

Although I understand the importance of living St. Paul's words, I struggle like most moms at making the choice to give and do out of love. An obligation may be fulfilled but due to a sense of duty rather than love. A concrete, simple example is when I present someone with a gift. When I give the gift from my heart, I feel much more gratified than when I give the gift because I feel obligated to do so. Another example is from my early parenting years when the boys were younger. I remember those evenings when I was exhausted and all I wanted was some quiet time and a break from being Mommy. Joe may have been on call and I was handling the home front alone. (I learned that when Joe was on call at the hospital I was on call as well.) By eight o'clock all I wanted was for the boys to be bathed, stories read, prayers recited, and all of them quickly tucked into bed. When the odds are not in your favor—one adult to two, four, six or more—fatigue, feelings of frustration, and self-pity can easily suppress feelings of love. It became a matter of survival at that point in my day. What I gradually learned, though, was that if I didn't stay calm and handle the boys with tenderness, quiet might have enveloped the house once they were in bed, but peace was not present in my heart.

Love: To Will the Good of Another

If we follow St. Thomas Aquinas's thinking of "to love is to will the good of another," love then also means making choices that enable each of the boys to reach his full potential and be a better person in the eyes of God. With this approach, choices that may seem difficult become much easier because

I ask myself, "Will this movie, this television program, this computer game, this activity, this school, or this friend be in the best interest of my son?" If I do not feel the movie, program, activity, friend, etc., are appropriate, then "No" becomes a loving word because the decision was made out of love just as the "no" was with Danny and the PG-13 movie. Likewise, when I am asked to commit my time outside the home, I ask myself whether the commitment is in the best interest of my family and myself. As I address meeting the physical, emotional, intellectual, and spiritual needs of the boys in later chapters, the importance of making choices out of love becomes even more obvious and relevant to their development and growth.

The Principle of Respect

Respect is paramount to the success of a relationship and to building a home of love. Respect flows from the principle of love being a choice. If I love someone, I choose to respect that individual in my interactions with him as well as appreciate the dignity that is inherent in him.

Communicating with Respect

One way I express respect is in the way I verbally and nonverbally communicate on a daily basis. My touch whether loving or harsh, or my expression, whether of pride or disgust, exemplifies respect. Likewise, the words I choose to say and the tone of voice I say them in when communicating with each son are powerful. I have to consciously think about what I'm saying and how I'm saying it—put my brain in gear before my mouth starts running. "Please" precedes a request and "thank you" follows a thoughtful statement or act. Joe and I, even after thirty-five years of marriage, still say "please" and "thank you" to each other. It may sound simplistic, but I believe it demonstrates appreciation and affirmation, whether speaking to each other or one of the boys.

Too often we underestimate the impact our words and our tone of voice has on others. Joe once attended a pediatric conference where he heard a psychiatrist tell them that for every negative comment a child hears, it takes seven positive comments to undo the one negative. I believe each of us wants to be spoken to and treated respectfully, especially at home. If one family member is speaking in a demeaning or derogatory manner to another family member, that individual will not feel loved and secure in his own home. And I strongly believe that each of us has a right to feel loved and secure in the home environment. Words should build up another person not tear them down, even when disciplining.

Every day situations lend themselves to ways to show respect and teach communication skills. When the garbage needs to be taken out, I can order Matthew, "Matty, TAKE OUT the garbage. I'm sick of looking at it!" Or, I can calmly state, "Matty, please take out the garbage for me." Ordering versus respectfully requesting makes a difference. (Notice, I didn't form the request as a question, "Matty, will you take out the garbage?" because he could respond "No." When it's non-negotiable, you don't leave room for an answer.) Matty really doesn't want to take the garbage out in any case, but being asked respectfully, I find, makes a difference in his reaction to the request. I would react negatively, too, if Joe walked in the door at the end of his day and made demands, "Why isn't dinner ready?" "What have you been doing all day?" "Why can't you keep this house clean?" "You sure look a mess." Instead, I have a completely different reaction because Joe will come in the door after work, give me a kiss and ask about my day. He will then jump in to help me with whatever needs to be done. His actions and words express love and respect and make me feel loved and respected. My sons are no different.

In the same manner that Joe and I demonstrate respect to each other and to the boys, the boys are expected to treat each other with love and respect. Too often in families, the children are allowed to say and do mean, unkind things to each other. I repeat, each of us has a right to feel loved and secure at home. When a sibling is allowed to talk or to treat in a demeaning way a sister or brother, that child will not feel loved and secure. I am responsible, as the mother in the home, for assuring each child is treated with love and respect. Whenever I hear or see one of the boys treating his brother inappropriately, I act quickly and firmly to handle the situation. The boys know that being unkind to a brother is unacceptable behavior in our home. If my sons don't learn this concept at home, how can I expect them to treat others outside the home with respect? Children learn through repetition, so if they are consistently taught what is acceptable or unacceptable from a very early age, they will learn to treat others with love and respect. Respect becomes a habit.

People assume because I have a house full of boys that our home is a free for all. My home may not be quiet and serene, or smell like a flower garden, but it is not a mad house with wild, undisciplined boys roaming the halls, beating each other up or knocking holes in the walls. (Although we have had a few soccer balls careen through windows over the years. Our insurance agent finally recommended that we drop the "broken window" clause from our policy.) I couldn't have survived with any degree of sanity, if that had been the case. I may be considered crazy by a lot of people, but it can't be attributed to undisciplined, rowdy boys. There is a lot of wrestling and jostling throughout the day, what I learned to be normal male interactions. I grew up in a family of girls; jostling and wrestling were not a part of our daily routine. I remember Timmy telling a preschool friend that he couldn't wait for his brothers to come home from college because they could "fight," "fight" defined as rumbling on the floor in a big pile of brothers. Fist fighting is not and was not a part of the day. Anyone who knows my sons knows that to be true. Our children rise to the level of expectation we have of them, a statement made in the movie *Stand and Deliver*. I expect respectful behavior from the boys and the majority of the time they deliver. Boys may be boys but that doesn't give them the right to be disrespectful.

If my sons witness on a daily basis respectful interaction, verbal or non-verbal, between Joe and me, they are more likely to learn and understand the importance of respect in the way they speak to and treat us, as well as their brothers, friends, teachers, and others. The boys see Joe respect me as a woman, his wife, and the mother of his children. I want my sons to witness a respectful relationship so that they will exemplify the same respect in their relationships. If a son sees and hears his mother being spoken to or treated disrespectfully, he learns that behavior. He accepts it as the norm, the way a woman is treated. If we want our sons to become loving, caring, and compassionate men, they need to learn how to become loving, caring, and compassionate at home while growing up. Being strong does not mean being abusive, just as being loving, caring, and compassionate does not make you a wimp. Tolerating abuse in any way, shape, or form is not a loving choice by you. The old adage, "Children learn what they live," holds true. In addition, respect for others begins, ultimately, with respect for self. If I allow someone to abuse me physically, verbally, or emotionally, then I am not respecting my self. I must have self-respect and then teach the importance of self-respect to my sons.

Respecting Each Son's Uniqueness

The other aspect of respect that is integral in creating a home of love involves appreciating, affirming, and celebrating each person's individuality. Each of us from mom and dad, from Tony the oldest son to Timmy the youngest son, is an individual blessed by God with unique strengths, personalities, interests, and abilities. The boys may have the same mother and father, yet each one is gifted uniquely: intellectually, creatively, athletically, socially, and spiritually.

When I described the boys in an earlier chapter, I gave a glimpse into their individual personalities, interests, strengths, and talents. Although each may be gifted in more than one area, not one of them enjoys the whole package. My challenge and responsibility as their mother is to recognize and appreciate each of them for the individual God made him. To expect all my sons to receive all A's or be the 4.0 student is unrealistic, just as it is unrealistic to expect all of them to be the gifted athlete. If I respect and appreciate each son for his individual God-given talents, each son will more likely accept who he is and what he can accomplish. I feel sibling rivalry is minimized in our home as well, a big source of dissension in many homes, because each of the boys knows he is loved for who he is. He is not competing with his brothers for my love and attention or Joe's. He knows he is loved for himself.

I have to realize, too, that while the boys may share some of my interests and talents, they are not carbon copies of Joe or myself. I need to support the boys' dreams and aspirations. Although Joe is a physician and I was a teacher, it doesn't mean all the boys have to be doctors and teachers.

When Tony decided to pursue a career in medicine, people were quick to assume that David would follow suit. David enjoys the written word and creative writing; he tolerated math and science. He had no desire to study the sciences in college or become a physician. David made choices in his best interest, just as Tony's choices were in his best interest.

I became acutely aware of how different a child can be from his parents one afternoon with Danny. Like David, Danny is creatively gifted, although in a different vein. Danny loves to draw and create. He would spend hours building with the mass of Legos we have accumulated over the years. As a room freed up with older sons heading off to college, Danny would dump the bins of Legos on the floor of this room and build to his heart's content. Unfortunately, with the Legos strewn all over the floor, no one could get into the room for any other purpose. I'm convinced it is easier to walk on water than it is to walk on Legos. I suggested to Danny that we "organize" the Legos by putting them in Ziplocs maybe by color or shape. (As the mother of ten sons I have to be "The Organizer.") Danny looked at me, ready to burst into tears as he told me, "It won't be fun anymore. The fun is in looking for the piece I want." I assure you looking for pieces would not be fun for me. I like things in their right place. I realized in a way I hadn't before that our thought processes were different. The solution to the problem, because I did need to use the room, took some creativity. Danny, with help from his dad, built a box the width and length of the bed in the room for the Legos to fit into that would slide under the bed, allowing Danny to still look for that definitive piece. Danny was pleased with the solution, and I could again walk in and out of the room. Respecting Danny's individual needs allowed us to solve the problem instead of create new ones, and I didn't have to squelch his creativity in the process.

As I shared a little about each son in an earlier chapter, I hope you can appreciate the diversity of the boys. The differences in the boys create challenges for me as a mother. It means I have to attempt to understand how each of their individual minds work, their personalities, their strengths, and struggles while gelling as a family. It is probably my most difficult challenge and my most satisfying reward. **I want the boys to appreciate**

that differences don't have to pull people apart but are opportunities to make everyone stronger.

Joe and I may share the same values and goals, but Joe and I are two different people with our own individual strengths and weaknesses. We often approach a similar situation from different angles. For example, if one of the boys brings home a paper to be signed on a Monday and needs it back on Friday, I would most likely sign it right then and there. Joe would probably wait until Thursday night to sign it. Same task—different approach to completing it. The boys know which parent to ask to help with different assignments. The boys, for example, rarely ask me to help them with science homework. Why? Because they know they would probably get it wrong. Science and technology are not my strengths. But they know I can help them with almost any other subject.

The boys as well know which of their brothers to call in different situations. David and Mark are the go-to brothers when looking for a book suggestion or understanding a concept in a book; Danny provides computer and creative input; and Joe Pat is definitely the technical advisor regarding any cell phone decisions and issues. We use our differences to our advantage as a family. Likewise, I am convinced that appreciating and respecting diversity in the home is the springboard for appreciating and respecting diversity in society.

The Principle of Commitment

Commitment: A Choice

What do my sons need to flourish? I believe most importantly that they need my love, time, and attention. They need to appreciate my commitment to them in what I say and in what I do—in the choices I make every day. Even young children can discern when someone is committed to them. They just sense it!

Parenting is not a part time job with responsibilities to be fulfilled only when we feel like it. From the moment of conception on, a mother has the responsibility to nourish a child's physical, intellectual, emotional, and spiritual development. My sons' needs precede my needs—not eliminate my needs but precede them. In his book *The Art of Loving*, Erich Fromm says: "When you truly love, you want what is best for that person, sometimes at the expense of what is best for yourself." That is not an easy concept to embrace in today's society where the emphasis is too often on the "me."

Each of us has many commitments to fulfill: God, marriage, children, family, career, community, friends, church, and schools. Where I fit these commitments into my daily life demonstrates to my sons the importance and significance I bestow on them. I can talk about how much I love them, but if I am not living the talk, then the words mean nothing.

Living these commitments entails making choices. I need to ask myself some questions. What are the priorities in my life? What commitments do I have? How do I prioritize these commitments so I will continue to grow as an individual and, more importantly, so my sons will continue to grow? I ask myself these questions over and over again; they are not questions to be asked once and set aside. Why? Because change is an inevitable part of life. There are many ways change enters our lives, and we need to focus on our commitments and priorities with each new experience: a new job, the loss of a job, a new career, each new child, financial challenges, the illness or death of a family member or friend. If we understand what our priorities are and what we want for our sons, the changes that inevitably happen are easier to adjust to, allowing us to stay committed to what we deem priorities.

The importance of balance is essential. While work and careers may be necessary, they become a negative if they dominate every waking thought, action, and minute. Although my sons may enjoy the material things a job provides, I know from experience that the boys prefer the time and attention to the material goods. It's easy to convince ourselves that we are good providers because we have bought many "things." But have we provided for their emotional and physical needs in the process? "Things" cannot replace our love, time, and attention. M. Scott Peck reinforces this concept with this statement: "When we love something it is of value to us, and when something is of value to us we spend time with it, time enjoying it, and time taking care of it."

The Commitment of Time

The valuable commodity of time seems to be in short supply in today's world. I don't believe, though, that lack of time is the only problem but, rather, the distribution of our time. Too many of us are rushing around chasing the wrong dreams. Work, social functions, and the accumulation of wealth and things are more important than time spent with our children. We also need to honestly evaluate how we spend our discretionary time because it too reflects our priorities. For example, am I watching television or working/playing on the computer instead of reading to my son, playing ball with him, or just wrestling around? The term *quality time* often comes up when discussing good parenting. I define *quality time* as any time I'm with one of the boys: nursing him, bathing him, changing a diaper, reading with him, driving him to practice or school. I learned to take advantage of each activity to interact with the boys. But it's also important to ask, how much quality time can there be if there's little quantity time?

How I choose to spend my time is my choice. I can choose to read a magazine or read with Timmy. I can choose to go shopping on Saturday morning or attend the boys' soccer games. When it comes to how I spend my time, I choose to be involved with the boys' lives and activities. At the same time, I have to admit, I enjoy being a part of their lives. My choice to attend the soccer game or the school program may mean I'll be folding clothes or completing paperwork late at night—a fair trade-off.

At the boys' high school, the freshman class participates in a three-day retreat. The upperclassmen organize and run the retreat. One evening of the retreat, parents are invited to a session on communication building. The boys and the parents are divided into small groups; a parent is not assigned to his or her own son's group. The time is spent answering similar questions and then sharing the answers. I've attended nine retreats to date and, during each one, at least one of the boys will comment on how he wished his dad would spend more time with him. I've learned that whether the son is six days old, six years old, or sixteen years old, he wants and needs to feel his parents' care.

I remember the time Joe Pat was in second grade and performing in a Thanksgiving program for Grandparents Day. It was the November following the birth of Danny, our eighth son. The play was scheduled for 9 A.M., which would give me plenty of time to get to the school. The night before, I was up with the baby several times. Joe, trying to give me a few extra minutes of sleep, turned off my alarm clock; he had forgotten about the program. When I awoke, it was already 8:30. Panic ensued. I have never thrown myself and a baby together faster than I did that morning. Joe Pat had been very excited about the program; there was no way I could miss his performance. I was late, but did make it in time to hear Joe Pat proudly announce, "I am Chief Massasoit, and these are my people."

I remember Chris's first college soccer game at Trinity University. The game was scheduled on a Tuesday evening in September in San Antonio. I could tell he hoped one or more of us would attend even though he was a freshman and uncertain as to whether or not he would see any playing time. I debated whether or not to go. San Antonio is three hours away and it was during the week. Finally my heart won out over my head, and I decided to take Timmy to see the game. An hour or so outside of Houston, I began questioning the sanity of what I was doing: driving three hours to San Antonio, watching a two-hour soccer game, and then driving three hours back to Houston. Was I as crazy as people think? Timmy and I arrived at the game as the Trinity soccer team was warming up. When Chris saw us, he ran over to give us big hugs and kisses. I will always remember the smile on his face that afternoon. That smile made the three-hour drive to campus, the two hours at the game, and the three-hour drive home worth every minute. There was no doubt in my mind that he appreciated Timmy and me being there. As a bonus Chris did play that game, but even if he hadn't, the smile was reward enough.

By contrast, I'll never forget the mom who arrived at a middle school basketball game to pick up her son as the game was ending. Her son had played exceptionally that afternoon and made a difference in the game. A dad went over to compliment her on her son's performance and added, "Oh, you should have been here!" The mom matter-of-factly answered, "I watched enough middle school basketball games with his older brothers. I'm not sitting through any more." I knew I never wanted to be like that mom.

I witnessed many changes in parental commitment over the twenty years the boys attended St. Francis de Sales Catholic School. When our older sons were there, parents participated in school activities at a much higher rate. Parents took the hour or two off of work to watch the Thanksgiving performance, the Christmas pageant, or the Living Stations of the Cross. It wasn't any easier then to take time off from work than it is now. Yet, at the Living Stations of the Cross when Timmy was in eighth grade, there were six parents present. During the older boys' years, the school had to reserve several rows to accommodate the parents. The absence or presence of a parent sends a message to the child of the importance you place on what he does. I know only too well how quickly the years go by. Some experiences can never be recaptured.

Playing with the boys—building blocks, Play-Doh, cars and trucks, Big Wheels, swings, swimming, kicking or throwing the ball—reading to them, attending school functions, swim meets, and soccer games shows them I care about them and enjoy being with them. I'm often asked, "Doesn't it get boring after a while?" Sure, playing Candy Land for the umpteenth time gets old, but I remind myself that it's about being with my son that's important.

When I attended open house at Strake Jesuit College Preparatory this past spring with Timmy, people asked and wondered why I was there again since all the other boys had attended the school. I reminded them that it may be my tenth time for open house but it was Timmy's first. I made the commitment for Tony, David, Chris, Joe Pat, Matty, Mark, Tommy, Danny, and Jamie, and it was important to make that same commitment to Timmy.

I know the commitment of my time, love, and attention made an impact because the older boys are now making that same commitment to their brothers. With the exception of Tony and Tommy who were out of the country, all the boys and their families made it home for Timmy's graduation from St. Francis de Sales School.

Financial Commitments

Choices regarding financial commitments also impact our children. Unfortunately, our society places too much emphasis on material possessions. A person's level of success is often determined by the kind of car he drives, the house he lives in, the clothes he wears, and the possessions he owns. There is pressure to have the latest television, iPod, phone, computer program, or video game. Financial demands stress the average household, even more so lately with the increase in energy and food prices.

What helps make the financial stresses easier for my family and me is continuing to live within our means. Joe and I work together to prioritize our financial commitments. Although our income may be higher than the average family, the financial commitments inherent in a large family are also significant in comparison to an average family. For example, the boys drank four to five gallons of milk a day when they were all home. We not only have one or two sons who have required orthodontia, but eight. With six sons having completed college, two sons still in college and two more to go, it is imperative that Joe and I continue to remain focused on our needs and our goals.

One financial goal that has remained constant is educating the boys in the Catholic school system since it offers a strong academic program in a faith-filled environment. This choice entails making additional choices. In order to pay the tuition, we maintain a simpler lifestyle, focusing on necessities versus wants. Cars are driven for many years. At one time, I am convinced Joe was driving the oldest car, a minivan, of any physician in the city of Houston. All it took to understand why was to notice all the university decals on the back. Obviously we were making tuition payments, not a car payment. Appliances are repaired rather than replaced whenever possible. My first Maytag washing machine lasted twenty-six years! We are not compelled to buy every new gadget or technological invention that becomes available. I am still using the mustard colored blender and hand mixer that I received at my wedding shower thirty-five years ago. I haven't heard any complaints from the boys on the quality of my brownies or mashed potatoes.

Our children model our behavior. If they witness me chasing "the more, the bigger, and the better," they are likely to do the same. It is important for them to distinguish between needs and wants and to learn to prioritize. A recent news story depicted a young mother struggling to make ends meet. During the interview, a big screen television set was in the background and a new pickup truck was in the driveway. She, unfortunately, bought into the media's perception of need, creating additional financial stress on her household.

If I've learned any financial lessons over the years, they are to prioritize my family's financial goals and live within our means. The boys may not have the latest and greatest gadgets or drive their own cars, but they are well educated, well fed, and well loved.

The Principle of Faith

I am often asked, "Cathy, how do you do it?" I know where the question comes from because being a mother is hard, whether you are the mother of one or many. Most of us want to be the best mother we can be to our children, so when we struggle with the demands, challenges, and constancy of motherhood we think we're the only one struggling. How far from the truth!

But how do I do it? The moms who usually ask the question have fewer children than I do and usually have a son or two. They also see that, for the most part, I am able to successfully handle the myriad responsibilities associated with raising ten sons and seem content and at peace with my life.

My simple but truthful answer: "It is not about how **I** do it but rather how **we** do it: Joe, myself, the boys, and our God." I commented earlier that I don't believe that God just gifts us with our children and then wishes us good luck. I believe He walks with us providing the wisdom, strength, and courage we need to successfully raise our children to reach their full potential **if** we invite Him on the journey. My faith is an invaluable source of strength, inspiration, and guidance in my mothering efforts. "Unless the Lord build the house, they labor in vain who build it" (Psalm 127:1).

My faith is based on my relationship with God and what I discern He wants from me. It's an active faith laced with prayer, moments of solitude, good deeds, and the virtues of faith, hope, and love. When I was in middle school at St. Paul Catholic School in Jacksonville, Florida, we sang a responsorial song that to this day remains in my heart: "God is love, and he who abides in love abides in God and God in him" (1 John 4:16). St. Paul's letter to the Corinthians reminds us we are nothing without love, and that of the virtues of faith, hope, and love, the greatest of these is love.

The love, respect, and commitment principles that I've already espoused are all interwoven into my faith. I don't believe I can consider myself faith-filled without choosing to love and strive for what is in the best interest of each of my sons. I don't believe I can consider myself faith-filled without treating each of the boys with the respect they deserve as a child of God. I don't believe I can consider myself faith-filled if I don't make the commitments necessary to enable the boys to reach their full potential in the eyes of God.

In society today, the different facets of our lives are often compartmentalized, faith included. People want to believe that, although they attend church on Sunday, their choices and decisions the rest of the week are irrelevant to their spirituality. They want to believe that their personal spirituality shouldn't affect their business decisions, their relationships, or their lifestyle and choices of activities. Many people are comfortable with their faith until it interferes with societal values and personal decisions. Faith isn't integrated into their lives; it is a separate entity.

I believe that faith needs to be integrated into my thoughts, words, and actions to be meaningful. The boys need to witness my faith in order to appreciate its richness and worthiness. In other words, if I want the boys to embrace faith, I have to embrace it and live it. "What good is it to profess faith without practicing it?" (James 1:14).

Our young people know hypocrisy when they hear or see it. They can discern whether we mean what we say and/or say what we mean. So how can I say I love God and then turn around and treat Joe or the boys disrespectfully? How can I teach the boys that God is a God of love and then not find time to spend with them to show I care about them? How do I teach them that God is forgiving of our sins if I hold a grudge or won't forgive a wrongdoing? How do I show the boys that God is first in my life if I'm primarily focused on gaining wealth, power, or esteem? Do I attend church services once a week where I publicly praise God and then leave

Him behind at the church door the rest of the week? Do I attend religious services at all? Do I take time to pray, individually and with the family? The answers to the questions tell where faith ranks in my life.

I mentioned that part of my faith journey encompasses discerning God's will in my life. Where I am today is not the plan I laid out for myself thirty-five or forty years ago. But as Father Donovan once reminded me: "If you want to make God laugh, tell him your plans." Upon graduation from high school, I attended Loyola University New Orleans in order to pursue a degree in education. I wanted to teach young children and, ultimately, go into educational administration. Marriage was somewhere down the road. Then I met a young medical student, Joe, who led to the first change in my plans. I graduated from Loyola University on a Monday; we had rehearsal on Tuesday; our wedding was Wednesday evening. We moved to Houston where Joe was completing a pediatric residency. I taught first grade at Corpus Christi Catholic School and began work on a masters degree. When Joe began a neonatology fellowship, we decided to start our family. Following Tony's birth, I decided to stay home. As hard as it was to give up the classroom, I felt it was the best decision for me, leading to another change in my plans. The birth of David followed the next year, and since I wanted my children close in age, Chris, Joe Pat, and Matty were not far behind. Although my career plans were changing, having five sons was a fulfillment of another dream. I was at peace!

During my pregnancy with Matthew, a major change came into my life. One Sunday morning at the end of Mass, Father Donovan invited and encouraged every one to sign up to spend one hour a week in the new perpetual adoration chapel opening in the parish. I will always remember that morning because I was sitting at the back of church with four squirmy boys under the age of five. I laughed inside when Father made the request, thinking where would I find one more hour in my week to spend sitting in a chapel. His final words that morning, though, changed my life: "I guarantee you one hour of peace and quiet." Now, I was the mother of four sons under the age of five. Peace and quiet was not a part of my day. I signed up from eight to nine o'clock on Wednesday evenings. I may have been seeking an hour of peace and quiet, but I received so much more.

I was not prepared for the difference that one hour of peace and quiet in the presence of the Lord would make in my life. I began to appreciate the importance of silence in my prayer life. I realized that during most of my prayer time up to this point I was doing all the talking; I never really took the time to sit back and listen to what God might be saying to me. As it turned out, He had a lot to say to me, especially in regards to the direction of my life.

In my early years of parenting, although I loved being a mother, I often felt that I couldn't love and give the way I was expected to. I had good days and not so good days. Growing up, the Holy Family was held up as the model family to emulate. I found it hard, though, to relate to the Holy Family. I couldn't envision Mary and Joseph ever having a disagreement, a frustration, being angry, impatient, or stressed out, or Jesus not being the "perfect" child who did everything he was expected to do and with a smile on his face. Plus, Mary and Joseph had one child, and I had four going on five. Quietly sitting in the chapel week after week, I grew in my understanding of the example of the Holy Family. It was their love, devotion, commitment, and support of each other that I needed to emulate on a daily basis. I needed to strive to mirror Mary's attitude, choices, and acceptance of what life brought her. I had to choose to love and support Joe and the boys. My attitude and approach to loving would make a difference in their lives and, ultimately, in mine. I learned that when love is in my heart, the activities of the day are filled with joy, whether I'm washing eight loads of clothes, cleaning bathrooms, running the boys to soccer, or striving to meet the individual needs of each son. I took to heart the words of Mother Teresa: "It is not how much we do, but how much love we put into the doing."

Likewise, the example of the importance of the Holy Family's faith life encouraged me to strengthen my prayer life. Mary and Joseph lived in the true presence of Jesus. Jesus needed to be present in my life as well. It was my choice. To this day when I find the emotional and physical stresses and demands of my life overwhelming and affecting my relationships, I have to reexamine whether my prayer life is adequate or if I have pushed it aside due to the stresses. When I refocus and reinstate God first in my life, everything—and I mean everything—falls right into place. I've learned that when I have God, I have everything I need. "It is not the absence or presence of problems that determines our peace of mind; it is the absence or presence of God."

It was also during my weekly hour that I felt called to have more children. At first, I rejected the notion that God could possibly want Joe and I to have more children. I came up with every reason imaginable not to, but I came to realize, after much prayer, that Joe and I would be irresponsible to not have more children. If this was God's plan for us, Joe and I had to trust and believe that He would strengthen and support us in the upbringing of all our children. How grateful we are that we trusted Him because that trust blessed our lives with Mark, Tommy, Danny, Jamie, and Timmy. The story doesn't end there. I am often asked why we stopped at ten children. We didn't; I had an eleventh pregnancy that I miscarried and have not conceived again. It was God's plan that we have ten children—ten sons! The acceptance of His will brings a sense of peace to my days. "I can do all things through God who strengthens me."

Creating a home of love filled with laughter, love, respect, and faith depends on the choices I make each and every day. It is simple, as Mother Teresa often reminded us, but not always easy.

Chapter 3

Boys are Boys—Thank God!

Life is either a daring adventure or nothing.
—Helen Keller

Boys are God's way of telling you that your house is too neat.
—Author Unknown

If I thought creating a home of love was a challenge, understanding boys was an even higher-level challenge. I assumed my challenge was greater because I grew up in a family of girls, but even moms I know who had brothers feel just as daunted by the experience. I should have put two and two together, though, because my husband, Joe, and I are very different. God, in His infinite wisdom, created male and female—not one and the same but male and female. It is easy to appreciate the obvious physical differences between us, but appreciating that male **and** female also differ emotionally, mentally, and socially seems harder to grasp.

Being married to Joe for thirty-five years and raising ten sons, I can attest that there are gender differences in the way males and females think, act, and communicate. This is not a bad thing—God intended it this way. And different does not mean better or worse than a female—just different. And within that framework of maleness, each of my sons thinks, acts, and communicates in a unique way.

After the birth of their second son, my daughter-in-law Megan called one morning to share a conversation she had had with Joe Pat. Joe Pat had recounted some of the mischief he and his brothers had gotten into over the years: pasting baseball cards with green dyed glue all over their bedroom walls and furniture or competing to see who could pee the farthest, outside at least. She wanted to know if the stories were true. When I confirmed that they were, she commented, "I would never even have thought to do those things." My response: "Of course not, Megan. You're a girl."

Although I would never claim that I think like a male, after parenting a few sons I did learn to anticipate some mischief in advance and deter the possible consequences. One example that vividly comes to mind is during the construction phase of the addition on our home. I was pregnant at the time with our seventh son, Tommy, and the plan was for the five older boys to share rooms in the upstairs addition. Steve, the contractor, noticed that the laundry hamper being built upstairs was directly above the laundry room. He suggested installing a laundry chute to make the chore of gathering dirty clothes easier. I vehemently rejected the idea. Steve couldn't understand my reaction until I shared a story from Teresa Bloomingdale's book *I Should Have Seen It Coming When the Rabbit Died*. Teresa was also the mother of ten children. In her home, dirty clothes were not the only items sent down the chute: bowling balls, toys, and even younger siblings. I decided walking up the stairs for the laundry was indubitably in my best interest!

Appreciating these gender differences, even when I don't fully understand them, goes a long way in successfully raising a son because then I am not trying to undo or remake his maleness. I accept him for who he is—a boy.

I affirmed earlier that my objective is to raise strong sons who are loving, caring, compassionate, responsible, respectful, well-educated, and faith-filled individuals. I understand these characteristics to be human traits—not male or female specific. And, being caring, sensitive, and compassionate does not mean a boy is a sissy. At the same time, I must appreciate that I am raising sons, not daughters.

Communication

Gender differences are especially evident in the way men and women communicate. Studies show that areas of the male and female brain develop differently due to the influence of testosterone. In an article "his brain, her brain" by Walt Larimore, M.D., he states: "The fact is that his brain and her brain perceive the world quite differently and communicate in very different ways. We speak and hear language differently. We mean different things by what we say. As a result, a significant communication gap can open between us and divide us if we're not aware of our design differences and why they are there. To bridge this communication gap, we need to understand not only how we say what we say but also what the other gender's brain hears." I clipped a *Houston Chronicle* ad out a few years ago and posted it on my refrigerator: "Score one for exasperated women: New research suggests men really do listen with just half their brains." Dr. Larimore confirms it and I live it.

I remember reading an article that related how, even at a very young age, girls and boys communicate differently. The article mentioned that when you listen to girls interacting you usually hear words, whereas with boys, more often than not, you hear just sounds—sirens, car sounds, explosions, and random noises. I started observing whether or not this was true. I was amazed when I listened to Jamie and Timmy playing, for that is exactly what I heard—sounds. And remember, sounds are usually louder than simple words, which means boys playing and interacting will most likely create more noise. I never said I have a quiet home. A neighbor gave me a plaque that reads: *Boys—noise with dirt on them.*

Girls, on the other hand, tend to screech at a high pitch, so there's a trade off. Our family was down in Galveston one weekend, and the boys were out in the water jumping the waves. A group of ten-year-old girls came running down to the beach screeching all the way into the water. Tony came up to me, pregnant with Danny at the time, and sighed, "Please assure me you're having a boy."

As the mother of boys, I adjusted to the high-spirited atmosphere that was ever changing as the number of sons increased. That does not imply, though, that I allowed the boys to raise the roof but that I accepted their way of communicating, whether playing alone or with brothers. One example is when Tommy, around five years old at the time, would play basketball with a small basketball hoop that his older brothers had given him and Mark for Christmas one year. He did not quietly shoot the basketball but would provide a play-by-play as he exuberantly reenacted a Duke basketball game: "Bobby Hurley passes to Laettner. Laettner turns and shoots. Duke wins!" I have fond memories of these performances. The commentating was half the fun—for Tommy and me. To have asked Tommy to shoot quietly would have shown a lack of understanding of the importance the commentating factored into the whole experience.

At the same time, the boys had to learn to play quietly when younger brothers were napping. They chose games and activities that did not entail making a lot of noise or played outside where pandemonium was more acceptable. It is important that they learn that there are times when making noise is acceptable and times when they need to have inside voices or no voices, as I used to tell my students. This is a skill that transfers from the home to school, to church, and to other activities. If my son has learned to be quiet at home when expected and appropriate, he is more likely to be quiet when the situation dictates, whether in the classroom, in church, or eating in a restaurant. It is also an issue of respect for others.

Non-verbal Communication

Communicating goes beyond the decibel level. When we think about communicating, speech is usually the first method that comes to mind. We communicate, though, in many different ways: through speech, touch, our eyes, the written word, and body language. They are all effective means of communicating and evoke similar reactions, positive or negative, as does the spoken word.

Each son learns from my touch and from my voice as well as from my smile. My touch, whether gentle or rough, telegraphs my feelings towards him—a non-verbal form of communication. My touch stimulates him and lets him know that I love him. The cuddling and holding won't spoil him. Studies abound on the importance of touch in a child's development.

Children deprived of physical contact manifest slower rates of physical, mental, and social development. I believe that touch continues to be important at all stages of their development. The hugs, kisses, and gentle touches reflect my love for them and foster an unspoken sense of security. Fortunately, my husband and I both grew up in families where physical expressions of affection were acceptable.

The boys are comfortable sharing their feelings through touch. When I am visiting the schools, they will come over and give me a quick hug and a peck on the cheek. Talk about warming a mother's heart. I love their hugs and kisses when they return home from school or work each day. Moreover, they are comfortable expressing affection to each other and friends with big bear hugs. The hugs communicate a feeling of acceptance and love. As the boys got older and friends would come over, a handshake may have been the initial greeting but, usually after that, hugs took precedence. Since I'm only a little over five feet, some of their taller friends had to decide whether to kneel down or pick me up, but one way or another, they were receiving a hug.

Although most of the boys have gone through a period, usually the middle school years, when they understandably preferred not to give or receive a hug or kiss in public, they eventually move back to appreciating this simple expression of affection. When Chris gave me a hug and kiss on arriving at a Trinity University soccer game, the "oohs" and "aahs" from the crowd followed. It didn't bother Chris one bit.

A smile and other facial expressions are additional non-verbal means of communicating. Recent research emphasizes the bonding that takes place when a mother and baby share a smile. I begin communicating with each son through these smiles and interactions. A baby will respond to a smiling face with a smile in return, just as a frown will appear when I have a stern expression on my face. The boys learned to read my facial expressions and moods. They knew when I was pleased with them and when I expected a change in their behavior. One afternoon in the car when one of the younger boys was fooling around, Chris asked, "How is it, Mom, all you do is look at him and he stops?" The boys knew that piercing look meant "cut it out." Sometimes a pat on the shoulder or the calling of a specific name evokes the same result—a change in behavior.

The boys communicate without words as well. I remember the evening that Danny was invited to attend a birthday party that I decided was inappropriate and told him "no," he couldn't go. He stomped upstairs and slammed the bedroom door. Talk about communicating! He communicated loudly and clearly that he was not pleased with my decision. A scowl, a grin, or a smirk also conveys how they are feeling.

I learned to read their facial expressions and body language. I realized that the boys' body language or their moods transmit many messages that the boys don't realize they are sending. I could usually tell when I picked them up from school how each of their days had gone, and how then to temper my questions about their day. Observing and "listening" to the boys, even when they are not speaking, is a beneficial and essential mothering skill. At the same time, the last thing you want to do is start pounding them with questions: "What's wrong? What happened? Are you all right?" Sometimes just a simple acknowledgement: "Rough day?" lets him know that you care and understand.

An incident that comes to mind regarding observing a child who has something on his mind is our son Tommy at 10 years of age. It was the middle of June after a week of emotional events in my family's life: I had miscarried our eleventh pregnancy on a Wednesday and then on Saturday Timmy, three years old at the time, was rushed to the emergency room with a ruptured appendix. Because the appendix had ruptured, Timmy needed to remain in the hospital to receive several days of antibiotic treatment. The family routine was significantly disrupted since I spent the majority of the day at the hospital with Timmy. When I was home I noticed that Tommy was unusually quiet. At first I assumed it was due to the different routine, but after a day or two of similar behavior, I felt something else must be bothering him. I made the time to sit and talk with him to try to determine what was on his mind. After a few minutes of sharing and talking about the events and routine of the past week as well as their effects on each of us, Tommy looked at me and said, "I know this is a bad time, but do you remember my birthday is next week?" Tommy was afraid that with everything going on in our lives that Joe and I had forgotten about his upcoming birthday. After some reassurances that we had not forgotten his special day, a relieved Tommy reverted back to his peppy self. Even in the midst of busy days, I must be cognizant of the messages the boys are sending me.

Likewise, the boys grew to be observant of my moods. I remember the afternoon when Chris, Joe Pat, and Matty arrived home from school to find me sitting on the sofa with their five sick younger brothers sprawled all over me. They could tell it had been a long day. They grabbed a brother or two, allowing me a few minutes to regroup. Or on other days they would arrive home and suggest I take a walk—a long walk—so I could de-stress.

Verbal Communication

Learning communication skills, whether verbal or non-verbal, begins at an early age. My ability to communicate with my sons didn't happen overnight. A relationship develops over time. When the boys are babbling in the early years, I listen as if I understand every word. When they find a "treasure" outside and are excited about their find, I share my excitement as well. That's a real stretch for me when they show me a disgusting bug or a weed that makes me sneeze. We interact, laugh, and talk over a board game. Jamie and I shared many afternoons playing Sequence while Timmy was napping. When Mark brought home a "creation" from preschool, I listened to the story behind it, always fearing he'd ask me the dreaded question: "What do you think it is?" before he told me what it was. When Danny sits at the counter and shares every detail of his day while I peel a dozen potatoes, my simple responses and nods let him know that I care about what he is telling me. I find that establishing communication lines early with the boys minimizes the pitfalls later as they enter the middle school and high school years. If a child constantly hears: "Just a minute," "Later,"—with the "later" never materializing—soon he won't take the time to share at all.

Too often parents expect a child to instantaneously start communicating in the middle school or high school years when they haven't made the effort in prior years. Or they still aren't taking advantage of opportunities to talk and relate. During a parent-student session at a freshman retreat held at the Jesuit high school, the six boys in our group voiced their desire to spend more time with their parents. They wanted to share their aspirations and desires with their parents but felt the feeling wasn't mutual. One freshman said, "My parents always say there's not enough time. But we're in the car a lot. Why can't we shut off the radio and spend the time talking?" I've heard similar scenarios during the other nine retreat sessions I've attended. The assumption is usually made that young men don't want to communicate, but that's not my experience. They may not want to be involved in an hour-long conversation, but they do want to convey their thoughts and feelings and feel like someone cares enough to listen.

I appreciate being available to the boys after school because so often an excitement, an achievement, a frustration, or a disappointment during the day is shared during the car ride home or in the time immediately upon arriving home. One afternoon when I picked up the boys from school, Chris, in fourth grade at the time, was visibly upset. On arriving home, I asked if we could talk in my bedroom, the usual place we migrated to when we needed privacy. Chris shared that some of the girls were pressuring him to tell them who he liked, and he didn't know what to say. I advised him to tell them that he likes soccer, he likes basketball, and he loves his mother. Chris chuckled and then proceeded to go outside to play. (I then called the teacher to ask her to handle the situation at school, which she did.)

I garner tidbits about the boys' days and moods from listening to them talk to each other, often on the ride home from school or to a sport's practice. I don't need to say a word; I just listen.

When asking a son about his day, I frame the question so he cannot respond with a simple "No," "Yes," or one word answer. Not: "How was math class today?" but rather: "What did you do in math class today?"

Talking face-to-face can prove awkward at times for the boys, especially if it's a touchy subject. Side-by-side conversations, whether walking along or driving in the car, seem less intimidating. It may take more effort on my part, but the payoff is worth it.

Conversations over meals are an additional and essential way to keep connected. Dinnertime has proven to be one of the most important times in our family's day. And we do eat together as a family most nights of the week. We laugh, share our day's experiences, discuss current events and sports, and just enjoy being together. Anyone who isn't used to a big family's dinner table may be taken aback by the ping-pong nature of the conversations: Multiple conversations going on one minute before reverting back to one conversation the next only to return to multiple conversations again. I am always relieved, too, to be able to get through the dinner without too much "bathroom" talk—fart, poop, etc. I know my sisters and I did not resort to this level of conversation—another gender difference. As the older boys started bringing young ladies to dinner, I just prayed that after eating with a household of boys they would consider coming again. I guess the experience wasn't too daunting since five of the boys are married.

Bedtime was another opportunity I found to talk to the boys. For some of them it was a diversionary tactic to stay up a little longer—ask mom a question or two. But for me it was another chance to interact with them, usually one-on-one. I treasure those moments and some of the conversations. One momentous bedtime talk was with Timmy and Jamie shortly after Timmy started first grade. Timmy was having a hard time adjusting to being in school all day. Those first nights he cried going to bed. One of the nights, through tears, he looked at me and said, "Mommy, I don't get it. You're a teacher. Why can't you just teach me at home?" Jamie didn't miss a beat. He excitedly jumped up agreeing, "What a great idea!" Although a few of the boys had had questionable first grade teachers, I knew Timmy was in great hands with Marilyn Megow, and I didn't need to homeschool him.

As the boys headed off to college, differences in communication styles among the boys came front and center. Cell phones and emails were not available when the older boys went to school, so we depended on dorm phones. Tony called almost every Sunday evening. He'd usually talk to Joe and me and then to each of his brothers, depending on time. David called whenever; there was no rhyme or reason. In fact, when Joe and I hadn't heard from him for over a week after dropping him off at Creighton University, we became concerned. Finally, I received a message on the answering machine: "Mom, I'm still alive." Chris called fairly regularly, as did Joe Pat. Joe Pat often called during the day so he could talk with Jamie and Timmy.

Timmy would carry the portable phone around the house describing every nook and cranny to Joe Pat, I assume so Joe Pat wouldn't forget his home surroundings. I found Timmy one day trying to call Joe Pat using speed dial. He was mad because the lady kept telling him Joe Pat wasn't home. The "lady" was the voice on the answering machine.

It was during these years that I realized even more than in years past that males and females communicate differently. Conversations with Chris are a prime example. Chris would call and talk to both Joe and me. When we got off the phone and shared our conversations, you would have thought that we had talked to two different people. Joe knew every detail of the soccer games Chris had played in that week. I knew only whether Trinity had won or lost and how well Chris had played. I talked to Chris about his classes, his professors, and his relationship with Stephanie.

I find the boys talk to Joe about certain issues. They discuss other things with me. And I'm sure they talk to their brothers about other topics. In fact, knowing the boys have each other is a blessing to me. They can turn to each other to share the ups and downs of their lives. There have been those times when I sense something has happened at school or with sports. It's reassuring knowing that I can ask one of the boys to talk to the other without getting directly involved. After high school soccer games, the younger boys usually call one of their older brothers to rehash the game. I want them to be comfortable sharing what's going on in their life and their feelings, whether with Joe, their brothers, a friend, a mentor, or myself. With cell phones now, the boys stay in touch on a regular basis. Even when Tommy studied abroad in Lima, Peru, we talked every couple of weeks. He usually talked with Joe and me for a while and then spent the next hour catching up with Jamie and Timmy. I am grateful that they **want** to spend an hour talking with a brother.

I grew to appreciate that some of my sons talk more openly and in more detail while some of the boys tend to keep more to themselves. Each son has his own style. Accepting and respecting each son's style is important. I remember talking to David while at Creighton about an upcoming dance being held on campus and asking him who he was taking. There was dead silence on the other end of the line. Laughingly I teased, "David, you could tell me Susan, or Karen, or Linda. I'm not going to fly up to Creighton to check out your date. I'm just making conversation."

Then there's Tony, who despised talking on the telephone. He once commented when he was very young that he thought he'd be a priest so he wouldn't have to talk on the phone. We have no idea where he got the idea that priests don't talk on the phone.

One of the more comical stories regarding communicating is when Jamie was in the preschool program for three year olds. One day early in the school year he asked, "Mommy, when can I talk?" I was confused by his question and reassured him he could already talk. "No, Mommy. When can I talk?" I decided that someone at school must have said, "No talking," and he took it literally. I found out that Lucy Gomez, his preschool teacher, heard his voice only on the playground when he played with his friends. She finally heard him speak to her when he answered questions during the oral evaluation she administered at the end of the year.

Healthy Communication

Another aspect to communicating is appreciating that there are healthy and unhealthy ways to communicate. Developing these skills enable a young man to relate amicably and respectfully with others, male and female. These skills are learned at home by observing and hearing how the people around him interact. And the learning, I repeat, begins from day one.

Joe and I have been involved in our parish's marriage preparation program for twenty-six years. One entire session of the program involves discussing communication skills and their impact on the relationship and, eventually, the family. Since we learn these skills in our families of origin, Joe and I assessed the skills we learned growing up and then made the necessary changes and adjustments that would enable us to communicate in a healthier manner.

Conflict and disagreements in a family are inevitable. How we resolve them, though, is a matter of habit and choice. We can resort to healthier ways: discussion, compromise, or collaboration. Or we can yell and scream, manipulate, pout, give-in, withdraw, or avoid the conflict all together. If all I do is yell and scream at the boys whenever something happens, they will assume that is how you resolve a problem, instead of sitting down and working through the issues. I understand, too, that nothing is usually accomplished by yelling and screaming or nagging because they tend to tune you out.

Healthy communication skills denote respect. When I respect Joe and the boys, I will speak to them in a respectful manner whether I am pleased with them or not. Name-calling, belittling or demeaning comments, or yelling and screaming are never appropriate. I addressed respectful communication in a prior chapter. A home that embraces healthy communication provides an environment that allows each family member the opportunity to share their thoughts and feelings and work through differences. If the boys are afraid of what Joe or I will say or do, they'll eventually stop sharing their thoughts and ideas with us, and they definitely wouldn't turn to us in time of need—and I'm not talking about only the high school years but even when they are young.

Although I didn't reason or argue with a two, five, or eight year old, I did explain why I did allow or didn't allow them to do something. For example, I might say: "We wear seat belts in the car at all times because you can get seriously injured if we're in an accident. I love you and don't want anything bad to happen to you" or "We don't play on the stairs because one of you might fall and get hurt" or "No, you may not have ice cream now. It's almost dinnertime."

As they get older, I continue to explain our reasons behind our decisions. I don't argue about whether they can or can't do the activity. For instance, I may say: "You may not watch that program. The content is inappropriate and immoral" or "You may not go to that movie because you're thirteen years old and it is R-rated."

The boys do know, though, that they can discuss issues with us. My husband Joe felt strongly about keeping communication lines open because he grew up in a family where what his dad said was final, no discussion allowed. He often says: "There was God and then there was my dad." One issue needing discussion arose when one of the college-aged boys brought home a Nintendo. Joe and I had gone out for the evening, and when we returned, the boys had it hooked up to the television and were all playing games. We did not allow electronic games in our home, and for a reason. Many of the games are inappropriate and many hours are spent playing them instead of pursuing other activities, especially playing outdoors. Joe and I were not pleased with the boys and asked them to remove it. Chris and Joe Pat respectfully asked if we could talk about the restriction. They presented some options about when they could play and which games were appropriate. An acceptable compromise was reached.

People assume that, because ours is a household of boys, foul language is freely spoken. Foul language is unacceptable—no discussion allowed. Fortunately, Joe sets the standard; the boys never hear him cursing. If they don't hear it, they are less likely to make foul words part of their working vocabulary. On a segment of *The Oprah Show* that my family was also featured on, a mother and grandmother wanted guidance in curtailing the three-year-old son/grandson from calling them both "bitch." A few techniques were presented to help the young boy change his language but— I'm convinced—unless the adult in the home stopped using the word, the time spent implementing the techniques would be wasted. The word is part of the three year old's vocabulary because he has heard it repeatedly.

I expect the boys to use appropriate language with Joe and me as well as with their brothers. "Shut up," "stupid," or any other inappropriate name or word is not tolerated. One afternoon when the older boys were much younger, the family was outside working in the yard. All of a sudden, Chris, who was four years old, yelled at the top of his lungs, "I need to go piss." I knew Chris didn't realize he had said something wrong, and I knew he hadn't heard the phrase from either Joe or me. After explaining to Chris that he was not to repeat those words, I took Tony and David aside. They may not have been guilty of saying anything wrong at the time, but they had obviously used inappropriate words in front of their brother at another time. If I wanted to curtail inappropriate language in the future, then it was important to make an impression now. Tony and David were disciplined! By setting the standards early and with the older boys, Joe and I established what is acceptable language in our home.

Back talk and sassiness are dealt with similarly. Determining what is acceptable and what isn't pays off in less confrontations. It is easy to get caught up in the back and forth comments that escalate into arguing even at very young ages. I finally realized that if I don't feed into the negative flow or feel determined to have the last word, the impetus to continue by one of the boys dissolves. It took practice catching myself and then consciously choosing not to retort; the natural inclination is to do so.

Healthy communication skills will benefit the boys in all their personal and professional relationships. What a gift to share with our sons!

Socialization

I'm always amazed at the people who ask me if I think my parenting experience would be different if I were raising ten daughters rather than ten sons. From my teaching experience and having grown up with four sisters, there is no doubt my life would be quite a contrast.

I remember coming home from college and sitting around the kitchen table talking to my sisters for hours. When the boys return from college, they usually end up on the den floor in a heap or outside shooting baskets. My sisters and I spent most of our time chatting; the boys spend most of their time just interacting.

The boys rarely walk by a brother without touching him in some fashion. Television commercial breaks are not spent quietly waiting for the show to resume. They are spent tackling and wrestling with each other. As long as they don't destroy the room or each other, I let them be.

Playing is mostly how the boys interacted. It is while they were playing that they learned social skills: to compromise, to resolve conflict, to appreciate different skills and abilities, to handle frustrations, to be tolerant, to lead, to follow, to win, and to lose. Dare anyone try to convince me that playtime is wasted time whether playing with a brother or friend or alone. I used to be intrigued watching the boys play at recess when I was teaching. I learned a lot about each student through these observations from the classmate each one chose to play with to what activity he was involved in.

The boys learned to distance themselves from someone who didn't play fairly, was bossy, or had to win—brother or friend. The advantage at my home is that if you don't want to play with one brother you can usually find another one to engage in an activity. Another advantage I have is that the boys do have each other. Boys need other males to interact and relate to. There's no getting around relating with other males in our house.

The boys began to appreciate each other's uniqueness and interests. Danny, for example, loved creating with Legos and would spend hours doing so. Once in a while, though, his brothers needed him to join in a game outside to even up the teams. Sometimes Danny chose to play with them and other times he was engrossed in his latest creation and didn't want to stop building. His brothers wanted me to "make" Danny play with them. How fair would that be? They wouldn't want me to force them to play with Legos if they weren't in the mood. So they figured out ways to compromise or play a game that didn't require even teams.

I was impressed to see how they became inclusive in their choice of activities, picking a game that the majority of them could play even though another game might have been more fun. Remember, there is an eighteen year age span from youngest to oldest son. The older boys gave the younger boys a little slack, but just a little. One afternoon Timmy was outside playing with his brothers and wasn't having a good day. He sat on the curb moping. Tony, who was in medical school at the time, drove up, got out of the car, and went and sat by Timmy. Timmy looked up at Tony and lamented, "You don't know how lucky you are. You don't have nine big brothers." Tony smiled and teasingly responded, "You don't know how lucky **you** are. You don't have nine little brothers."

The social skills the boys learn at home follow them to school and their other activities. How they interact with classmates, teammates, and teachers reflect what they live at home. If we want our young men to be polite and respectful outside the home, they must learn to be polite and respectful at home, not only to mom and dad but to brothers and sisters as well. "Please" and "thank you" are appreciated whether directed to a peer or an adult.

Teaching my sons to interact respectfully helps them to adjust socially. I do my sons no great service if I allow them to act and speak disrespectfully. No one likes to be around a bully, a braggart, a name caller, or a rude individual. Resorting to name calling, bullying, teasing, and bragging usually reflect low self-confidence and self-esteem whether in first grade or tenth grade. Setting high expectations of social skills when the boys are young reaps rewards for them and me. In addition, they learn not to tolerate this behavior in others.

During a junior year interview at the high school, Matt was asked if he had witnessed any bullying on campus. He answered yes and recounted an incident that happened during soccer tryouts. One of the less athletic boys was being unmercifully teased, to the point where the young man was ready to burst into tears. The counselor asked Matt how he handled the situation. Matt, his face turning beet red as he recalled the emotion at the time, said he yelled at the boys to "Cut it out." The counselor was surprised and wanted to know what followed, expecting to hear that the boys turned on Matt. Perplexed by her question, Matt matter-of-factly responded: "They cut it out!"

Socializing with girls requires this same level of respect in a relationship. (Additional thoughts on boy-girl relationships follow in a further chapter.) Joe exemplifies the standard for the boys in how he talks and treats me. Our sons learn what they live and see transpiring every day. That is why it is so important for me to expect to be treated and spoken to respectfully. It is also important that, while Joe sets an example, I also teach the boys appropriate etiquette and courtesy from table manners to opening or holding the door for another. When I taught school, I was aware from day one those students who had learned manners and common courtesy at home and those who hadn't. Respect, whether just a simple "please" or "thank you," communicates a lot.

Many teaching opportunities naturally present themselves. For example, we are at church and an elderly couple arrives late to standing room only. Out of respect, a couple of the boys will relinquish their seats to the elderly couple. One Easter, we were out of town and attended services with our son and daughter-in-law who was obviously expecting at the time. Although we arrived early, the church was already filled. Not one person, young or old, male or female, had the courtesy to let her sit down even after I asked one young father if he could hold his toddler so she could sit. I was appalled, especially being in church. The boys received a refresher course on the ride home on what to do in a similar situation. I remember the forty minute bus ride to my college job when I worked in the District of Columbia one summer. An older woman got on the packed bus. I waited for one of the gentlemen to surrender their seat, but it wasn't happening. I finally stood up to allow her to sit. Most men avoided eye contact after that, hiding behind newspapers or looking out the window. I have heard the equality argument, but I don't think any of these situations involve equality but, rather, respect and common courtesy. I think a few mothers would have been disappointed in their grown sons that morning.

Personalities Reflect Social Styles

Each of my sons has their own God-given personality. It is fascinating— same mom and dad yet ten unique personalities from day one. Their individual personalities play into their sociability. No one style fits each of the boys. Tony and Mark are more introverted and enjoy small groups of friends; they've never been known to be loud and boisterous. In fact, at Strake Jesuit the teachers thought Tony was the quietest of the boys until Mark attended. David, Chris, Joe Pat, Danny, and Timmy are more outgoing and adapt easily to most situations. Matt, Tommy, and Jamie are a little of both.

Accepting each son's personality is important in helping each of the boys develop socially and feel good about himself. I was extremely shy growing up (hard for the boys to believe today) and appreciate how intimidating attending a new school, launching into a new activity or sport, or making new friends can be. I understand that each one of them adjusts in his individual time frame. Some of the boys walked right into school on their first day without a fear in the world. A few of them had a harder time separating and being away all day. When Tony was in first grade, he felt left out of the at-home activities when he was the only one in school all day. That was one long year, for him and me. The next year was a little easier because both he and David were in the same boat. Some of the boys took longer to make friends while some made friends right off the bat. The different styles didn't mean they were maladjusted or socially inept. Unfortunately, society tends to define what is "best," and when someone doesn't fit the mold, they are labeled.

Allowing each of the boys to be who he is and mature individually has proven worthwhile. They don't feel they are inferior because they are more gregarious or more introverted. They are comfortable in who they are and in social situations, still within their individual styles. Tommy, who had a difficult time separating each morning through preschool and kindergarten, spent his junior year in college abroad, one semester in Managua, Nicaragua, and the other in Lima, Peru. He lived with two families and traveled throughout South America. If you knew him in his early years, you would not imagine him to be so adventurous.

One of Tony's high school state swim meets was held in El Paso, my husband's hometown. Joe's parents still lived in El Paso and attended the meet. Joe's eighty-year–old mother was the team's most energetic cheerleader. She stood at the edge of the pool exuberantly encouraging each Strake swimmer. She pressed Tony to join her poolside. While energetic cheering was her style, it was not Tony's way of supporting his teammates. He would have felt awkward following his grandmother's example.

I find there is a fine line between encouraging the boys socially and pushing them. I want the boys to have good friends and be comfortable in social situations. I want them to know how to shake hands firmly and look someone in the eye—a social skill that should be practiced from preschool on. When the boys are introduced to company at home, we use the opportunity to reinforce these skills. One by one the boys walk up to the guest, shake hands, and say their name. If it's the first time meeting the guest, they often provide their birth order number as well.

While I want the boys to be socially adept and well liked, I have not set being "popular" as a goal. I never mention popularity as one of the qualities or characteristics I want the boys to attain. I worry about parents who desire that for a child. Being popular has no reflection on his character or values, and, I believe, it puts pressure on a young man to be what he thinks others expect him to be instead of being his true self. He will tend to live up to societal values instead of familial values.

Friends

"A faithful friend is beyond price; no sum can balance his worth" (Sirach 6:15). A true friend helps you grow and move through the different phases of your life. A true friend is one who makes you a better person. A true friend encourages and motivates you to be the best that you can be.

I want true friends for my sons who will enrich their lives. Friends play a huge role in our sons' socialization—often in what they choose to do and choose not to do. That is why the choice of friends is of utmost importance, and sometimes one of the most difficult parts of their life to monitor.

I feel blessed many times over with the friends in my life. They laugh and cry with me during times of joy and sorrow and are there for me in the ups and downs of life. My best friends growing up were my sisters. I was fortunate as my family moved around the world to have my best friends move right along with me. I see the same close relationships develop with the boys. They are each other's best friends; they may be closer to one brother than another but overall they are all close-knit.

When Tony and David were in high school, they joined a volleyball league at our church. Tony played from the very beginning and David joined a few weeks into the season. During the week after David joined the team, the new youth director approached me to find out more about Tony's friend who had joined the team, unaware that they were brothers. He noticed how well they got along, laughing and having a great time together. When I told him they were brothers, he was shocked. He figured they were best friends—and, in fact, they are.

Matt's senior year in high school, he took Mark, a freshman, under his wings. He never hesitated to include him in after football game activities with his friends or take him to a school function. He encouraged him in his classes and his soccer. They bonded that year in a way I would not have imagined. When Matt left for college the next year, there was a definite void in Mark's life. The bond that developed in that one year continues today.

The relationship between Joe Pat and Timmy, thirteen years apart, is special as well. From the earliest days of Timmy's life, Joe Pat and he were inseparable. Timmy adored Joe Pat. Timmy took Joe Pat to preschool for show and tell wrapped in a sheet. He tucked Joe Pat's photo under his pillow each night after Joe Pat left for college. He wrote a touching essay about his favorite brother for a fourth grade assignment. And the love flowed both ways. Brother Casey, SJ, at Strake Jesuit recounts an afternoon soccer game when Timmy, playing on the sideline, fell. When Joe Pat heard his cry, he immediately stopped warming up and ran over to cuddle Timmy.

The boys coach a summer swim team together. The team started with Tony as head coach. Then David joined him as an assistant the following year. When Tony moved on, Chris teamed up with David, then Chris with Joe Pat, Joe Pat with Matt, and so on. This year, I appealed to David (Tommy and Danny were not returning home from college in time to coach) to coach again with Jamie as his assistant. Jamie learned not only swimming techniques from David but also positive approaches to encouraging and motivating the swimmers while still having fun. Over the years, many parents were surprised the coaches were brothers. One parent commented to me, "I've never seen brothers have so much fun working together." The boys are not just brothers but close friends.

Their brothers are not their only friends, of course. They made friends through mother's day out programs, preschool, school, Sunday school, sports, and other activities. They played with boys **and** girls. Their friends shared similar interests and activities. With the boys close in age, many friends were mutual friends of the boys. They went and did things together. Rob, for example, may be Tony's best friend but he and David also spend time together. Bryant is a friend to all the boys although he is closest in age to Chris. One recent Sunday he stopped by and spent the whole afternoon with Jamie, the only one home that day.

As I said earlier, the boys' friends influence many choices they make about what they do or don't do and what they accept as appropriate or inappropriate behavior. There is no denying the force peer pressure exacts on a young person's life. I want them to find friends that share our values and expectations. I often remind the boys: "If a friend leads you astray, is he really a friend? A true friend wants what's best for you." And this applies both ways. "Are you being a good friend, if you lead a friend astray?" There have been those times when Joe and I felt obligated to step in and reevaluate whether a friendship was a positive in our son's life. I think it is one of the most difficult situations to deal with. While you want to be supportive, at the same time the responsibility to assure our son's well-being takes precedence. Discouraging a friendship when a son is young is much easier because you have much more control of who they are with and where they are. As they enter the middle school and high school years and become more involved in activities outside the home and make new friends, often from families you do not know, the challenge becomes more daunting. These years require more diligence than ever before, especially with the societal influences that continue to evolve. I can attest that raising a son today demands more vigilance on my part than when raising my five older sons, especially with access to computers, cell phones, and cable television.

Getting to know the boys' friends when they were young and in preschool was easy. I knew most of the children in the class and their parents. The same held true from first through eighth grade. I volunteered in the schools, providing additional opportunities to become acquainted with students and parents. I am a strong believer in parents developing support systems. It's through talking and sharing that we learn from each other, during the toddler years or the teenage years. Having fellow parents know my feelings on different activities proves beneficial. Joe Pat and a friend decided they wanted to attend a dance that Joe and I had already vetoed. The boys were determined to go; they figured if Joe Pat spent the night with his friend, not mentioning to us they intended to go to the dance, Joe and I wouldn't know. His friend's mom was aware of our attitude on attending dances in sixth grade, so was surprised by the boys' plan. Confused, she called me. Needless to say, Joe Pat didn't attend the dance, and he didn't spend the night. Instead, his weekend was filled with "hard labor"—cleaning gutters, working in the yard—to remind him of the importance of trust and honesty.

I find the high school years much more challenging in getting to know the boys' friends and parents. The school draws from all over the Houston area so their friends live all over Houston. If their friends are involved in similar activities and sports, then parents usually meet during these times. But if they aren't involved in the same activities and live on the other side of town, the challenge grows. Making the effort pays out rich dividends: I get to know the boys' friends and in addition enrich my life with their parents' friendships. One wonderful blessing of being the mother of ten sons is my ever-widening circle of friends.

Appreciating the long-term effects of positive socialization for the boys encourages me in my day-to-day interactions with them. My efforts are rewarded when a teacher shares a story of Mark stopping to help a classmate pick up his dropped crayons; or a physical education teacher touched by Jamie's first choice of a teammate, not athletically gifted, when he was captain for the day; or Marilyn Smith's words of gratitude for the boys' ability to work with children of all ages and dispositions; or one of my daughters-in-law thanking me for my son. Studies show that the ability to socialize well trumps intelligence when determining success in all areas of our life.

Intellectual Development

Studies continue to show that boys' and girls' mental development differs. This becomes a touchy subject when "different" is interpreted as more intelligent or less intelligent. I believe the difference is in how knowledge is attained and processed rather than the ultimate level of intelligence. Again, studies show that the male and female brains are wired differently.

Watching my ten sons learn and develop has been fascinating. Yet each of the boys didn't follow the exact pattern or rate of learning or enjoy the same types of activities. To this day the boys' interests, strengths, and learning styles vary. Tony had a photographic memory. Joe Pat was methodical. Danny leaned toward detail. Matt lined up the little *Matchbox cars*. Tommy put puzzles together.

My boys tended to be hands on learners: building, mixing, creating, chalking, exploring, and experimenting—often making messes and taking risks. Bath time wasn't just about getting clean but about pouring water in and out of cups and over the side of the tub, splashing the water to make more soapsuds and watching the soap get slimy sitting in the water. Building towers, whether with cans from the pantry or wooden blocks, involved construction and destruction, usually quickly and rarely quietly. The homemade Play-Doh started out as four colors but ended up as one; the same with paint. Painting was usually more about creating designs than drawing an actual picture.

Language skills developed at different rates as well for the boys. My experience has been that those sons who were more rambunctious and physically active developed verbal skills later. The more active sons as toddlers were less likely to want to sit and read a book for any length of time. They needed to be in motion. Their vocabulary developed around their activities and our interactions.

I was fascinated, and still am, with the boys' problem solving skills. They usually see and solve a problem in a way I wouldn't have dreamed of. Joe is the same way. We may end up with the same solution but arrive at it differently.

I also think the boys get into mischief more often than not because of their thought processes—thinking about how to do this or that or what happens when he does this or that. His curiosity may lead him to try something I would never think of doing. He's not necessarily thinking through the consequences of his action. That is why, when I ask, "Why would you do such a thing?" he answers, "I don't know." He probably truly doesn't know.

Accepting their different learning styles and approaches allows each of the boys to develop at their own rate. Unfortunately, our schools provide for little leeway in this development but rely primarily on chronological age to determine grade level. As a first grade teacher I am extremely cognizant of the variance of intellectual, physical, and social development on the first day of school. Students with later birthdays, especially boys, usually (not always) lag behind in one area or another. Many times it is not being ready to face the structure of the typical classroom. Most preschools allow for flexibility of physical activity during the day. The typical elementary classroom does not, making it harder on physically active boys. Recesses are being cut back or eliminated completely in many school systems, intensifying the problem.

With two of the boys, Joe and I chose to wait a year before entering them into kindergarten. My philosophy is that school is twelve long years. If waiting a year will provide a more positive experience, then the learning that takes place will be more effective and enjoyable. If we accept that children walk and talk at different times, why is it so hard to appreciate that some of our children are ready to read and add at different times? Pushing a child into formal education before he is developmentally ready, academically or socially, sets him up for failure as soon as he walks through the classroom door.

Bridge classes have been established in many of the preschools in my area to meet the needs of students with late summer and early fall birthdays. The bridge classes provide an extra year of development before thrusting him into the structured classroom. Chris's birthday is late August. There was no question in my mind that the extra year in preschool would be beneficial. If he had been born two days later, the decision would have been made for me with the September 1st cut-off date for school admissions. Tommy has a late June birthday, but I also chose to wait the year for him. He needed the year to develop socially and feel more secure being in a non-home environment. Both decisions were made with the individual son's best interest in mind. I have no regrets with either decision.

Since I believe one of the greatest gifts we give our children is an appreciation and respect of knowledge, I devote another entire section on instilling a lifelong love of learning in our sons. My point in this section is to reinforce that the learning style of a son may differ from that of a daughter or yourself. Accepting and appreciating these differences enable our young sons to achieve to their fullest potential.

Another observation that concerns me is how many boys are diagnosed with ADHD and prescribed psychotropic medications. Recent studies indicate 10% of male students are diagnosed with ADHD. In addition, there is an increase in the number of children being diagnosed and medicated in preschool. I worry that parents and educators alike are too quick to identify an active boy as ADHD when in reality he may be just that an active boy or one who needs a little more structure or discipline. I worry that our educational programs are demanding unrealistic expectations of our children, academically and socially, at earlier and earlier stages of their development. Our children are in much more structured environments today at earlier ages than in years past.

I worry when a mom at a recent presentation shared that she wanted her first grade son to be more focused so he was on medication. She enrolled him in a very competitive school and, I believe, felt the pressure for him to achieve. I worry when the mom of a second grade boy continually makes excuses for incomplete homework assignments when he is capable of doing the work. Even when a child has been diagnosed with ADHD, he needs structure and discipline in his life. It is important to establish realistic expectations of him and follow through with appropriate consequences. I taught over fifty children in the years I taught. Only one student was diagnosed with ADHD and on medication, and he was diagnosed prior to entering the school. I had a couple of students with learning challenges, but I would not have classified them as ADHD. I know as moms we want the best for our children. Sometimes medication is what a child needs, and other times alternative approaches may be useful or maybe even a combination of both.

Boys are boys and our acceptance and appreciation of their God-given gifts enable them to grow and mature emotionally, physically, intellectually, and socially as the boys they are meant to be. I wouldn't want it any other way.

Chapter 4

Meeting the Needs of My Sons: To Be or Not To Be a Responsible Mother

We are what we repeatedly do. Excellence, then, is not an act but a habit.
–Aristotle

Be what you want your children to be and watch them grow.
—Leo Buscaglia

I will never forget the first weeks and months of Tony's life. I was exhausted. Not only was I exhausted from the pregnancy and labor and delivery, I was amazed at the commitment of energy and time required to meet his basic needs. I always wonder if someone had told me, at that point in time, that I would eventually be the mother of ten boys, if I would have chosen to go into a multi-year hibernation.

The reality is, though, that raising a child entails a major commitment on the mother's part from day one. It is not a nine-to-five commitment or a commitment made only when I'm in the mood or it's convenient. A child needs a mom day in and day out who appreciates the importance of being responsible.

Raising responsible sons begins with being a responsible mother. I just love it when someone infers by a condescending look or by a tacky comment that I am not a responsible mother because I have ten sons. I do not define responsible parenting by the number of children a parent has but, rather, by how a parent raises the children they do have, whether one, two, four, or ten. If responsible parenting was defined by the number of children we have, then we would have one of the most responsible societies that has ever existed with 1.9 children per family. Unfortunately, that is not the case.

A responsible mother meets the physical, emotional, intellectual, and spiritual **needs** of her children. I believe that is what God asks of us as mothers—how He will hold me accountable. Responsibly fulfilling these needs is a gift I give my sons. It entails choices—some difficult and others less so, such as what they eat for dinner or where they go to school. It more often than not entails placing my sons' needs before mine. What mother hasn't foregone much needed sleep to care for a newborn or for a sick child? That's just one simple example of choosing the child's needs over your own. Making these choices continues throughout the parenting years.

Physical Needs

Physical needs encompass eating, sleeping, physical activity, safety, acceptance of one's physical attributes, and sexuality. Some aspects of my sons' physical needs were similar, but each one was born with a unique body and nature. Although I was more experienced with each son's birth, I quickly learned that what may have worked or been appropriate for one of the boys wasn't necessarily appropriate or worked for another. I was kept on my toes; there was no room for complacency, even with Timmy.

Eating

I breast fed all ten sons for varying lengths of time. I was fortunate that most of the boys latched on right in the delivery room, and there was no stopping them after that. David, though, had a slow start due to some medical issues. I ended up pumping and then feeding him for about six weeks. The hand-held breast pumps in the mid 70s were primitive compared to the pumps my daughters-in-law use today. The time commitment became overwhelming, especially with Tony only a year old and Joe's hours extensive. I made the switch to formula; we both survived.

I knew that breastfeeding was good for the boys, but I wasn't prepared for the physical and emotional benefits it would provide me. I grew to appreciate that breastfeeding gave me the freedom to stop and take time with the baby. I didn't have to feel guilty for postponing other chores because I was the only one who could satisfy the baby's hunger. For me, breastfeeding offered time to be alone with the baby, not necessarily meaning no one else in the family was around—a near impossibility except at the late night and early morning feedings—but in the sense that the baby and I were together as one. I realized, with each son's birth and the additional responsibilities, how important it was to find one-on-one time with the baby. I know how easy it would have been to have used bottles and passed the feeding on to whoever was home at the time, whenever I was busy with someone or something else. What a blessing when Timmy came along that I could justify stopping whatever I was doing, sit for a few minutes, and feed and nurture him. The same, of course, can be replicated when feeding with bottles, but I know it would have taken a lot of discipline on my part to follow through.

I am a big proponent of breastfeeding, but at the same time a mother must determine what works best for her. Feeding time should be a time that allows you to **be** with your child. Whether you breastfeed or use formula does not define you as a good or bad mother or affect bonding with your child. You want it to be a peace-filled time.

From breastfeeding to solids, eating and meal times continue to be main events in our house. What the boys eat is much more important than how much they consume. With childhood obesity at epidemic levels, I make the difference in the boys' health by my choice of what they eat. A two year old, a six year old, or a ten year old does not buy the food he eats. It is up to me to make healthy choices for my sons. From an early age they ate fruits and vegetables: baby food first then to the real thing. I do not cook with a lot of salt, so the boys are not predisposed to salty food. (I begged off salt during my first pregnancy when I gained 7 pounds one month. Cutting out the salt and sugar made for a normal and steady weight gain the rest of the pregnancy. I never went back to cooking with salt or putting a saltshaker on the table.) I also watch the amount of sugar in their diets. When they were young, they rarely ate sugarcoated cereals or store-bought cookies. I didn't buy them, so they weren't in the house for them to even choose from. I convinced them that fruit was God's candy—a natural sweet. When Timmy was in preschool, he had a friend over to play. For a snack I gave them grapes. His friend looked at the grapes and told Timmy he didn't eat those things. Timmy was surprised: "You don't like God's candy?" The word "candy" prompted his friend to try them, and he liked them.

I am often asked if I fix different foods for the boys at night to accommodate their individual likes and dislikes. I decided early on that I would not be a short order cook. For breakfast, the boys chose from the various cereals that I had available. But if I made French toast, pancakes, or eggs, then that was the breakfast of the day. There were some choices for lunch, depending on what was prepared. But dinner was whatever I prepared that evening. If dinner wasn't to a son's liking one night he could hope for something more delectable the next. I think not catering to their individual likes and dislikes made a difference in their eating habits. I knew too many mothers who fixed three different meals each night, sometimes even fixing hot dogs every night because that is what the son wanted. Caving in to a son's whining or demands when the choice is not in his best interest is not being responsible. I assure you that none of my sons starved.

Danny was one of my pickier eaters early on. He would often look at the food on his plate and make a grimacing face conveying: "You really don't expect me to eat this?" And he wouldn't eat much of it, to the delight of an older brother who gladly finished off Danny's plate as well as his own. I rarely had leftovers. Danny, then, would wake up in the morning and eat a couple bowls of cereal, usually oatmeal, and some toast. He is no longer a picky eater and remains, like his brothers, a bottomless pit.

Boys are bottomless pits. Coming from a family of girls, I am amazed at the amount of food the boys can eat in one day. I'm sure my food bills over the years rivaled the cost of weddings for my sisters and me. When all the boys were home, they drank five to six gallons of milk a day. They ate three pounds of meatballs and three pounds of spaghetti. French toast entailed two loaves of bread and me getting up an hour early to prepare it. We went though peanut butter by the jarfuls each week. Bananas disappeared almost immediately on arrival from the grocery store, especially when Tommy was around. They could eat a full meal at six o'clock, turn around a couple hours later and have a "snack"—snack defined as equal to a meal, just not eaten at meal time. That's after having a "snack" at four o'clock when they arrived home from school. I gradually bought bigger pots to accommodate the increasing portions of spaghetti and soups required to feed the gang.

I didn't worry about whether the boys ate enough fruit and vegetables each day. I tended to follow their eating habits over the course of the week. That is a better judge of their nutritional intake. I also don't give up on a food when they reject it the first time. Sometimes preparing it a little differently will prove more appealing. For example, cauliflower with melted cheddar cheese proved edible over plain cauliflower. Tastes change over the years as well, so I continually reintroduce foods.

What you don't want happening is for meal times to become times of friction or for food to become a big issue, a bargaining point, or a reward. Meal times are times to nourish the body, mind, and soul. It is not just a time to feed the body but also a time to interact as a family while thanking God for the blessings on the table as well as the other blessings in life. Even if one of the boys wasn't eating what was placed before him, he was required to sit at the dinner table until everyone had finished eating. If a child is not eating much at meal times, especially when they are young, watch what he is eating between meals. Maybe those cookies or glass of juice at four o'clock curbed his appetite.

Fast food and prepared foods are major contributors to the obesity epidemic. Fast foods and prepared foods tend to be high in sodium, fat, and calories. The documentary *Super Size Me* convinced my older sons of the negative impact fast food has on the body. In addition, the boys participate in sports and are learning the benefits of a healthy diet on competing. At an early age, though, I am the one who determines their diet. I remember the first grader finishing his Coke and potato chips one morning when I was opening car doors in the carpool line at school. Not a healthy start to his day. I **choose** to restrict the potato chips, soft drinks, cookies, or pizzas not to be mean but because I love them and want them to remain healthy in the long term.

Sleeping

Sleeping through the night—a parent's dream from day one. I love the quote: "The joy of motherhood—what a mother experiences when all the children are finally in bed." We shouldn't feel guilty when we sigh with relief that our children are asleep—we mothers earn that joy.

Sleeping issues are a primary source of frustration for many parents. My sons began to sleep through the night from three months to six months. They were all early risers, so sleeping through the night for us meant until around six o'clock in the morning. Even after they slept through the night on a regular basis, there were many nights when they still woke up, maybe with an earache, fever, or due to a developmental milestone. When a son was able to pull himself up or began to walk, he would often wake up in the middle of the night wanting to "practice" his new skill. Shortly after Matthew was born, I was nursing him in my bed when thunder shook the house. A few minutes later, we were joined by Tony, David, Chris, and Joe Pat. Joe and I looked at each other and laughed—just what we wanted, a slumber party at three o'clock in the morning.

Adequate sleep is essential for healthy development. There is a point in time when the child needs to sleep through the night for his own well being. He will respond differently to life experiences when rested. When I've had enough sleep, I am more cheerful, attuned to the needs around me, and react more positively. My sons are no different. I am convinced that many discipline problems we face as parents are due to the inadequate sleep of our children. A three year old who has had a nap during the day is going to be a much more pleasant three year old at four o'clock in the afternoon. A toddler who has slept through the night will be better prepared to face the day.

The boys had quiet time or a nap every day until kindergarten. They needed it and I needed it. Even during the summers I implemented quiet time. The older boys read or played quiet games in their rooms while the younger boys slept. Our routine was simple: we ate lunch and then had quiet time. Moms tell me that their children don't want to rest. It isn't about what they want but, rather, about what they need. Of course, I had the son or two who challenged the routine by not wanting to rest, but I remained firm in my conviction that we all needed the quiet time. A child may give up the nap at three years old, but they still need time to unwind and rest—that's why I call it quiet time and not naptime. Naptime implies sleeping whereas quiet time implies just that.

Sleep needs differed from son to son. Tony required less sleep than David. Joe Pat required silence while Chris slept through anything. Matt fell asleep almost immediately upon his head hitting the pillow. Joe Pat went through what we called his last hurrah—crying a couple of minutes before crashing for the night. I had to figure out each son's sleep pattern and needs and then determine how to merge his needs with the routine already in place.

I found having a bedtime routine helped the boys unwind and ready themselves for the night. Before the boys were in school and sports, the routine rarely varied: we had dinner, the boys played for a while, baths were given, teeth brushed, stories read, prayers recited, and by eight o'clock they were in bed. Since they shared rooms, the boys usually talked for a while before one fell off to sleep. As long as the interactions were reasonable, Joe and I allowed the boys this time. The routine was adapted as the boys entered school and homework and sports entered the picture. Bedtimes were extended as well.

I found it a challenge at times to determine when to move one son in with another. This is less and less an issue than it used to be with most families comprised of only a couple of children. Most children never share a room with anyone until they head to college. At Seattle University during a parent orientation session, a mom expressed concern because her daughter's roommate had arrived first and monopolized the entire room. The roommate did not feel obligated to move her things. The dean then asked the five hundred parents in attendance how many of their children had **never** shared a room. Almost the entire room stood up. He would have been wiser to ask how many students had shared a room, because there were only a handful. In our home, the boys share rooms. Jamie and

Timmy still share a room, even though there are four other bedrooms available. Tony and David were already sharing a room when Chris was born. Chris and Joe Pat made the transition fairly easily. Moving Timmy in with Jamie took a few tries; Timmy's excitement at being with his brother kept Jamie from falling asleep.

As an aside, there are advantages to the boys sharing rooms. They learn to work with each other, adapt to different approaches, and share space. I recommend it, even if you have enough bedrooms for each child to have his own room.

Sleep patterns and the amount of required sleep changes with the different stages of a child's life. A toddler will sleep more hours than a ten year old. A teenager tends to go to sleep later but then sleeps longer in the morning, at least on non-school days. They need the sleep in the teenage years. When the boys do not have a commitment on a weekend or non-school day, Joe and I allow the boys to sleep in. If they choose to sleep later, the boys know that they must still fulfill their responsibilities. I also believe that some of us are morning people and some of us are night people. Determining which your son is proves helpful. My main goal was to assure that the boys had adequate sleep for whichever phase they were in. I reap the benefits in better behaved sons. Teachers teach more attentive students. Coaches train more alert athletes. Life is just easier.

Physical Activity

Boys are motion extraordinaire. They need to be active. They need to climb, jump, slide, run, crawl, build, skip, wiggle, and squirm. My role is to provide the environment that allows them to do just that.

The mother of a boy must, I emphasize **must**, appreciate his need to be in relatively constant motion. Physical activity provides an outlet for their energy levels and emotions. Whether at home or in day-care, a boy needs to have toys that recognize these needs: tyke bikes, balls, big trucks, building blocks, etc. He needs space to run and jump and be a boy. When Tony and David were little, the duplex we lived in was not exceptionally big. I made use of the space I had for Tony to crawl around and play with his toys. One of the best purchases I made over the years was a wooden slide. It had four steps up, an enclosed area underneath, and a short slide. Tony took advantage of all the facets of the slide. He climbed up the stairs and slid down, crawled underneath the slide playing peek-a-boo at times, raced cars, trucks, and balls down the slide, and even learned to crawl up the slide. The slide often kept him busy when David needed to be fed or cared for. As they got a little older, they would use it to make a fort or play with their stuffed animals on it. Every one of the boys benefited from the slide. It could be used rain or shine, all day long—but it provided a simple physical outlet for their energy.

The duplex had a small porch with steps on two sides. Tony loved going up and down and around on those steps. It kept me busy following right behind him, a growing challenge as my pregnancy with David progressed. We walked to the park at the end of the block where he could run and climb some more. We played with balls, went swimming, and explored the neighborhood. He slept well at naptime and at the end of the day—another benefit of physical activity.

The need for physical activity continues through each stage of the boys' development. The swing set in our backyard was another great purchase. One side of the set had a climbing apparatus and a fireman's pole down the middle. The boys played every game under the sun around the set. They made forts, played pirates, and made up game after game. They never seemed to tire of playing in the backyard.

The boys had tyke bikes, big wheels, and eventually graduated to tricycles and bicycles. I trained ten sons to ride a bike, running alongside each of them, holding on to the seat to provide needed stability, and picking up bruised bodies (sometimes mine) and egos off the sidewalk. (And people want to know how I stay slim.) While some of the boys learned quickly, a few had a harder time staying balanced and on track. But riding a bike is a skill that once learned stays with you forever. Every child should know how to ride a bike. Maybe that's one reason I love the programs that provide bikes to children in the community. I remember the fun and freedom a bicycle provided me growing up. The boys rode their bikes to school when they attended a school close to home. They rode their bikes up to the baseball card store to check out available cards. Jamie and Timmy could ride their bikes to both Matt's and David's houses when a car was not available.

The boys began organized sports around kindergarten or first grade. The older boys played sports in rotation: soccer in the fall, basketball for a church league in the winter, baseball at the YMCA in the spring, and swam on a neighborhood swim team in the summer. The younger boys chose to play soccer year round as that became more available. They also swam on our neighborhood swim team; their older brothers were the coaches and that's what we did for the month of June. The boys needed the physical outlet that sports provide. Even with the organized sports, the boys still played outside.

For many years, the front yard was more of a dirt pile than a well-manicured lawn. I remember the day someone asked me if the yard had a fungus that destroyed the grass. The "fungus" was actually the boys playing on it continuously—a small price to pay in my eyes. As one older dad in my neighborhood wisely advised me: "Be more concerned with growing kids right now than with growing grass." I have grass again in the yard with the boys older, but I miss all the bodies running, sliding, and having a great time together. When the boys are all home, I get to relive those days as they are still inventing new games to play in the yard.

I did not allow the boys to sit around and watch television all morning or afternoon. With computers and electronic games increasingly becoming the "toy" and activity of choice for most of our children, the challenge to move them outdoors or into another physical activity increases. Even with the advent of computers and other stationary games, I **expected** them to go outside and play. It was a given. At the same time, they **wanted** to go outside and play. They raced up and down the sidewalk on their big wheels, kicked the soccer ball around, and shot baskets on the portable hoop that Joe set up by the driveway. The older boys taught the younger boys different games, including them in most of the activities. During the summer, we headed to the neighborhood pool once morning chores were completed or after quiet time in the afternoons.

They learned the difference between healthy competition and unhealthy competition—playing for fun, a novel concept in our increasingly competitive world. In our first book, *Good Families Don't Just Happen*, David and Tony wrote: "As we've grown older, we've learned that when playing sports, especially with our brothers, our goal isn't winning or losing, but having a good time. Now in our friendly soccer games at the neighborhood field, we have an unwritten rule: We never keep score. The games are still competitive, but they always remain fun, because it doesn't matter whether or not the last goal counts or who wins or loses."

Unfortunately, in my eyes, I think organized sports have become too organized and too competitive. The idea of playing for fun is slowly becoming a thing of the past. If a young person wants to stay competitive, he is expected to practice three or more nights a week, attend games every weekend, and compete in tournaments throughout the season. While trainers and coaches talk about developing age-appropriate skills, more and more the emphasis is on developing the player to compete at higher levels, dangling the possibility of playing in college, being the next pro athlete, or an Olympian. The commitment demanded becomes all encompassing at too young an age. This is from a mother's perspective. I enjoy sports and know the value of team involvement and the physical outlet sports provide. At the same time, I am witnessing the negatives of this increased emphasis on higher and higher levels of competition. I have watched the change evolve over the years and strive to find a balance in my family. At times I feel the balance is not shifting in my favor.

While I provide physical outlets for the boys' energy at home, I depend on the schools to meet their needs during the school day. Recess is essential! Physical education is essential! The boys need to run around for a few minutes at different intervals during the school day. A power walk can be the best thing a teacher can do for a restless class. Not only is a power walk an opportunity to release some of that built up energy, the exercise increases oxygen to the brain. As the mother of boys, I monitored the amount of time the boys spent in motion, and moving from class to class didn't count.

Safety Issues

Another responsibility I have in meeting my sons' physical needs is to assure they remain physically safe. The concept seems simple and straightforward enough but following through requires a conscious choice on my part.

Each son came home from the hospital in a car seat. When Tony was born in the mid 70s, Joe had to buy the car seat at the dealership. The car seats available then would not meet the standards of today. The requirements keep changing and being refined as new technology is developed and crash tests performed. I was impressed and pleased to see that the hospital required my daughter-in-law, Rita, to partake in a car seat safety check before they dismissed our grandson, Matías, from the hospital.

Appropriate car seats at each age are a must, as well as assuring each person in the car wears a seat belt. It drives me crazy when I'm driving around Houston and witness a toddler not in a car seat or even belted in. A minor fender bender, not to mention a major accident, could change the child's life and the family's life for years to come. I didn't spend all that time belting all the boys in because it was easy. I did it because I love them and didn't want anything to happen to them. When we had five of the boys under the age of six, I carefully planned any trip in the car—whether across town or across the country—because traveling anywhere was a major commitment just getting them all belted in the car.

When Tony and David were in high school, they had a car accident in which the Suburban flipped and landed upside down. The boys and two other young people in the car were uninjured. The emergency medical technicians who arrived on the scene were amazed that all four of the teenagers were wearing seatbelts. The young woman in the car later lamented to her mom, " Why do I always learn the hard way? I don't usually wear a seat belt, but Tony asked all of us to put our belts on when we left Astroworld." The EMT's were convinced wearing seat belts had protected them from serious injury.

When I drove carpools to school, games, or other activities, I insisted everyone wear a seat belt. I teased that the GP cars didn't run unless all the seat belts were clicked. Inevitably I heard a few more clicks. The boys used to give my dad a hard time when he didn't put his seat belt on. The same rule applied: The car didn't run unless all the seat belts were clicked. Wearing seat belts becomes a habit. Because our sons have always worn them, they accept the practice as part of riding in a car.

Along the same lines, Joe and I expect the boys to wear protective gear when riding a bike or in-line skating. With all the information on head injuries that could be avoided by wearing protective equipment, I can't imagine why a loving parent would allow her children to ride a bike or go skating unprotected. Setting a good example is important, too. If I expect the boys to wear protective gear, I must do the same, signifying to them safety is important at all ages. So when I am biking, I wear a helmet, even in hot and humid Houston.

Water safety is another area of concern, especially living in an area where water sports are plentiful. The boys learned to swim at an early age. But water safety also entails being careful with a child in the bathtub and around other water sources at home: the toilet or buckets of water used for cleaning. And boys love water—anywhere and anytime. Give them a puddle and they will walk through it, not around it.

In spite of safety precautions, we have made many trips to the emergency room or doctor's offices for one injury or another. The boys play hard, and injuries happen—at all ages. We've had our share of stitches, broken bones, muscle pulls, dislocated body parts, and head injuries. Teaching first grade prepared me a little for the myriad injuries possible and that head wounds bleed profusely. For someone who had no desire to go into the medical field, I was thrown into "nursing" by way of being the mother of boys. Although I'm always saying, "Be careful" and mean it, I wouldn't prevent them from being active to avoid injury. Boys (and our husbands) take risks that I would never take. I believe it is in their nature. Does it scare me? It scares me to death at times, but it comes with the territory.

Medical Needs

I am a person who believes that prevention is the best medicine. The boys visit the pediatrician for annual check-ups and the dentist twice a year through college. Of course, we visited the pediatrician more often than once a year. The boys are healthy but not immune from every thing floating around the community. In fact, one of the biggest challenges of a big family is that viruses go right through the family. So when one got sick, I could usually count on a few more catching the bug. I most dreaded when one of the older boys got sick because I knew I had a long run in front of me. When a younger son got sick, often it was with a virus that the older boys had already endured so they were immune, and I only had five sons to nurse back to health.

One of my worst memories involved chicken pox. The day I was due with Mark I received a call from the school. The secretary teased that the staff had pulled straws to determine who would call me, not a good sign. They knew I was due any day with our sixth child. She informed me that they thought Tony had chicken pox. She was right. I spent the last week of the pregnancy nursing Tony through the chicken pox. He was only the beginning. For the next six weeks, I nursed Chris, Joe Pat, Matt and, finally, David through the ordeal while caring for a newborn. Fortunately, Mark received immunity from me since he was breastfeeding, for the time being anyway. Six months later, Mark had shingles. I experienced a second round of chicken pox with the younger four boys. Aren't I lucky?

I also found it interesting that each of the boys has a different pain threshold. I cringed when a few of them got sick because I knew it would be a tougher few days. They were "needier"—no names mentioned here. But like everything else, each one had individual needs that required individual attention.

The annual check-ups included information on growth patterns and developmental progress, as well as the appropriate immunizations. Our pediatricians provided me with useful parenting tips and advice over the years. Dr. Plessala provided me with up-to-date information on the pros and cons of circumcision before the birth of Tony. They are, and continue to be, an excellent resource for physical, emotional, and intellectual developmental milestones. I appreciated Dr. Curtis taking the time to talk to them about sex or remind them of the responsibilities entailed upon obtaining a driver's license. (Although my family has been with the same practice for thirty-two years, we're on our fifth pediatrician. That's what happens when you have sons that span eighteen years. With Timmy fourteen years old, I anticipate seven more years with the group.)

In addition, the boys' doctors diagnosed a thyroid condition in one of the boys and a heart condition in another. They referred us to subspecialists when needed. They were there for us in emergencies. One of our more memorable emergency stories involved Joe Pat and the battery. While eating dinner one Sunday evening, Joe Pat, then three years old, blurted, "I almost choked today." "What do you mean you almost choked?" I asked. "A battery was in my mouth," responded Joe Pat. "What battery—and where is the battery now?" I quizzed him. "In my tummy!" Joe Pat answered, explaining, in his words, that it was a small, nickel-sized cadmium battery from a hand-held game. Joe and I glanced at each other, and I proceeded to call Poison Control (an essential phone number to have handy in a home with children, especially ten boys). The kind soul on the other end of the line, in as calm a tone as he could muster, said, "Ma'am, call your doctor and get to the nearest emergency room immediately."

What was supposed to be a relaxing evening was spent in the emergency room taking X-rays of Joe Pat's "electrified" stomach. When Joe Pat found out he would get to see his buddy, Dr. Curtis, and lots of ambulances, he was thrilled. Dr. Curtis assured us, after viewing the X-ray, that yes, a battery had been swallowed.

Each morning at 7 A.M., until the battery passed through his system, Joe drove Joe Pat to the hospital to check the status of the battery. Although it was extremely inconvenient, we counted our blessings, because the recommended procedure not too long before had been to remove the battery through abdominal surgery. The incident still lives on for Joe Pat when he is teasingly reminded: "Had your battery charged lately?" "Is your charge low?" or "Joe Pat can take a lickin' and keep on tickin.'"

Physical Attributes

I continue to emphasize the individuality of each of my sons. Nowhere is that more evident than in their physical attributes. Ten sons and no two are exactly alike, although they resemble each other. A few of the boys have curly hair, a few have straight hair. A few have light complexions reflected in their Irish and Spanish heritage, and a few have darker skin coloring inherited from the Italian and Mexican sides of the family. Matt is over six feet tall but the other boys range in height from 5'7" to 5'11". They all have brown eyes, although some are deeper browns and others lighter shades. The point I am making is that even with the same mother and father each of our sons has been created differently. If God wanted them to be exactly alike, He would have created them exactly alike.

We live in a society that puts excessive emphasis on our physical characteristics. We are judged by our height, weight, the color of our skin, beauty, sexual appeal, and athleticism. We are deemed inferior if we are lacking in any of these areas.

My responsibility is to help each of the boys to appreciate that there are some things we can change about ourselves and there are some things that we cannot change. I am only a little over five feet tall. Nothing I do will stretch me to 5'6" or 5'8", so why worry about it. Their father is also small in stature. If Joe were given four or five more inches, twenty-five more pounds, and rippling muscles, the increased height and bulk would not make him a better husband, a better father, or a better physician.

Having grown up in a family of girls, I understood the role outward physical characteristics played in a young girl's self-esteem. Until I became the mother of boys, I did not realize that our young men also are impacted by this "need" to meet societal standards of physical perfection albeit the criteria are different.

Even when the boys were toddlers, mothers were comparing the physical size and agility of their sons, as if being a higher percentage on the growth chart made them superior in some way. I couldn't believe the comments made about my own sons by other moms, often in front of the boys. "Oh, my gosh, Danny is taller than Tommy," as if we hadn't noticed. In response to ridiculous comments like that, I usually calmly answered, "If God had wanted Tommy to be taller, He would have made him taller. He's a great kid just the way he is!" Comparisons begin so early. My simple advice: Don't get caught up in comparing your children, within your own family or with other children, on any level. It serves no purpose.

As the boys entered school, I continued to be amazed at the role athleticism (and competitiveness) played in who was accepted and who wasn't. Joe wanted the boys to each have a sport that would carry them through high school because he knew, from his own experience, the role athletics played in a young man's life. I had a hard time understanding this emphasis at first, and in some ways still do; I valued physical activity from a different perspective. When I played outside with the boys when they were little, whether riding bikes, kicking the ball around, swimming, or playing tee-ball, I was not preparing them to play a sport. I wanted them to enjoy playing and being outdoors—period!

The craziness continues because then the issue becomes which sport is manlier. The more contact the sport engenders, the manlier it supposedly rates. I find that approach such a narrow and inane way of thinking. Each sport requires different skills and, often, body type. Michael Phelps was gifted with unique physical characteristics that, along with his competitive spirit, provided him an edge in swimming. The results may not have been the same if he had competed in gymnastics. Soccer requires different skills than football and golf. Height plays an important role in basketball. I haven't noticed a 200 pounder running on the cross country team since the boys have been at the high school, yet the team has won numerous state titles over the years.

Like so many areas of our sons' lives, they need to find their niche, a sport that they enjoy. Mom (and dad) needs to be supportive of the son's choice, even when we would prefer a different choice. Tony, our oldest son, asked in fourth grade if he could swim year round instead of playing soccer and baseball. He enjoyed swimming and found success within the sport. In high school, he swam and played water polo. He continued to swim for St. Louis University. The other boys enjoyed soccer, Chris and Joe Pat playing in college. The other boys chose to participate in intramural sports during their college years.

If a son would choose to participate in non-sport related activities such as music or debate, I would support that as well. It means finding a different physical outlet for him, especially in the younger years. Playing outside or riding a bike just for fun is a physical outlet. It does not need to be an organized sport to qualify as physical activity. Providing an outlet for all the boys' energy was my focus and goal.

When Matt was in third grade, his teacher, Jane Cassidy, commented on how Matt released his pent up energy at recess. He would be quiet and attentive during class but then play his heart out when he had the chance. He needed this outlet, as do all our sons, at home and at school.

I also observe the restlessness in the boys when they are injured and unable to partake in physical activities. They are testier, moodier, and tend to pick at their brothers more than usual. Exercise is a healthy way to release all the pent up energy and emotion a boy faces each day.

Sexuality

From an early age, I want the boys to appreciate and respect their sexuality. I want them to learn appropriate terminology for body parts and functions. I remember one of the boys' teachers, who was responsible for teaching the section on family life, struggling to say penis and sex. Not a positive sign that she was comfortable teaching the subject.

An appreciation of their sexuality is a gradual process, learned as they mature physically and emotionally. The three-year-old son might wonder and ask why I don't have a penis, even feeling sorry for me because I don't. Or he may wonder why I have breasts to feed the baby and daddy doesn't. He's learning that I am physically different from him. A desire for privacy in taking a bath came at different ages for the boys. I innately sensed when it was time to step back, respecting each son's individual needs. At the same time, they learned to respect my privacy and knock before entering my room or bathroom.

The boys did things that I would never have dreamed of coming from a family of girls. I was flabbergasted the morning I walked outside to witness Tony and David, two and three years old at the time, having a "peeing" contest from the swing set. They thought it was great fun. Joe assured me that this was normal male behavior. Okay! That wasn't the last contest I witnessed over the years.

A friend shared a story of her mother babysitting her son one day. She kept asking him if he needed to go to the bathroom because he was fooling with his penis. After the fourth time, he indignantly told his grandmother, the mother of girls, that he just needed to fix his crooked penis. Some things we moms learn through day-to-day experiences.

I felt fortunate that our sons' school taught family life in religion class. The program is taught in conjunction with parents. Parent books are sent home prior to the classes so a parent may review the content. A parent may opt her child out of the class, if so desired. Each lesson is read and discussed at home first, providing Joe and me the opportunity to delve more deeply where needed. I found the program and curriculum age appropriate and allowed an easy way for us to discuss the physical and emotional changes he was experiencing. Some of the boys asked questions, and some did not.

The older boys grew to appreciate what a woman experiences during a pregnancy, from mood changes to body changes. They learned a lot in the school of life, an insight that I know will be helpful when their own wives are pregnant, or another woman, as one pregnant teacher shared with me on a morning when she was feeling exceptionally nauseated. Chris obviously recognized the look because he walked up to her before class started and asked if there was anything he could do to help her. She appreciated his concern.

Unlike my sons, most teenagers do not have mothers who are pregnant. I believe, though, that young men are curious about a pregnancy but are uncomfortable asking. At a swim meet when I was about eight months pregnant with Tommy, a swimmer on Tony's team asked a simple question about how it felt when the baby moved. That one question opened the door to more questions by other swimmers. They asked excellent questions about labor and delivery, intent on hearing my answers. I didn't talk down to them but answered in a way they could understand, remembering all too well my learning process with my first pregnancy. It was definitely an unplanned but an incredible teaching moment. Later, a few moms asked if I had been uncomfortable with the boys bombarding me with questions. I realized I wasn't at all because it was a true learning experience without any disrespectful tone on the part of the boys. They really wanted to know.

Another issue to discuss with your sons regards inappropriate sexual contact, never allowing anyone to touch them in private areas. The challenge is to discuss this topic in a way that does not cause unnecessary fear, especially in the younger years.

Sexuality is an uncomfortable subject for many of us to discuss. In a later chapter, I delve more deeply into the sexual pressures and challenges that face our sons.

Intellectual Needs

One of the greatest gifts I give my sons is an appreciation and respect for knowledge. When you have knowledge, it is yours forever—nobody can take it away. My goal is to instill a lifelong love of learning in the boys.

The Early Years

Lifelong learning begins from day one of a child's life. We, the parents, are the first educators of our children. An education degree is not required or needed to teach them. It is my total interaction with the boys as they experience their daily lives that creates this love of learning. Because learning begins long before a child enters school, a parent's role in the learning process is vital and fundamental.

An article "Rethinking the Brain" published by the Families and Work Institute, states: "New insights into early development point to one key conclusion: the experiences children have and the attachments they form in the first three years of life have a decisive, irrefutable impact on their later development and learning."

From the beginning our sons learned from using their senses: hearing, touch, smell, sight, and taste. In newborns, all the senses are activated; they need us to stimulate them. "A great deal of new research leads to this conclusion: how humans develop and learn depends critically and continually on the interplay between nature (an individual's genetic endowment) and nurture (the nutrition, surroundings, care, stimulation, and teaching that are provided or withheld). Both are crucial." (Rethinking the Brain)

Using the senses, I began each son's learning process. My touch, whether gentle or rough, conveyed to each son my feelings towards him. The cuddling and holding stimulated him and let him know he was loved. With my belief in the importance of touch, my younger sons have truly been blessed, because their older brothers, in addition to Joe and me, held and rocked them endlessly.

Touch and physical contact should not stop at a certain age. The hugs and kisses Joe and I continue to bestow on the boys reflect our love for them and foster an unspoken sense of security. Being loved and feeling secure has a positive effect on learning and development. Fortunately, both Joe and I grew up in families where physical expressions of love were acceptable. The boys are comfortable with the hugs between each other and us, whether it's been a day since they saw each other or months. When Tony would come over for dinner during his medical school years, his brothers welcomed him home as if he had been away an entire semester.

From the moment of birth, a newborn also learns from what he hears. Your voice teaches him about his world. The age-old practice of singing lullabies soothes a restless child and often relaxes a restless mom as well. I have always been amazed at how quickly a baby recognizes his mother's voice. This used to frustrate the older boys when I entered the room while they were holding their baby brother. As soon as the baby heard my voice, he wanted me.

Talking to the boys from the earliest moments set in motion the important wheels of language development. It is through the repetitive hearing of words that children master language. Children usually understand the meaning of words long before they are able to speak them. I learned to take advantage of every opportunity to "talk" with my sons. When I nursed the baby, I talked to him, even though I knew he didn't understand one word I was saying. If I read a story to one of the boys while I was nursing, the baby heard my voice and language. I often wonder if Tony acquired his strong command of language because I read out loud to him—*Time, National Geographic*, and novels—while I rocked him. Looking back, not having a baby swing at the time was a blessing because I spent extra time holding and reading to Tony.

The opportunities to speak to our children are endless. I took advantage of every moment: during the baby's bath, when he nursed, while he sat in his infant seat and I prepared dinner or folded clothes, and especially during the never-ending diaper changes. I sang songs, nursery rhymes, and the ABC's, counted, and told stories. The baby didn't have to comprehend the words I was saying for the time to be meaningful and stimulating. My son's response—the smile, the giggle—rewarded me time and time again, just as my responses and interactions encouraged and motivated him.

Music is another wonderful avenue to develop a baby's hearing and language. I love music, so some kind of music was usually heard around the house. I played *Raffi* cassettes (no CD's back then) and other children's music in the car. The younger boys spent a lot of time in the car carpooling their older brothers to school and games. The music made the time more fun, and the repetitive tunes and words helped develop their memory, just as counting and singing did during diaper time.

Joe and I spoke to the boys using normal vocabulary, not baby talk. We used correct terminology and sentence structure. Children learn to understand and speak the words they hear on a regular basis, and their vocabulary will reflect that. If we never speak to our children above the first grade level, how can we expect them to speak above that level? Children usually don't realize a word is too difficult for them to speak. We adults are the ones who assume they can't say a word. The whole family was amazed at times at the vocabulary that Jamie and Timmy used. They were repeating words they heard from all of us.

I experienced a similar experience when I taught first grade. It was February and the class was making valentines. I realized the students thought their hearts were shaped like a Valentine's Day heart. Taking advantage of the opportunity, I contacted the American Heart Association and obtained some wonderful materials appropriate for first graders: a model of the heart and hands-on materials for the children to manipulate. My students became fascinated with the circulatory system, and I was fascinated at how quickly they grasped the concepts and appropriate terminology. They weren't intimidated by the unfamiliar words:

circulation, arteries, veins, and valves. The experience reinforced for me how young children absorb knowledge like a sponge—we provide the information and they soak it up.

I didn't look at learning as a structured time in the day. Learning happened as we scurried through the day. When I attended Loyola University New Orleans, Mrs. Egan's favorite phrase in a child psychology course was "Bombard the environment"—provide stimulating surroundings for your children, constantly expanding the environment with new stimuli as they develop.

I hung a colorful mobile over the baby's crib, played soft music, and situated bright-colored toys and pictures where the baby could see them. My favorite toy was a red plastic apple with a smile-face that wobbled and rattled when it was touched. I have a photo of each of the boys trying to mouth the apple, an inexpensive toy that stood the test of time. Now my grandchildren are enjoying this same happy apple.

The boys didn't need expensive toys to play with. They had fun banging on the kitchen pans, putting the metal juice tops in and out of a plastic bowl, and stacking small cans or boxes—all items readily available in a home.

I looked for toys that would develop their mental and physical skills. Push toys and pull toys are great for toddlers. Shape sorters, puzzles, and blocks develop spatial relationships and can be played alone or with others. I made Play-Doh rather than buy it (see the recipe at the book of this book)—it is softer and more pliable, making it easier for small fingers to manipulate. Using cookie cutters and other small kitchen utensils, the boys created an assortment of items.

I kept art supplies readily available, enabling the boys to artistically "express" themselves while developing fine motor skills. I supervised the younger boys' use of non-toxic markers and glue. (I prefer markers to crayons at first because a child can draw using less pressure and see immediate results.) Finger painting and water coloring are other creative activities. Mixing the different colors together taught the boys how colors are formed. Gluing pieces of colored paper or small items together and pouring rice in and out of a dump truck enthralled the boys. They enjoyed chalking or designing with shaving cream on the sidewalks—the Garcia-Prats's sidewalks were spectacularly decorated year round. Keeping these times unstructured allowed the creative juices to flow. I framed and hung their works of art; one bedroom wall and hallway are still covered with the boys' art.

I also took advantage of the learning opportunities provided outdoors. The outdoors is a classroom unto itself, and the boys loved being outdoors. We observed ants crawling along the sidewalk, collected and counted acorns, watched airplanes flying overhead, pulled up weeds to see the roots, planted seeds and watched them grow, and talked about the different shapes and colors of leaves. The boys rode their tyke bikes, played ball, climbed trees, and made mud pies. The playing, whether indoors or outside, stimulated their innate curiosity.

Children learn by doing, and the more movement the activity involves the better, especially for boys. I encouraged and planned hands-on activities. The boys helped add and mix the cake ingredients, rolled the cookie dough, stirred the food coloring into the icing, and scrambled the eggs. I allowed them to play and experiment with water, sand, and the combination of both—mud. We fertilized and mulched plants, mulched leaves to add to the compost pile, and planted seeds. The boys made secret potions mixing dirt, leaves, and other assorted materials. They used scissors, hammers, and screwdrivers. Even as the boys got older, I used the multisensory approach to enrich their learning experiences.

Fortunately Houston offers many activities for children, and the weather allows us to be outdoors most of the year. In addition, we took advantage of the art, science, and children's museums, the parks, the zoo, and the beaches on Galveston Island. Even the grocery store provided learning experiences—counting the apples, weighing the potatoes, describing the different fruits and vegetables by name and color. During one excursion to the grocery store when David was eighteen months old, he amazed me with his ability to infer association. My mom used to send the boys care packages—usually homemade goodies packed in colorful coffee cans. Walking down the aisle stocked with coffee, David pointed and demanded, "Cookies! Cookies!"

Each new experience I provided the boys increased their vocabulary, understanding, and awareness of their world. (In addition, the time spent with them during these activities had value in and of itself.) No matter what the boys were doing, I was indirectly "teaching" them: it's a red truck, green grass, blue sky, yellow flower, or a round ball. I counted climbing up and down the stairs, placing silverware in the kitchen drawer, or putting toys away. I didn't need fancy flash cards to teach them their colors, numbers, shapes, and letters. They learned them by hearing the words and seeing the objects over and over again.

One amusing "color" story happened when Tony was eighteen months old. His favorite color was "orange." Joe drove an orange Volkswagen Beetle at the time. When we would ask Tony what color Daddy's car was, he would quickly respond, "Orange!" Friends were so impressed with his precociousness until we asked him what color was the grass or sky. "Orange!" was his inevitable response. Everything was the color orange for a while.

I learned to use the time in the car productively, whether driving to the grocery store or across town. The car in many ways became my mini-school on wheels, more so for the younger boys than the older ones. When Tommy was in first grade, a friend nicknamed him "Flashcard Tommy"—Tommy could rattle off math facts with incredible speed and accuracy. One mom asked about the secret of Tommy's success. I explained we played mental math in the car. I proposed a math problem and the boys solved it. I also kept crayons, paper, and pencils in the car so the younger boys could write numbers and letters, sound out words, or draw pictures. I would call out a letter or a word while five-year-old Jamie wrote the letter or the beginning or ending sound. Gradually, Jamie wrote words. He thought we were playing a game, yet his reading and writing skills continued to improve. He was learning *and* having fun—without a formal lesson or a worksheet.

When I started playing these games with the older boys, I didn't realize at the time the long-term benefits. It was a rewarding surprise when their brothers insisted on playing the same games—the trickle down effect at work. What a novel concept—to make the educational process fun so our children enjoy learning. One summer, while waiting for their next events at a swim meet, Tony and David were solving problems in a math workbook. A mother observing their efforts commented, "I can't believe you're making your sons work on math during the summer." I glanced at the boys and responded, "Now does it look like we're forcing them to do that?" Tony and David didn't consider the math drudgery; solving the problems kept them entertained during the monotonous waits between events. When Tony began swimming in United States Swimming competitions, the swim team members often whiled away the time reading wonderful books. Many of the books passed from one swimmer to the next. Maybe our own attitudes on reading, writing, and arithmetic imply that learning is work. A positive attitude and example shows our sons the value and satisfaction we derive from acquiring new knowledge at any age.

Dinnertime also proved another natural opportunity to "teach" the boys. Dinnertime was not just a time to nourish our bodies but also a time to nourish our minds and our souls. We discussed what happened in our sons' days and in the world. Soccer, always a favorite topic around our table, often led to locating a country on the globe or commenting on cultural differences or political issues between competing countries. The indictment of a local government official prompted a discussion on Watergate and the infamous Richard Nixon presidency. Fascinated by this unbelievable piece of United States history, the boys later read the book and watched the movie *All the President's Men*. As the boys moved into high school and college, the discussions evolved and covered the gamut of world affairs.

Read, Read, and Read Some More

I had a Mother who read me the things
That wholesome life to the boy heart brings—
Stories that stir with an upward touch
Oh, that each mother of boys were such!

You may have tangible wealth untold;
Caskets of jewels and coffers of gold.
Richer than I you can never be—
I had a Mother who read to me.
— "The Reading Mother" by Strickland Gillian

The most important and effective way to foster the boys' love of knowledge is by reading to them. No other activity enriches their love of learning more. Every one of our sons enjoys reading. They are constantly recommending books to each other, often discussing books over dinner. I feel the love of reading is one of the best gifts I gave them.

Reading to the boys developed their listening and memory skills, increased their vocabulary and language skills, provided experiences beyond their imagination, and enriched our relationships from the time spent together. We discovered books with the boys before they were even a year old. We started with books that have vivid illustrations of toys, trucks, animals, and household items. We bought several copies of many of Richard Scarry's books—we wore them out from constant use. Each of the boys preferred different books: Tony loved *Cars and Trucks and Things that Go*; David favored Dr. Seuss's books; Mark enjoyed *The Napping House*; Jamie's favorite book was *The Very Busy Spider*; Timmy couldn't get enough of *Brown Bear, Brown Bear*.

We traveled the world through the books we read together: to China in *Ping* to Boston in *Make Way for Ducklings*, or to England in *Lassie Come-Home*. We shared the emotions of friendship in *Amos and Boris* and parents' love in *Sylvester and the Magic Pebble*. They appreciated the struggles of Helen Keller, Harriet Tubman, and Lou Gehrig, and experienced racial injustice in *Roll of Thunder, Hear My Cry* and courage and devotion in *Island of the Blue Dolphins* and *The Cay*. Their imaginations soared reading *Castle in the Attic* and *The Lion, the Witch and the Wardrobe*. They laughed at the antics of the characters in *Wayside School is Falling Down* and the poetry of Shel Silverstein and Jack Prelutsky.

When I read aloud to the boys, the titillation found between the pages sprung to life. Why would a child want to pick up a piece of paper with a bunch of letters on it, unless he had discovered the excitement derived from those letters? We do our sons an injustice by not reading to them on a regular basis and put them at a disadvantage when they begin formal education. Children who have been read to are familiar with letters, words, and sentence structure, and children who haven't been read to aren't. Most books for children under five years of age take less than fifteen minutes to read. Those fifteen minutes are invaluable minutes spent with the boys.

At a PTO meeting, Sally Landram, the principal, strongly encouraged parents to find the time to read to their children every night. After the meeting, I was sarcastically asked if I read to the boys every night. When I responded that I did, many parents were surprised Joe and I had the time with so many children and commitments. We found the time because we didn't allow the television and computer to dominate our lives. Instead, we chose to spend the time reading to the boys. I assure you, from my years of experience, the time invested was well rewarded.

I know the impact reading had on my life. I learned important lessons from the heroines and heroes in the stories I read. I was touched by the courage of Karana in *Island of the Blue Dolphins* and the bravery of Johnny in *Johnny Tremain*. I was motivated and inspired reading *Quo Vadis, Cry, the Beloved Country, Profiles in Courage, Uncle Tom's Cabin,* and *Anne Frank*. Because of the powerful influence of my parents and teachers **and** the books I read, I have always felt confident that I can do and be whatever I choose. I want the boys to experience that same level of confidence.

Even after the boys learned to read, Joe and I continued to read to the boys. Children are able to understand books at a higher level than they are capable of reading on their own. Our reading to them beyond their reading level helped to open their world and to increase their vocabularies and understanding of the English language; it also provided us with special moments together.

A comment five-year-old Jamie made after a close friend's sister-in-law and nephew were killed in an automobile accident reinforced the importance of story time. The mother left behind two other young children. Jamie, when he heard about the children, sadly said, "Oh, Mommy, who will read them stories now?" I had always cherished the time spent reading to my sons, but with Jamie's comment, I valued the experience even more. Joe often teases that at first he missed *Monday Night Football*, but the choice to read to the boys became a "no-brainer" as Chris leaned on him from one side and Joe Pat from the other, reminding him that the time was more than reading words from a page in a book. It is obvious the boys treasured this time as much as we did.

I used the interests of the boys as a springboard to choose reading materials. When Danny was in second grade, Mrs. Jackson read *Mr. Popper's Penguin* to the class. Danny's curiosity about penguins soared. We read *National Geographic* articles and probably every book in the library on penguins, including rereading *Mr. Popper's Penguin*. He drew penguins and created a family of penguins by decorating toilet tissue rolls. Next came his fascination with the sinking of the *Titanic*. We read the book *Exploring the Titanic* and watched the *National Geographic* video on the efforts to locate the sunken ship and its treasures.

If you find yourself at a loss at which books to choose for your children, ask a teacher or a librarian for suggestions. One of the best resources I used was *The Read-Aloud Handbook* by Jim Trelease. The book provides an extensive list of excellent children's literature as well as why, when, and how to read to your children. Another resource is the recommended books from the National Endowment for the Humanities. I had an excellent list of NEH recommended books published before 1960. Their website now has recommended summer reading lists and *We the People Bookshelf*, a program that suggests books at the different grade levels that share a theme important to our heritage such as courage, freedom, or equality.

There is great pressure on our children to read at an earlier and earlier age. Like all developmental skills, each child will learn when he is ready. Some children walk at nine months while others are fifteen months old before they walk. Reading is no different. Just because a child is in first grade does not mean he is ready to read on day one or day 100. One summer I tutored a young boy in reading. In a few short weeks, he had moved from sounding out every word to fluent reading. His parents gave me credit for his tremendous strides. Although I had strengthened his phonetical skills,

I was convinced his reading clock had clicked on.

As the boys grew older, I wouldn't allow them to see a movie before reading the book. When David was in seventh grade, the movie *The Hunt for Red October* came out. Joe and I told David he could see the movie once he had read the book. Motivation kicked in and David engrossed himself in the novel. He couldn't put the book down, and on his recommendation most of his friends borrowed the book to read as well. The boys agree that the book is almost always better than the movie. I also believe that the boys would have lost interest in reading the book after seeing the movie: the experience in reverse is never the same. (The boys helped compile a list of books that they enjoyed over the years that I have placed at the end of the book.)

Formal Education

Our children spend seven to eight hours in the school environment. Joe and I wanted that environment to enrich the lives of our sons and to build on the love of learning that we instilled in them at home. We wanted schools that provided a stimulating and challenging curriculum. We wanted our sons in schools where respect for oneself and others is integrated into the daily experience. We wanted our sons in schools that appreciated their individuality and encouraged them to reach their full potential. And we wanted our sons to grow in their love and appreciation of God. I don't think that's too much to ask of every school in our country— whether in the most affluent or the poorest section of town. If you have a choice of where your child attends school, make a wise choice because it has a tremendous impact on the life of your child. Even many public school districts have options within their systems. Try to make a choice based on the needs of each child, which may differ from child to child. Joe and I chose to move the boys from one school to another during the elementary school years when we decided the educational experience and environment at the one school was not what we wanted for the boys.

Success in school is not solely dependent on the school. Research has shown that a major determinant of a student's success in school is the support, involvement, and encouragement of his parents. Joe and I demonstrated our commitment to the boys' education when we took the time to ask about their day, reviewed their schoolwork, assisted with their studies, read with them, helped them stay organized, and participated in school activities. If all a parent does each day is drop off her son in the morning and pick him up at the end of the day, that parent is not fulfilling her parental responsibilities. If parents expect the school to shoulder the entire responsibility, their children will pay the price.

The school day can be a difficult time for a young boy. Students are expected to sit still and be quiet during class, not an easy task for most boys. I found some teachers were more "boy" friendly than others, meaning they understood boys and maintained realistic expectations of them. Girls, for example, might like to sit and color all the pictures on a phonics sheet, but most boys don't. The coloring has nothing to do with whether they know the phonetical sounds, and yet they are usually expected to sit there and finish coloring the sheet.

The more structured the environment, the harder it is for many of our sons. While I didn't want a school where chaos reigned, I did want an educational environment that respected boys' needs. With the pressure on schools to produce academically, many schools choose to reduce recess time and physical education classes. Those choices are not in the best interests of our sons. At least in middle school and high school they move from class to class.

Homework is another controversial issue, but would be less so if it were reasonable and realistic for the grade level, and the work served a purpose. There is definitely a place for homework. Fr. Leininger, a high school math teacher, used to remind the boys and parents of the importance of nightly review of information learned during the day. He told us that if not reviewed in three days, 65 percent of the information is forgotten. A student will be taught math concepts and facts in class, but when a child reviews them for five minutes a night, the progress and sense of accomplishment advances much more rapidly. The same progress can be experienced reviewing spelling or vocabulary words, or re-reading social studies and science notes a few minutes each evening. Requiring a student to pre-read material, answer questions, or write an essay are not unreasonable assignments. Study after study of successful students and schools reflect the benefit of homework and outside learning activities. Education is a discipline, and it takes discipline to attain success.

When the boys completed their assignments differed for each of the boys. The boys at all ages took a break when they arrived home from school. They would get a snack, watch a little television or play outside. If one of them had a sport's practice that day, he would work on his homework earlier rather than later. When practice was not on the schedule, the boys usually completed homework after dinner, and often worked on the kitchen table. I could be reading with one of the younger boys but still be aware of or accessible to the older boys, if needed.

Joe and I fully understand the time commitment reviewing homework entails. We usually finished with the boys around 9:30 in the evenings; we started with our younger sons and moved up the ladder. There were nights when an older brother would help out a younger brother by calling out spelling words, practicing math facts, or listening to them read in order to reduce the time before Joe or I could assist him. During the elementary years, we provided oversight, but as the boys moved into middle school and high school, they became more self-sufficient. They organized their materials, took responsibility for completing assignments, and read and reviewed for quizzes and tests. If they needed assistance, they knew we were available.

We attended teacher conferences from pre-school through high school regardless of whether the grade was an A or a C. They boys were aware of the value we placed on their education by our continuous concern and involvement. We emphasized from an early age the importance of attending college. They knew this was the next step in their education. They also knew that they had to do their part scholastically to make it a reality, especially if they had a certain college in mind.

Whenever we determined one of the boys needed additional help in a subject, we sought it. Assimilating and retaining information came easier for some of the boys than it did for others. Instead of having one of our sons struggle and feel incompetent, we made sure he received the appropriate help. Self-confidence and self-esteem play a major role in educational success. When a child continually performs poorly or below the standards he sets, self-esteem and self-confidence plummet. My experience teaching first grade convinced me that no student wants to do poorly. So when one of the boys struggled academically, we determined what it would take to break the cycle and get him back on track. Recognizing that each person learns in a different way encouraged us to present information from different perspectives, using different teaching techniques. If it meant finding an additional program or tutor to fill in the gaps, then that's what we did. The additional commitment of time and money sent a clear message that Joe and I cared and wanted the best for them.

Many parents are intimidated by the school environment and are afraid to approach a teacher about their child. It is important, though, to establish a good relationship with the school, and to work with them in meeting the needs of your child. Most teachers provide conference time to meet with you on the progress of your child. Take advantage of these opportunities or set up a time to discuss your child's progress, academically, physically, and socially. If a situation arises that causes you or your son concern, don't hesitate to address it so your son's school day will be the enriching environment he deserves.

In addition to providing our sons with a strong formal education, we supplemented their schooling with enrichment opportunities. We looked for programs that enriched and enhanced their natural abilities and interests: Space Camp, taking advantage of our proximity to NASA, art classes, sports camps, and the Rice University Summer School for Middle School Students. One summer I planned "field trips" with the boys where we explored Houston and Galveston. We discovered together the downtown tunnel system with our guide Mike Quiray, Timmy's godfather, the Water Wall near the Galleria, and even viewed the film depicting the aftermath of Galveston's 1900 hurricane.

By our example, Joe and I continue to show the boys that learning is ongoing and rewarding. The older boys also set a great example for their brothers. Often they were the ones recommending books to their brothers or engaging them in an activity. We've reached the point now where the younger brothers are recommending books to their older siblings. I still believe instilling a love of learning is one of the most enjoyable aspects of being a mother. For three decades I've had fun playing and interacting with the boys. All the stimulation has reaped countless benefits. The boys have developed their individual talents and interests while gaining an appreciation and respect for the gift of knowledge. My simple advice—talk, laugh, sing, hug, play, pray, and read with your children. They will learn—and you will both enjoy it!

Emotional Needs

Previously in the book, I outlined what I wanted for each of my sons. I wanted them to be loving, caring, compassionate, forgiving, responsible, respectful, well-educated, and faith-filled. Along those same lines, I wanted them to possess self-confidence and self-acceptance, appreciating who they are and the gifts God has given them. Not an easy task for a mother to instill in her sons in today's world, especially when we, as mothers, draw from different experiences and challenges that we faced while growing up. My greatest learning curve as I look back on my experiences in raising the boys was in the area of their emotions. I asked more questions and delved more deeply in how to best approach their individual emotional needs without them loosing their masculine identity. Too often a young man who is empathetic, responsible, and respectful is also deemed by society a sissy or a wimp. Finding the right balance was the challenge and the goal.

Emotional well-being is very dependent on how we think of ourselves and how we feel others perceive us, especially our parents. I've shared my views on creating a home of love where each family member feels loved and secure in his home environment, where we respectfully treat each other and talk to each other, where the commitments of our time, energy, and finances are appropriately focused, and faith is integrated into the day. Creating this home of love has a profound effect on the emotional well-being of a young man.

It is in the home that a young man learns love and acceptance. It is in the home that a young man learns kindness and compassion. It is in the home that a young man learns respect—respect for himself, respect for others, and respect for God. It is in the home that a young man learns responsibility for himself and others. It is in the home that a young man learns right from wrong, appropriate from inappropriate, and morality from immorality. It is in the home that a young man learns appropriate behavior and how to handle the emotional ups and downs of life. It is in this framework that our sons' emotional needs are met.

Societal pressures and expectations abound. Macho is still preached in too many arenas at the expense of the emotional fiber of our sons. I am still amazed at how often I hear, "Stop crying." "Boys don't cry." "Be a big boy." "Be tough." And the child may only be a toddler. I didn't want the boys to be crybabies, but if they fell down and needed a touch of TLC, then I gave it—and so did Joe. It is okay to hug and show signs of affection to our sons. We all need to feel loved. Affection is healthy, and needed, at all stages of our lives. If all that's been preached to a young man is be rough and tough, then a whole side of that young man has been shut off.

My sons constantly wrestled and mixed it up. I worried at times that the younger boys would get seriously hurt. The older boys would assure me that that wouldn't happen—and it never did. The boys proved you can be both tough and gentle—there is a time for both. But to act as if being loving and gentle are inferior traits does a disservice to a son. At the recent funeral of a dear friend, Marilyn, whom eight of the boys had worked for in the extended day program at St. Francis de Sales School, her husband Dick shared with me his experience on meeting my sons for the first time. He had heard all kinds of stories about the Garcia-Prats boys from Marilyn. His first reaction after meeting them was they were all "boy" **and** they were all "love."

A physical emotional support was also a benefit to my sons. Each one snuggled up with a favorite stuffed animal or pillow or blanket. The "snuggie" provided a sense of security or a touch of home when they were away. Although some of the blankets and pillows have become frayed over the years, they remain special to the boys. Timmy was gifted with a quilt by a volunteer organization during his stay in the hospital following his appendectomy; he still treasures that quilt or the fragment that remains of it.

Acknowledging and Expressing Feelings

A characteristic of good communication is acknowledging the feelings of the other person. I found it natural to acknowledge the feelings of the boys. Sometimes the acknowledgement was non-verbal—a pat on the shoulder or a simple look of understanding. At other times, words expressed my understanding: "Long day?" "That had to make you mad!" or "I can appreciate your disappointment. Sorry it didn't work out."

A boy needs to feel free to share his feelings and be comfortable expressing affection, not only when he's three or four years old but also when he's thirteen and fourteen years old. The affection of the three year old may understandably be more expressive, and that's to be expected. My sons naturally pulled away from me as they moved into the middle school and high school years, but they still **needed** to stay connected and assured of my love. Being a "helicopter" mom, always hovering over every move your son makes or nagging him with questions will, in my opinion, push him away further and faster. I don't think I was as aware of the distancing from me and connecting more with Joe with the older boys as I am with Jamie and Timmy. As I thought about why, I realize I was too busy taking care of the younger boys to really notice the changes in the relationship with the older boys. I think I'm glad I didn't notice. It can be a hard transition.

The boys released their feelings in many different ways, more often than not in actions rather than words. Danny might have banged on his drums, while David and Chris might have resorted to shooting baskets outside. We had a few lessons in how **not** to release feelings as well. Redecorating the room with additional holes in the walls, throwing toys or any item, or taking it out on a brother were unacceptable. Some of the boys' tempers had to be re-directed: that is, they had to learn how to deal with their anger in acceptable and non-destructive ways—a good lesson to learn at home rather than school.

My sons are sensitive young men who care for each other, with that care extending outside the home as well. **Our home provided them a safe place to be sensitive and caring without fear of being ridiculed or teased.** When Timmy fell and hit his head during an interview with the *Dallas Morning News*, four-year-old Jamie jumped up and ran into the bedroom. The writer, the photographer, Joe, and I couldn't figure out why he darted away, until he reappeared with Timmy's favorite blanket to comfort him. When eight-year-old Chris broke his wrist at a gymnastic party, Joe Pat insisted on being with him when we went to the hospital. When three-year-old Timmy suffered a ruptured appendix, the older boys assured Joe and I that they would take care of the home-front so we could meet Timmy's needs at the hospital. One summer ten-year-old Tommy won a ping-pong tournament at our neighborhood Fourth of July party. Tommy graciously accepted his first-place prize—two gift certificates for ice cream. His brothers teased about who Tommy would take with him to the ice cream parlor only to watch him walk over to his opponent and hand him one of the certificates.

The expectation in our home is for the boys to be kind and loving, emphasizing the adage: "Charity begins at home." You would not hear one of the boys tease a brother for being kind or going out of his way to help out. Again, Joe and I strove to provide a home environment that encouraged and accepted love and compassion as the norm, not the exception. The boys also received praise and acknowledgement from us when we observed a kindness, reinforcing the importance we placed on it.

Self-Esteem and Self-Respect

When you are comfortable in your own skin, you are much more likely to be emotionally stable. I stress as I do in other chapters the importance of self-acceptance. There are some things we can change about ourselves and there are some things we can't change. If I, as their mother, have grasped and accepted that concept for myself, then I can impart that understanding and acceptance to each of my sons. I must also maintain age-appropriate and child-realistic expectations for each of my sons, recognizing and appreciating each one's intellectual, emotional, and physical uniqueness.

Tony was gifted intellectually. He made straight A's, was a National Merit Scholar, and a member of Phi Beta Kappa. But not all the boys achieved academically at that level. Each of the boys has done well academically, but at his own, God-given achievement level. The expectation in our home was for each of the boys to reach his potential, not that of his brothers. It would have been unrealistic, and unjust, to expect all ten sons to achieve academically at Tony's level. That was not the gift that God bestowed on each one of them. When an expectation is unrealistic and unattainable, self-image falters, no matter how hard you try. Joe's and my goal is that each of the boys strives to be the best he can be in all areas of his life. That may not transfer into **the** best, but instead into **his** best. Understanding that difference has a major and significant impact on a son's self-esteem.

The same holds true physically. If a son senses that his parents think he is inadequate in his physical appearance or athletic ability, he will think less of himself. I have attended too many athletic events over the years from pee-wee squads to NCAA competitions where I've witnessed a parent deride a son for his less than stellar performance—as if the son intentionally struck out, deliberately missed a game winning free throw, bounced a penalty kick off the soccer goal post, or swam slowly at the season's final meet. I cringe when I remember a father yelling at his son after a high school soccer game: "You embarrassed me!" as his son's shoulders drooped lower and lower. That dad cared more about his own feelings than those of his son.

Keeping expectations age-appropriate and child realistic helps to build a child's self-image. Positiveness begets positiveness. If I praise my sons for their accomplishments and encourage them in their efforts, my sons will be happy and confident in who they are and what they do. If I constantly point out how many are wrong on a work sheet, instead of how many are right, my son feels more like a failure than a success.

At the same time, false praise can be just as detrimental as no praise. I believe that each of us knows when praise is deserved. If I tell Mark, "Great game!" when it wasn't one of his better games, he knows that. Or if I tell Mark, "That's great!" but without enthusiasm in my voice, he will never believe it's great. Just as an adult can detect from my tone of voice what I imply, my sons can do the same.

Encouragement goes a long way at all developmental stages to build a strong self-image. If you praise your son honestly, he will feel special and loved. Learn positive words and phrases to show your support and encouragement: "You're special." "Great job cleaning up. Thanks." "I knew you could do it." "How creative." Don't be afraid to show your love, pride, and understanding at any age. Ours sons need to hear and feel our love. How quickly positive words and actions make a difference in a child.

I sing the boys' praises. They need to know I am proud of them. You can talk about a son's accomplishment without being boastful. Speak highly of them and take pride in their achievements. If **you** don't, how can your sons expect others to? So much of our self-esteem is determined at an early age by parents. To quote Viktor Frankl: "True self-esteem and a true sense of identity can be found only in the reflected appraisal of those whom we have loved." With that in mind, build your sons up; don't tear them down.

Joe and I are our sons' loudest cheerleaders—their advocates not their adversaries. I am comfortable sharing with the boys positive comments people make about them, or my pride when a teacher comments on the kindness one of the boys exhibited to a classmate or teacher.

They have been each other's cheerleaders as well. It was not uncommon to hear one of the older boys encouraging a younger brother in his efforts, whether it was swimming, soccer, reading, guitar, or drawing. Since the boys admire and look up to each other, younger to older and older to younger, it means so much to have the praise and encouragement of a brother or two. When Matt and Jamie received the Principal's Award upon graduation at St. Francis de Sales, their brothers were the first ones out the door to congratulate them. At Tony's graduation from Strake Jesuit, Joe Pat commented on feeling "puffed up" after hearing Tony's salutatorian address. People often ask, "Aren't they jealous of each other?" I can honestly say no. They respect each other's talents, are proud of each other's achievements, and share in each other's disappointments. Again, because Joe and I have reinforced that each of us is blessed with unique gifts from God, they understand that each of them will excel in his own special way, if he develops the gifts he has been given. You aren't trying to be someone else if you're pleased with the person you are.

Responsibilities Augment Self-Confidence and Self-Esteem

The more a person can do for himself the more confident he becomes. I struggle, for example, with technology. I am a visual learner as well as a hands-on learner. For me to retain a skill on the computer, I usually have to repeat the task several times or have it written down so I can follow the necessary steps. I've slowly built up my confidence working on the computer and am less and less dependent on Joe and the boys for help. That's a good feeling and a sense of accomplishment.

Our children are no different. With each new task they learn, they become a little more independent, self-reliant, and self-confident. Teaching the boys to tie their shoes, dress themselves, put away the silverware, take out the trash, or clean their rooms may have been a help to me, but more importantly, they were skills they needed to learn. In addition, the sense of accomplishment they felt when they finished these tasks augmented their self-esteem. Accepting responsibility for their soccer or swim equipment or their homework and school supplies taught them the importance of organizing their belongings and putting them in their proper place.

I believe in teaching responsible behavior at an early age. I guarantee you that our sons don't wake up on their twelfth birthday, look at Joe and me and say, "Today I think I'll become responsible!" It doesn't work that way. Children first learn to be responsible by helping and being involved at home. We found appropriate chores for the boys at different stages of development. With an increase in age and ability, Joe and I increased the level of responsibility. As the boys matured, we also increased their privileges and freedoms, emphasizing that with these new freedoms came responsibility. This approach worked for our family because the younger boys saw firsthand their older brothers accepting responsibility and that, as they got older, they too would be granted more privileges. A two year old is capable of putting his pajamas away each morning or his clothes in the hamper at night. A three year old can help put the silverware away, dress himself, put his toys away, and empty small trash cans. They graduate from setting and clearing the table to cleaning the kitchen after dinner. The boys designed a rotating schedule for kitchen duty, glad to have so many helping hands. From picking up pinecones and piles of leaves, they move to mowing and edging the yard. In the mornings they made their beds before going to school. In addition, a couple of the boys straightened the kitchen, and a couple made sure their bedrooms and the upstairs bathroom were picked up. When they began to drive, they helped us drive their younger brothers to school on their way to the high school. And they willingly baby-sat their brothers when needed.

At a presentation I gave several years ago, a mother told me that she only had two children, a maid, and a yardman. She implied her children didn't need to make their beds, wash the dishes, or mow the yard. That may be the case, but she still needed to instill responsibility in her sons for their benefit, not hers. Just because you can do something for them doesn't mean you should. If making the bed isn't the responsibility of choice, decide on ones that fit your lifestyle. What is important is to teach your children responsibility that, again, augments their self-esteem.

When one of the boy's friends stopped by during Christmas break, I asked him how his first semester in college had gone. He moaned a little; I assumed the academics were more challenging than he had expected. He went on to tell me that classes were the easy part; he struggled with all the day-to-day needs: changing sheets, washing clothes, and organizing his time to fit all those needs into his schedule. He added, "I was embarrassed when I had to ask my roommate how to change my sheets. Your sons are lucky. You teach them how to do these things while they are at home."

With only Jamie and Timmy presently at home during the school year, I could easily include their clothes with Joe's and mine each week when I launder. But I know the benefit they gain from taking on this responsibility and refrain from doing so. The two of them are still responsible for the yard, even though there are only two of them and not five, six, or seven of them to divide the labor as in years past. They still are responsible for cleaning the kitchen each evening and setting and clearing the table, although Joe and I jump in a little more often because we're not bathing or reading stories to younger brothers.

In our home, chores are not gender specific either, and not just because we have all sons. The expectations would have been the same whether a sister had been in the mix. We embrace a philosophy that whoever has the time or the ability to complete a task does so. I remember the evening we had some guests for dinner. At the end of dinner, Jamie and Timmy started clearing the table. As Jamie took his plate, one of the gentleman stated: "Jamie, isn't it a shame you don't have a sister so she could be cleaning up." Jamie didn't know how to respond. I clarified for the guest that if we had had a daughter, she would be in the rotation right along with the boys. He was a little surprised, expressing how in his home the girls were responsible for certain chores and the boys responsible for others. My daughter-in-law, Rita, quickly piped in, "I thank Cathy every day for teaching the boys how to help out. It makes such a difference having David's help!"

I wanted my sons to learn to be responsible for themselves and their things because they need to do so. And, can you imagine the nightmare for me if I had tried to ready each backpack every morning, make eleven beds, or clean the kitchen alone? But, I reiterate, whether you have one son or ten sons, they need to have responsibilities. At a soccer game one morning, a young player came screaming and demanding of his mother, "Where's my blue jersey?" The flustered mom went searching for it, only to realize she had forgotten to put it in his soccer bag. The son was extremely angry and the mom felt embarrassed and guilty. Standing next to me, she asked, "How do you keep it all straight with so many of your sons playing soccer?" I explained to her that the boys, from eight to eighteen years old, are responsible for their soccer uniforms and equipment. I make sure the uniforms are washed and ready, but they must prepare and organize their soccer bag.

Teaching the boys to be responsible, again, augments their self-confidence and self-esteem. Too often we moms rate ourselves by how much we do for our children, instead of considering the long-term impact of our doing so. We have young men who don't know how to make a bed, cook a meal, or launder clothes—and then expect their wives to pick up where Mom left off? They also need to appreciate the time commitment of each of these chores—or they end up not appreciating the time demands incurred by their wives.

When I was invited to give a presentation on responsible parenting in California, I forwarded to the woman in charge, the mother of five sons, a handout I often distribute, "Age Appropriate Responsibilities." At dinner the night I arrived, one of the sons teasingly commented, "We have a lot more responsibilities around here lately," as his eyes shifted to the refrigerator and the responsibility handout. Then he added, "We never realized how much my mom did every day."

Actually, my older sons began washing their own clothes as a consequence of not appreciating the time commitment involved in laundering everyone's clothes. It was almost an all day job, twice a week. I sorted, washed, dried, and folded the clothes. Their responsibility was to put the folded clothes away in their drawers. Gradually, they weren't following through, as I noticed clothes in piles around their rooms. I reminded them of their responsibility, and when they didn't fulfill it, I told them I would no longer be responsible for laundering their clothes. A few lessons in operating the washer and dryer took place and, since then, the boys have been responsible for laundering their clothes from around the middle school years on. Have there been a few mishaps? Of course there have been. They had a load or two that went in one color and came out another color; they learned the importance of proper sorting. Black spots appeared on one load when a black marker was left in a pocket; they learned to check pockets before washing. The mishaps were rarely repeated.

Stress

I don't remember dealing with a lot of stress at a young age. Yet today stress is, unfortunately, a real part of too many of our children's lives beginning at too early an age. The stress they encounter affects them emotionally. My goal is to provide as stress-free an environment at home as possible, as well as buffer them from outside stresses.

Many stresses our children encounter are home-grown—from relationship or financial difficulties to having unrealistic expectations of them to succeed, academically, artistically, athletically, or socially, or, the other extreme, too little expectations of them and letting them run wild. Creating a balance in their lives or reducing stressful situations is a challenge, but possible.

Creating a home of love is the first step in keeping stress at a minimum. When the people in the home treat and are treated with love and respect, the atmosphere is radically different from a home where love and respect are absent. When children live in a peaceful environment and not one where yelling and fighting are the norm, they gain an unspoken sense of security. A stressed home breeds stressful children. They end up worrying about issues that a child shouldn't have to worry about.

Buffering the boys from outside stresses and teaching them how to deal with stress is the next step in guiding our sons' emotional state. When I have too much to do and not enough time to complete the tasks successfully or am not able to carve out a few minutes for myself each day, I am stressed. When the boys have too much to do or the activity or task at hand is too demanding, they begin to feel overwhelmed. It is up to me to help them balance their days, and I work hard to do so, often choosing to live counter culturally.

When a mother of a five year old rattles off all the activities he is involved in, and then wonders how I can possibly accomplish everything with ten sons, I let her know that my sons are **not** in multi-activities at an early age. They pick one activity until middle school and high school when school and church activities enter the picture. Tony and David taught me that lesson. When they were six and seven years old, they played the rotation of sports: swimming, soccer, basketball, and baseball. I decided I wanted them to learn to play the piano, so I enrolled them in piano lessons. The afternoons became full for them, either a sport's practice or piano. One day they came to me and said, "We never have time to just play." They were right, and they loved to just play. They finished the piano lessons and then each was allowed to choose one activity at a time. I never looked back.

I hear every "reason" for having children in multiple activities, from wanting a child to be well-rounded to not wanting them to be bored. I want my sons to be well-rounded too. You can still provide your children with different activities, just don't feel compelled to do them all at the same time. You will slowly sense what activities he enjoys and which ones are drudgery for him. When you enjoy what you do, you tend to be more successful and happy. In addition, for each activity a son is enrolled in, I'm responsible for getting him to and fro, ratcheting up my stress levels as well. I, the boys, and Joe, can attest to the affects on the household when I'm stressed and worked up. I'm constantly reminding myself and the boys that we can't do it all. I believe it is better that our sons grow up relaxed and secure than overwhelmed by the demands placed on them, especially if they are expected to be the best at whatever activity they are engaged in.

Learning ways to deal with stress are important life lessons. I wanted the boys to learn positive and constructive ways to reduce stress: By organizing and prioritizing; by maintaining realistic expectations of their time, energy, finances, and abilities; by establishing goals for the day, week, and year; and by trusting in God.

Joe and I teach through our example of dealing with the stresses in our lives. When I focus on what's really important at that moment in time—prioritizing—I reduce my stress. Since fatigue aggravates stress, I make the effort to get adequate sleep. Since time is a precious commodity, I try to take advantage of those little five and ten minute blocks of time that pop up in the day: write a thank-you note, start or fold a load of wash, make the salad for dinner, or open and sort the day's mail. I keep a tote bag in the car with reading materials, stationery, notecards, and pen and pencil to make use of the time waiting for a son to finish practice. The boys had their special bags, too, if they accompanied me. My Christmas cards for years were completed during the long intervals between Tony's swimming events. I took advantage of any opportunity to exercise. I often spent the time prior to one of the boy's games walking, since the team is usually required to be there forty-five minutes before the game starts. When I'm down in the dumps, I try to determine why I feel as I do and then work to change my mood. I turn to prayer, music, physical activities, or maybe a call to a friend or sister.

These same techniques work with the boys: change of pace, physical activity, adequate sleep, realistic expectations of themselves, and prioritization and organization. If, for example, they complete an assignment that was assigned two weeks ago in a timely fashion instead of waiting until the last minute, they will experience less stress and probably produce a better outcome. If they organize their schoolwork and supplies the night before, they will have less to do in the morning and won't be running around looking for a missing shoe or math book. If they choose to stay up late playing the computer or talking to friends, they need to understand the implications. If they're feeling restless or moody, choosing to go outside and shoot the basketball or kick the soccer ball around can make a difference. Stress can't be completely eliminated but it is controllable.

Social and Peer Pressure

Our sons also experience societal and peer pressures that add to their stress levels. They hear Joe's and my beliefs on what is acceptable, and then they hear what society deems appropriate. The two usually don't mesh. Joe and I choose to live counterculturally—obvious from the mere fact that we have ten sons. We choose to live simply versus feeling obligated to buy every new gadget or upgraded item. We've lived in the same home, although with an addition along the way, for thirty-one years. We still have one television in our home—without cable. We drive our cars until they aren't safe to do so. I often tease that Joe drove the oldest car of any physician in the city of Houston for many years. It was obvious why when you looked at all the university decals on the rear window. With ten sons to educate, we chose to put our money into the boys' education rather than luxury cars; we couldn't do both and wouldn't, even if we could.

Joe and I had to demonstrate to the boys how to deal with societal pressures and peer pressure, so they could appreciate that happiness isn't based on material possessions or being "number one" or "Mr. Cool." As parents, we have to recognize that we are confronted with peer pressures, too. Peer pressure does not disappear once you are out of high school or college. The pressures continue in the many facets of our lives to be and do what society deems successful. How we deal with these pressures is the foremost teacher of peer pressure to our children. The old adage comes to mind: "Preach—and sometimes use words."

What example are we setting for our sons? Do they see us chasing the American dream of more, bigger, and better? Or do they see us living within our means and setting goals not based on material gains? Do they see us watching television shows or movies that contradict our beliefs and lifestyle? Or do they see us choosing according to the standards we set or the values we live at home? Do they see us drink too much or use illegal substances or abuse legal substances? Or do they see us respect our bodies and what we put in them? Do they see us develop relationships that use the other person for our own benefit? Or do they see the importance we place on true friendships?

Do we feel compelled to have the "best" birthday party, which usually translates into the most expensive? Do we feel driven to keep up with our son's friends even when we can't afford it? Are we pushing our son to be involved in activities that he isn't ready for or interested in because we want him to be in the "in" group and popular?

In his books *The Hurried Child* and *All Dressed Up and No Where to Go*, David Elkin expounds on the issue of pushing our children to grow up too fast and caving in, as parents, to societal pressures. We must live the values that we want our children to embrace, insuring that those values are in the best interest of our children. Living counterculturally can be challenging at times, but I have no regrets. Imparting my values to the boys has provided them, for example, the freedom to make career choices that someone more focused on material success or status would most likely not make. David and Matt, along with their wives, Rita and Mary, are teachers. They knew education would provide a different standard of living than that of an engineer or attorney. They accept that, and because they have lived simply, yet comfortably, over the years, they accept not driving the fancy car or living extravagantly. (Their students are the true beneficiaries of their choice.)

Spiritual Needs

"You have been told, O man, what is good, and what the Lord requires of you: only to do right and to love goodness, and to walk humbly with your God" (Micah 6:8). Simple but powerful words! As are the following words from scripture: "You shall love the Lord your God with your whole heart, with your whole soul, and with your whole mind. You shall love your neighbor as yourself" (Matthew 22:37,39).

The Influence of God in Our Lives

Instilling a love of God, self, and others is the most important responsibility I have as a mother. I can be successful meeting the physical, emotional, and intellectual needs of my sons, but without the integration of spirituality woven into their lives, I would have failed to develop the entire person, as God holds me accountable to do. Their outlook on their relationships and the world takes on a different meaning when God is or isn't a part of their lives.

I make no bones about the influence of God the Father, God the Son, and God the Holy Spirit in my life. My faith is an invaluable source of strength, inspiration, and guidance in my parenting effort. My religion is a liberating force in my life, not the binding, restrictive experience often portrayed by society. I want my sons to experience that same source of strength, inspiration, and guidance in their lives—as well as liberation and peace.

I recognize and respect that spirituality, faith, and prayer are unique to each individual, even to those who share the same religion. Faith practices, beliefs, celebrations, and religious holy days may differ from faith to faith. What is important is to embrace and practice the tenets of your faith so your children will appreciate how and why you live and believe what you do. It is also important for them to understand and appreciate that "it is not the absence or presence of problems in life that determines our peace, but rather the absence or presence of God in our life."

God loves us and wants us to be happy. I, too, as their mother want the boys to experience love and happiness. That doesn't mean letting them have and do anything they desire but, rather, providing them with what they need. I believe God the Father is no different. He provides guidelines for us to follow that strengthen us in our daily efforts and prepare us for eternal life. He bestows on each of us our unique talents and then expects us to use them to love and serve Him. He gifts us with a free will to choose whether to accept or reject His teachings.

Unfortunately, society pulls us in other directions, wooing us with dreams of power, wealth, and fame. We chase the wrong dreams in search of happiness. "Do not lay up for yourselves an earthly treasure. Moths and rust corrode: thieves break in and steal. Make it your practice instead to store up heavenly treasure, which neither moths nor rust corrode nor thieves break in and steal. Remember, where your treasure is, there your heart is also" (Matthew 6:19-21). Your children quickly discern where your heart is.

Who I am, what I do, and the choices I make for my marriage, the boys, and myself evolve from my faith. I strive to integrate my faith into the fabric of our lives. Faith, therefore, becomes an active part of our lives, not just something we put in a drawer and pull out only as we need it. We have to try to live and express it in our day-to-day interactions and experiences. Our faith and love of God is expressed in the love, respect, and commitment we demonstrate every day to each other and those around us. St. James tells us: "What good is it to profess faith without practicing it?" (James 1:14).

Society tends to compartmentalize all the facets of our lives. People want to believe that, although they may attend church on Sunday, their choices and decisions the rest of the week are irrelevant to their spirituality. They want to believe that their personal spirituality shouldn't affect their business decisions, their relationships, or their lifestyle and choice of activities. Many people are comfortable with their faith until it interferes with societal values and personal decisions. When this happens, faith isn't integrated into their lives but remains a separate entity.

How I live and love, therefore, is the best example to my sons and others of the importance I place on God's love in our lives. I realize, too, that my sons' first impressions of God stem from their experiences with Joe and me. It's scary and humbling to think that we are the face of God to our children and that the knowledge and love of God that my sons embrace begins with the love and respect we demonstrate to each other in our family and those around us. If I want my sons to appreciate that God is a loving God, for example, then I must demonstrate love. If I want my sons to understand that God is a compassionate and forgiving God, then I must be compassionate and forgiving in my dealings with them. If I want them to know the way of truth, then I must strive to seek truth and the will of God in my life. If I want them to develop a relationship with God, then I must have a relationship with God, showing them how my faith will grow and strengthen as I devote time and attention to it. If I want them to learn the Commandments and teachings of my faith, then I must embrace them, often rejecting societal values that contradict these Commandments and teachings.

Embracing my faith means teaching my sons right from wrong, good from bad, appropriate from inappropriate, moral from immoral, and ethical from unethical. It means teaching them that with the free will gifted from God, they are free to make choices about what they do or don't do. It also means accepting the consequences of their actions.

Let me give some examples of choices to be made. Choosing to cheat or not to cheat, whether playing a game with a brother or taking or giving answers on a test. Choosing to complete or disregard a homework assignment. Choosing to obey or disobey, whether a dictate from a parent, a teacher, or an authority. Choosing to watch or not watch an immoral television program/movie. Choosing to treat a friend or brother with respect or be unkind and mean-spirited. Choosing to share time, talent, and/or treasure with others or ignoring the needs of others. Choosing to respect one's body or abusing alcohol, drugs (legal or illegal), or tobacco. Choosing to be sexually active or choosing to remain abstinent. Consequences follow each choice: good choice—good consequence; poor choice—poor consequence. Our children have to learn that just because everyone is doing something or society deems it appropriate does not make it acceptable in the eyes of God. From my thirty-two years of parenting, I appreciate the challenge we face as parents in guiding our children to live faith-filled lives.

In order to face these challenges, I need to provide my sons with faith-based tools to assist them in making acceptable, moral, and ethical choices. They need to learn what our faith teaches is right and wrong, based on the Commandments and the principles and practices of our faith. The pressure is on me to assure they know the teachings of the Church. If they don't know them, how can I expect them to follow them?

I don't assume I can do it all myself. I appreciate the "village" concept—religion teachers, the Catholic schools the boys attend, friends, and family—all combining to influence our sons. Joe and I want them to be in environments that strengthen and foster the beliefs we embrace. People often question, for example, why we choose to pay tuition to send our sons to the Catholic Jesuit high school when public schools in the city offer strong academic programs as well. We choose to send them to Strake Jesuit College Preparatory because faith is integrated into each day. Classes begin with prayer; liturgies, prayer services, and the *Examen* (a methodical prayer that helps discern the movement of the Spirit in our daily lives as we reflect on our day) enrich their day; theology courses teach and broaden their understanding of their Catholic faith; retreats strengthen their relationship with God; service projects emphasize the need to be "men for others"; and the importance of community and family are experienced in the support and love given and received.

We can help our sons learn to discern what is right and wrong from our experiences and challenges. Opportunities arise every day, so *carpe diem*! One afternoon I stopped with the boys at the grocery store to pick up discounted movie tickets. When I returned to the car, I realized the young clerk working the service desk had give me an extra ticket. I told the boys we needed to go back into the store to return the ticket. Annoyed, one of the boys said, "It was *her* mistake," and another added, "It's only a three-dollar ticket, Mom." I knew it would be a hassle taking everyone back inside to return the ticket, but I explained that I hadn't paid for the ticket, so it was wrong to keep it. The girl had made an honest mistake, and she might be held responsible for the discrepancy in the day's tally. I asked them how they would feel in a similar situation. The boys learned firsthand a lesson in honesty and gratitude—the young clerk was most appreciative.

One of the boys' middle school theology teachers, Mary Ann Petru, created a teachable moment when she overheard a group of students talking about the night's upcoming episode of *Friends*. She was surprised at how many students watched the show on a regular basis. She assigned the students who typically watch the show homework based on what they viewed in that night's episode. The students were to list the Commandments broken during the half-hour segment. The next day she asked these students to share their answers with the class. The answers varied on the number of Commandments broken to which Commandments were broken. Mrs. Petru informed them, having viewed the show to the amazement of many of the students, that **seven** Commandments had been broken in that segment.

I think it's important to remember—garbage in, garbage out! What we watch, what we read, what we listen to, where we go, what we wear, and what we use do make a difference. We all—adults and young people alike—become desensitized to what's right when we are constantly bombarded with what's wrong. If our children watch immoral, unethical, abusive, or violent behavior on television programs or in the movies without guidance from a parent, they will begin to believe that behavior is normal and acceptable. I was amazed at how many pre-teens saw the movie *Titanic*, depicted as a wonderful love story. Yes, it is just a movie, but pre-teens are impressionable, and the impression given in the movie was that you meet someone, fall in "love," and have sex a few days later. Not the lesson on responsible sexuality or on a committed love relationship that I want my sons to learn.

Joe and I have been criticized over the years for being too restrictive and protective with the boys. The comments don't bother us. We made the choices out of love for the boys and what we believe God asks from us as responsible, Christian parents: to show them the way, the truth, and the life. It goes back to the peer pressure issue: Are we making choices based on right or wrong, or are we making choices because society deems them acceptable?

Prayer

We pray as a family. I grew up hearing, "The family that prays together stays together." Prayer was important to both Joe and me, so it was natural for us to want our sons to experience the power of prayer. From the time when Tony and David were little, family prayer became part of our home and continues today even with only a couple of sons home. We say grace at mealtime, reciting the traditional prayer before meals that Joe and I learned growing up. In addition, each family member and guest adds a personal prayer intention. (My father likes to tell people that he never gets a hot meal at my house—by the time everyone says their prayer, the food is cold.) At the end of each day, we all stop what we're doing and come together as a family and say evening prayers, again the traditional prayers of our faith: the "Our Father," the "Hail Mary," the "Glory Be," the "Prayer to our Guardian Angel," and the "Act of Contrition." At the end of the prayers, we ask God to bless each and every one of us by name (my Dad calls this time the Litany of the Saints), we thank Him for the day, and we ask Him to guide and help us to be good parents and good boys. The boys learned that Joe and I depended on God to help us parent and live our lives. We wanted them to know that we didn't try to do it all on our own. When people ask me, "Cathy, how do you do it?" I remind them that I don't do it alone. It entails Joe, the boys, me, **and** God working together. "With God all things are possible" (Mark10:27).

I pray **for** the boys each day as well. I have previously shared how I start my day by thanking God for the gift of Joe and the boys in my life. I also ask Him to keep them safe as they drive to and from school and work. I ask Him to protect them from harm. I ask Him to grace them with the courage and wisdom they need to make good choices. I ask Him to show them the power of His love and peace in good times and in bad times.

The boys realized we could pray anywhere, not just in the confines of our home or church. When we start a trip in the car, we pray for a safe and enjoyable trip, and we thank Him when we arrive. If we witness an accident or hear an ambulance, we pray that the individuals involved will be okay. Even when we eat out, we say a prayer. One night in between high school soccer games, we stopped at a fast-food restaurant for a quick meal. Even before we had our food, three-year-old Timmy vehemently insisted we say prayers.

The boys learned the traditional prayers of our Catholic faith by saying the prayers every day. When I taught preschool religious education, I asked parents to begin teaching their children certain prayers by reciting them daily—children learn through repetition: "Repetition is the mother of memory." One parent questioned the need to learn the prayers at that age, saying the words of the prayers mean nothing to little kids. I used the analogy of learning the alphabet to explain my reasoning behind reciting prayers with young children. Learning the ABC's is important for reading readiness. Most parents teach their children to sing the alphabet song long before they learn to read. Similarly, if children know the words to the "Our Father," they will gradually understand their meaning and relevance. I incorporate formal prayers with informal prayers so the boys learn and appreciate that there are different ways of talking to God.

I also want them to spend time in prayer on their own, recognizing the importance of silence in their prayer life. Mother Teresa often emphasized, when asked about prayer, the importance of silence: "In the silence of the heart God speaks." She continued: "Silence gives us a new outlook on everything. We need silence to be able to touch souls. The essential thing is not what we say but what God says to us and through us. In that silence, He will listen to us; there He will speak to our soul, and there we will hear His voice."

The boys have witnessed how Joe and I commit one hour a week to silent prayer in the presence of Jesus Christ in the Holy Sacrament at our church's chapel. We began this commitment over twenty-seven years ago when I was pregnant with our fifth son, Matt. I shared previously how our pastor at the time, Monsignor Donovan, asked each parishioner to commit one hour a week in the newly opened Blessed Sacrament chapel. At the time, I was overwhelmed with my responsibilities as a mother. I laughed inside when he made the request, thinking, "Where was I going to find one more hour in my week to sit in a chapel?" Father's next words, though, changed my life: "I guarantee you one hour of peace and quiet." As the mother of four sons under the age of five, I needed an hour of peace and quiet. I was probably the first person out the door to sign up, my motives questionable. But God works in wonderful ways. Little did I realize when I made the commitment how that one hour a week would affect my life from then on. I realized that, for most of my life, I had been doing most of the talking in my relationship with God. I hadn't provided God the opportunity to talk, or taken the time to listen to Him. In this newly found silence of my heart, God spoke. In this silence, then and now, I experience peace—His peace, the peace He promises. I am not bothered, for example, by comments made about the size of my family or the choices in my lifestyle. I am confident this is where He led me and that He will provide me the means to do what He wants me to do.

I want my sons to experience this same peace as they discern God's choices for them in their individual lives. I pray that they will have the courage to listen to Him, whether He asks them to be a physician, a teacher, an engineer, a priest, a coach, an attorney, a businessman, or a peacemaker.

My role is to provide opportunities for them to discern. Fortunately, the schools hold retreats as well as the religious education programs. As the boys got a little older, we organized family retreats once a year. We chose a retreat center in the area, asked a priest to join us for the day, and then planned a day to pray and play, intermingling soccer and canoe races with prayer services and Mass. The older boys organized the morning prayer service with Scripture readings and songs. The priests who joined us decided on a theme for the day and integrated the theme into two or three talks throughout the day. I remember the year Father Phi asked each of us to spend time in silence reflecting on his words. Timmy and Jamie were very young at the time; I was worried about them wandering alone on the retreat grounds. David and Tony gave me a reassuring look that indicated they would be with Jamie and Timmy in their "aloneness." I could tell, too, that they felt it was important for Jamie and Timmy to experience this aspect of the retreat along with the rest of the family. When we all came back together, Timmy excitedly shared how wonderful the silence had been. Even at a young age, he was able to reap the rewards the silence provided.

Incorporating prayer into your sons' lives is a gift that provides lifelong giving. Teach them the power of prayer: "I give you my word, if you are ready to believe that you will receive whatever you ask for in prayer, it shall be done for you" (Mark 11:24).

Sharing our God-given Gifts

Just being good and following the Commandments isn't all that is expected of us by God. He expects us to **love** with our whole heart, with our whole soul, and with our whole mind, and to put our love into action using our time, talents, and treasure. I again quote from St. Paul's first letter to the Corinthians 13:1-3: "If I speak with human tongues and angelic as well, but do not have love, I am a noisy gong, a clanging cymbal. If I have the gift of prophecy and with full knowledge, comprehend all mysteries, if I have faith great enough to move mountains but have not love, I am nothing. If I give everything I have to feed the poor and hand over my body to be burned, but have not love I gain nothing." Love and service to others, at home and in the community, exemplifies the teachings professed by our religion.

Each of the boys needs to know that he can make a difference in another's life using his unique gifts. Joe and I remind them that God expects those who have been given much to return much. I am often heard reminding them that God loves a happy giver. I want them to give from their hearts, not because it looks good—following the concepts espoused by St. Paul to the Corinthians that if done without love in their hearts, the act means nothing in the eyes of God.

This understanding begins when they are very young and at home. The opportunities abound at home to share ones' gifts: to be compassionate and kind, to help each other with schoolwork, to work together on chores around the house, to willingly accept doing chores, to help take care of their brothers, to encourage and support each other, and to be respectful in what is said and done. Little things matter!

Once the boys learn to love in the home then they are able to share this love with others: friends, neighbors, classmates, teachers, and strangers. They can include a classmate in an activity so he won't feel excluded. They can help a friend with an assignment that he is struggling with. They can mow a neighbor's yard when he's sick. They can bring food on Sundays to leave in the basket for the food pantry. They can draw pictures and cards for the homebound. They can collect school supplies for underserved schools. I was so proud of our parish school, St. Francis de

Sales, and my son Matt's school, St. Raymond in Downey, California, when the students raised money to send to an orphanage in Lesotho, Africa, where Tony is a pediatrician treating pediatric AIDS. The needs of these children are great—and for the students to reach out a world apart and make a difference in many children's lives was touching and rewarding. The giving students received as much, if not more, from the experience than the children of Lesotho.

As the boys mature, they discover additional ways to make a difference. During their high school years, Tony and David accompanied a dentist in our parish, Dr. Theresa Garcia, to Ocotlan, Mexico. Dr. Garcia returned to her hometown to provide free dental care. They assisted her in the dental office but, more often than not, they could be found interacting with the children at the orphanage, usually organizing soccer games. Tommy spent a couple of weeks between his junior and senior high school year in the Dominican Republic building latrines in a small village. Chris, Joe Pat, and Matt volunteered at the Muscular Dystrophy camp during the summer. What was originally part of a high school requirement to fulfill one hundred service hours became a commitment to service that extended into subsequent years. Mark tutored students at an elementary school during his Seattle University years. Tommy is doing the same in Providence, Rhode Island, becoming a "big brother" to some of the boys he tutors.

We are told in Matthew 5:16: "Your light must shine before men so that they may see the goodness in your acts and give praise to your heavenly Father." With this sense of giving instilled in their hearts, they are now free to shine their light through their chosen careers and volunteer endeavors.

Basing My Philosophy on My Faith

My religious beliefs and faith are the foundation of my parenting philosophy. One is indistinguishable from the other. God's influence, His grace, permeates all aspects of my life. God is the purpose for what I do and how I live.

My discipline is of God—teaching the boys that God gives us a free will to choose right from wrong. He is merciful but just. He holds us accountable for our choices—for what we do and for what we don't do.

The education of my sons is of God—providing my sons opportunities to learn, develop, and use their God-given talents to love and serve Him.

Respect is of God—teaching the boys that God created everyone; therefore, all people deserve to be treated with dignity as children of God. Respect begins at home with the people God has chosen to place in our daily lives. We must respect ourselves by fulfilling our physical, emotional, intellectual, and spiritual needs. Eating, drinking, and exercising appropriately and adequately, and not abusing food, alcohol, drugs, and sex demonstrate respect for ourselves.

My values are of God—teaching my sons to establish priorities with God being the number one priority. And I remind them that all things are possible with Him by our side.

Love is of God—I teach them to love God with their whole hearts, souls, and minds, and to follow His commandment to love others and ourselves. "The basic vocation of every person is the same: Follow the way of love, even as Christ loved you." *(Follow the Way of Love)*

I encourage you to embrace and live your faith, to rediscover it if it hasn't been a priority in your family. My faith provides the foundation to build and to strengthen my family as well as the grace I need to fulfill the responsibilities God has bestowed on me as the mother of sons. I take to heart St. Luke's words: "When much has been given a man, much will be required of him. More will be asked of a man to whom more has been entrusted." God has entrusted me with ten sons. I must now strive to help each one of them reach his full potential—emotionally, physically, intellectually, and spiritually. That is what I am called to do as a mother.

Chapter 5

Discipline Matters—
Garcia-Prats or Garcia-Brats?

And the beginning, as you know, is always the most important
part, especially in dealing with anything young and tender.
That is the time when the character is being molded and easily
takes any impress one may wish to stamp on it.
—Plato

Teach me, O Lord, your way that I may walk in your truth;
direct my heart that it may fear your name.
—Psalm 86: 11

"Boys will be boys!" How often do we hear that statement? Unfortunately, too many parents allow their sons to be unruly and irresponsible and then excuse their behavior by saying "Boys will be boys." Usually when I am asked, "How do you do it?" what is actually being asked, besides the time and energy commitment, is "How are you successfully raising ten responsible and disciplined sons?"

I want to enjoy my sons. No one, including a mother, enjoys being around a brat, whether one or ten. She may love him but not enjoy him. So I choose to raise sons who are responsible, respectful, and well disciplined—sons I enjoy.

How then do I do it? In a nutshell, it means starting early, establishing guidelines, boundaries, rules, and expectations of my sons' behavior, determining age appropriate and realistic responsibilities, and remembering that **the ultimate goal of discipline is self-discipline**. Then when the expectations are not met or the responsibilities fulfilled, consequences follow—discipline. Discipline is essential, not only to allow each member of the family to develop and mature, but also to avoid chaos and frustration. I do not want to spend most of my parenting time disciplining. What fun is that?

The concept sounds easy as I write it on paper, but establishing expectations and responsibilities, following through to assure they are fulfilled, and determining appropriate and relevant consequences is anything but easy. I'll be the first to admit that raising sons to be good men is challenging, demanding, and constant, but at the same time an achievable and rewarding goal.

Effective Discipline

After thirty-two years of parenting, I recognize there are several factors that foster effective discipline. Begin when a child is young. Be consistent, loving, firm, and fair. Acknowedge the different developmental and moral stages of a child. Talk, listen, and empathize with the child. Prevent and avoid potential problems. Implement appropriate consequences. Maintain a positive approach and attitude.

Does this sound like a lot of effort? It is, especially in the early years, but once I started reaping the rewards with my older sons, Tony and David, I knew the effort was a worthwhile investment of my time and energy. We could have fun exploring the museums, visiting the zoo, feeding the ducks, taking mini field trips around Houston, and enjoying picnics. We could go almost anywhere because they were well behaved. At home, they would play for hours without a disagreement. They learned to give and take and help each other. Physical fighting was not an option. (Although many people find it hard to believe, the boys did not reconcile their differences by clobbering each other.) The time I now spend disciplining is minimal—they are self-disciplined, not to be construed to mean perfect. The early effort paid off.

I am fortunate to have Joe's support regarding discipline. By working together we send a clear message to our sons about what is appropriate and acceptable behavior, imparting our values and morals in the process. We are gentle, firm, loving, consistent, and constructive in our approach. We do not discipline the two year old, the eight year old, and the fourteen year old in exactly the same manner because they are at different physical, intellectual, and moral developmental stages. It is important to have age-appropriate expectations of each son as well as age-appropriate consequences, disciplining each son according to his age and needs. For example, it may be appropriate for a twelve year old to sit in his room for a thirty-minute time-out to think about his behavior. It is not appropriate for a two year old to do the same. Thirty minutes to a two year old is a lifetime. I can expect the thirteen year old to mow the back yard as a consequence, but not the four-year-old. Instead, the four year old could pick up all the pinecones or twigs in the yard. I can talk to my sixteen-year-old son about the moral and ethical ramifications of a choice. A six year old may not be ready for a discussion at that level.

A Positive Approach

Discipline is two-fold: teaching the boys what is acceptable and teaching them what is unacceptable. My discipline in the first few years served to protect the boys. Children at this age don't do "bad" things, but they can get into trouble. I taught them through persistent reinforcement what they could and couldn't do. For example, they couldn't crawl upstairs, play with lamp cords, put objects in their mouths, run into the street, or throw toys—or temper tantrums. I tried to minimize the "No's" by arranging the house to accommodate their growing curiosity and mobility. Breakables were on high shelves, sockets were covered with safety caps, bathroom doors were kept closed, and certain cabinets and drawers had safety locks. With grandchildren now gracing our home, we are replacing many of the safety locks and caps around the house as well as teaching them the "Do's" and "Don't's" at Grandma's house.

Persistent reinforcement also entailed teaching the boys at an early age the correct way to politely and respectfully act and talk, not just correcting them when they slipped up but also preventing them from slipping in the first place. They learned to say, for example, please and thank you by hearing the phrases over and over again from Joe and me—as well as from older brothers. In addition, they heard Joe and I express words of appreciation with each other and them. Praise was consistently doled out when they helped out. Timmy liked to help me empty the trash cans, add soap to the washing machine, carry in the mail, and bag the raked leaves. I reinforced his willingness to help by letting him help. I know how much easier and faster it would have been to do these activities myself, but I wanted to instill in each of the boys the need and importance of working together. I did not want to squelch their early desire to help out. I did want them to know how much I appreciated their pitching in with the daily chores—and I accomplished that through continual positive reinforcement.

The positive reinforcement continued through each stage of development. I thanked the boys for their help in straightening up the kitchen and their bathroom each morning. Jamie and Timmy, both in high school now, don't need reminding each morning to put their cereal bowls in the dishwasher. It has become second nature. I remember a reporter visiting our home ten years ago when the boys arrived home, got snacks, and then cleaned up their mess. She was amazed that they did it all without one word from me. The boys learned early on the routine and the consequence when not followed—restricted snacks after school for a few days. I don't look at positive reinforcement and positive discipline as rocket science but, more often than not, just plain common sense and practicality.

The boys learned respectful and appropriate behavior on a daily basis. When we ate meals, they learned basic table manners. If a child learns table manners at home he will replicate them at a restaurant or at a friend's home. Learning proper behavior at home leads to proper behavior outside the home whether at a restaurant, school, or church. Children need to learn when they can play and when they need to sit quietly out of respect for others. I do not appreciate going to an adult restaurant only to have disruptive children in attendance. I do not appreciate attending church services only to be distracted by misbehaving children. If we don't teach and expect proper behavior, we won't witness it. At church while on vacation this summer I finally, out of frustration, leaned over to the three children sitting in front of me, ranging in age I guessed from ten to thirteen, and made a simple statement: "You are too old to be acting like this in church." They immediately stopped fooling around—and, to the amazement of their parents, behaved the rest of the service. The expectation had been set; plus they knew I was right behind them and not going anywhere for the next hour. I am tolerant of a squirmy two year old but am less so of a twelve year old who is old enough to know better.

One afternoon at the orthodontist office, two brothers were acting obnoxiously. Their mother asked them to stop several times to no avail. The receptionist finally felt compelled to step in. The embarrassed mother looked at me, obviously not realizing that the six boys interacting quietly in the corner were my sons, and then tried to justify their behavior by saying, "Oh, you know. Boys will be boys." The receptionist didn't miss a beat as she nodded toward my sons: "Mrs. Garcia-Prats knows about boys. She has ten." Teaching appropriate behavior and then reinforcing it makes a difference in your son's life and yours. It goes back to choosing to be a responsible mother or not.

Many opportunities arose to reinforce the behavior I wanted and expected from the boys. When they were playing a board game together nicely, I commented on how wonderful it was to see them play so well. If I noticed a kindness performed by one of them, I thanked them. Often praise to one son led to one of the other boys mirroring his brother's actions. I credit the older boys in setting a good example for their younger siblings. They made parenting the younger boys easier because the younger boys, fortunately, wanted to emulate their big brothers. I wanted respectful and appropriate behavior to become habit forming. I agree with the words of Aristotle: "We are what we repeatedly do. Excellence then, is not an act, but a habit." Behavior, good or bad, becomes second nature through repetition. I also believe positive parenting will become second nature through repetition.

The Preventive Approach

I find it much easier and less frustrating to avoid discipline problems from the beginning than to exert the time, energy, and emotions needed to resolve them. Many problems and confrontations are avoided and prevented by simply setting boundaries and establishing rules. Our home would be in a constant state of chaos without some semblance of what is allowed and what isn't acceptable. They knew that television after dinner was not allowed. Use of the computer was monitored to assure they were completing assignments and not just playing games or communicating with friends. They knew who was responsible for cleaning the kitchen each night. The boys decided on the schedule and then each son accepted the responsibility to complete the task. They were expected to keep their rooms reasonably clean and the bathroom straightened up with towels hung up and dirty clothes in the hamper. They were expected to be respectful to their brothers, Joe, and me.

I found understanding each son's physical, emotional, and moral developmental stages guided me in my approach and reaction to situations. Understanding a son's need for independence or a son's indecisiveness, for example, helped me patiently tolerate his need to exert control over the littlest decisions: choosing which color cup he wanted for his juice in the morning or how he wanted his sandwich cut—a triangle or a square, or open (no bread on top) or closed. Jamie used to "bump" his cereal in the morning—he wanted the Cheerios pushed under the milk. Timmy would only wear black shorts or pants to preschool, while Tony had his favorite corduroys to wear to preschool.

Learning to be flexible in handling the day-to-day activities prevented minor, and sometimes major, confrontations that can easily frustrate and wear us out. It's learning to pick the battles, deciding what is actually important and what isn't. An example is hair length and style. While they are in elementary, middle, and high school, there is a dress code. They will by necessity abide by the code. When they head to college, almost all the boys have come home less clean cut—some a little, some a lot. I'm convinced it is mostly due to exerting some independence being on their own, but also I'm convinced they did not want to waste any money on a haircut. I loved Timmy's first comment when David returned home the first time from Creighton University: "David, you look like Chewbacca!" Joe and I knew we weren't going to have to say anything about his hair; his brothers would take care of that. Joe Pat's hair resembled an Afro; the children at his apartment complex at Regis University called him "Wolverine." Interesting now to see that most of the boys have chosen close cut hairstyles. Hair—not a battle to pick.

Also appreciating that boys need to be "doing," I always kept an activity tote bag with me. I filled the bag with paper, colors, books, playing cards, toy cars, etc. So while waiting at the pediatrician office, getting the oil changed in my Suburban, or sitting at a swim meet or soccer game, the boys had something to do to occupy their time and their fingers. I just kept the tote bag in the car so I had it when needed. Matty supplied his own diversion. How well I remember him toting his Matchbox cars case with him everywhere. He was rarely bored or into mischief.

It is unreasonable to expect a young boy to sit and do nothing, and then get upset with him when he fidgets. By planning ahead, I avoided situations that could have easily evolved into chaos with four, five, or six sons in tow; I had to take all the boys with me places before Tony was old enough to babysit.

As the boys moved into the middle school and high school years, Joe and I thought through where the boys were going and with whom, whether it was a middle school party or the after homecoming party. We asked ourselves whether we thought the son was developmentally ready for an activity. For example, was he ready to drive a car? Just because a son reached 16 years of age and completed the driver education course didn't mean he automatically received his license. He had to demonstrate responsible behavior at home, school, and outside activities as well as indicate he understood the responsibilities inherent in driving a car.

The Three C's: Choices, Consequences, and Consistency

As I previously shared, I am a strong believer in teaching the boys about choices. You choose to go in; you choose to go out. You choose to go left; you choose to go right. You choose to listen to your mom; you choose to ignore your mom. You choose to complete your chores: you choose not to complete your chores. You choose to do your homework; you choose not to do your homework. You choose to act and speak respectfully; you choose to be disrespectful. You choose to speed; you choose not to speed. You choose to drink; you choose not to drink.

My responsibility as their mom is to teach and guide my sons to make good choices and for them to understand there are consequences when they don't. I look at discipline as a way to **teach** the boys appropriate behavior with, to emphasize again, **the ultimate goal being self-discipline**. With that in mind, I have to make responsible choices as well when guiding the boys. If one of the boys wants to have something, do something, or go somewhere, I determine whether it is appropriate based on his age, the time of day, who is going, and the location. This can be difficult when other mothers are allowing their sons to attend movies or participate in activities that I don't consider appropriate for the boys at a particular age.

When seven-year-old Joe Pat was invited to the movie I*ndiana Jones and the Temple of Doom*, I knew he could not handle the frightening scenes, so I didn't accept his friend's offer. The friend's mom was upset with me and took my "No" as a criticism of her movie choice. Joe Pat, on the other hand, did not question my decision; he knew I had his best interest at heart as I did when eleven-year-old Danny was invited to a PG-13 movie. I know I often go against the grain, but I know my sons and I have a responsibility to make choices that I believe are in their best interests. I also remember the time twelve-year-old Mark went with some families on a camping trip. One afternoon, one of the dads called to ask my opinion on the boys going to see the movie *Lethal Weapon 4*. I told him I thought it was a bad idea. He teased, "We all thought that's what you'd think." He didn't try to convince me otherwise or embarrass Mark by telling him and the boys that I had voted against the choice; the parents just chose a different movie for the boys to see. I was most appreciative of the parents providing me the chance to give my input.

Likewise, when one of the boys wanted to attend an after homecoming party at a ranch outside of Houston his senior year in high school, I asked some questions about the plans: "Were the parents of the young man going to be there?"—"No." "How many young people were invited?"—"A lot." "What time did he expect to be home?"—"Don't know." I turned the question back to him asking why he would want to go to a party without adult supervision knowing what might possibly take place—drinking, drug use, and sexual activity. He realized it would not be a good decision and, of course, the answer was going to be "No" anyway. Fortunately, quite a few other parents agreed; a group of friends got together after the dance and ended up having a great time. A few weeks later, this same son came to me and, without going into detail, shared that it was good that he hadn't attended the party. If I can help the boys learn to make appropriate decisions while they are still at home, hopefully they will carry what they have learned with them.

Joe and I set limits whenever we felt it was best for the boys. Sleepovers, for example, at too young an age usually left us with a cranky, irritable child because they didn't get to sleep at a reasonable hour. Not a good idea—the whole family paid the price of the night out. We also made a decision to restrict the boys from at home parties during the middle school years based on our gut feelings. They were free to attend parties at skating rinks, bowling alleys, or other more public venues. I remember the night David asked if he could go to one of these parties. When we told him we had decided we didn't think these get togethers were a good idea, he sighed—a sigh of relief. Joe, to provide a diversion from the party, picked up tickets to the Rice University versus Georgetown University basketball game for David and a few friends. I heard for weeks how we had ruined the party because, given the choice, the boys preferred attending the game rather than the party. We maintained this restriction for all the boys—and they survived socially intact. Knowing what I've learned about what happens at too many of these parties, I know without a doubt it is still a good practice. Not all parents share the same understanding of chaperoning. They may be in the house but not actually watching the comings and goings of the young people. We are throwing our children into situations they are not ready or mature enough to handle. I find many parents are still naïve regarding what their children know at this age and what their children feel compelled to participate in so as not to feel left out or uncool. These parties are not immune from drinking, drug use, or sexual activity. Yes, I am referring to middle schoolers. My advice: Parents beware. The "ban" was a blanket ban so the issue of which parents I trusted to host a safe party was not a factor in the decision.

Do the boys challenge these decisions? Sure they do. They may ask to go and question our reasoning or, in the case of Joe Pat, try to maneuver his way to one party. He and a friend decided they wanted to attend a dance Joe and I had already vetoed. They figured if Joe Pat spent the night with his friend, not mentioning to us that they intended to go to the dance, I wouldn't find out. What they didn't know was that I had shared with his friend's mom my attitude on attending parties in sixth grade. Confused, she called me. Needless to say, Joe Pat did not attend the dance, and he didn't spend the night. Instead, he spent the weekend in "hard labor"—working in the yard, cleaning gutters—to remind him of the importance of honesty and trust.

I strongly believe that our sons want and need guidelines; and they need us to establish and enforce them. If you love your children, do what you know is best for them, not what is easy. The word "No" is often the loving response to a son's request.

While I teach the boys early that there are rules, standards, and consequences, I also make it quite clear that I will implement and enforce them. If I begin early when they are ages two, four, and six, it's easier when they're twelve, fourteen, and sixteen. For one, they learn I mean what I say and will follow through as needed. I don't believe in "three strikes you're out"—the boys are asked once and expected to follow through. Frustration builds when you have to keep asking a son to do the same thing over and over again. Then you lose it. To avoid the frustration and anger—mean what you say and say what you mean. Set boundaries, and then keep them.

I also learned that I had to be consistent in my expectations and rules. If eating ice cream in the den was unacceptable on Monday, eating ice cream in the den needed to be unacceptable the rest of the week. If jumping on the sofa was inappropriate at ten o'clock in the morning, then jumping on the sofa at four o'clock in the afternoon should also be objectionable. If we are inconsistent on our rules or the time of day when we enforce them, we send a mixed message to our sons—at all ages. Inconsistency confuses them on what is acceptable or unacceptable. They are more likely to try to get away with something and take their chances on not getting caught if I'm inconsistent. It was hard to be consistent when I was tired at four o'clock in the afternoon after a long day. But holding to a rule or behavior at all times of the day began to pay off; the boys learned to follow the rules more consistently. My consistency fostered their consistency.

Once the boys understand the expectations, responsibilities, rules, and boundaries, then each of them has to choose whether to abide or not abide by the standards established, whether at home, school, athletics, or extracurricular activities. If he doesn't choose to pick up his toys at the end of the day, he may not have the toys to play with the next day. If he doesn't choose to work on his physical endurance and skills, then his coach may choose not to play him in the next soccer game. If he doesn't complete his reading assignment, his inaction will likely result in a lower grade than if he had read the material. If he doesn't clean his room, he will end up having additional chores to complete. If he breaks a window because he kicked the ball against the house (and obviously missed) when he was told not to, he pays to replace it. If he looses a textbook (we buy textbooks in high school), he pays for the new one. Joe and I don't argue with the boys. We don't nag the boys. Neither is effective. We establish the guidelines and then follow through.

I have frustrated parents share with me that their sons don't **want** to clean the kitchen or mow the yard. I assure you when it's Tommy's turn to do the dishes he doesn't jump up from the table, look at his brothers, and yell, "Yes! It is my night to do dishes." They would prefer to spend their time doing other things as well, but they accept their responsibilities. Whatever the chore or responsibility you have deemed appropriate, assuring the chore is completed or the responsibility fulfilled is the parent's responsibility. Joe often says, "While it's important to have expectations, you also need inspections"—meaning the parent needs to follow through and, if necessary, implement a consequence when the expectation was not met.

The boys need to appreciate that their parents aren't the only ones setting and enforcing boundaries. Teachers, principals, and law enforcement also determine what is acceptable and unacceptable. When Chris was in eighth grade he elected to enroll in a high school entrance exam preparation class being offered after school. One afternoon Chris and a group of friends decided it was too pretty an October day to sit in a boring prep class. They chose to go to the park across the street instead; the park was off limits during school hours. Unfortunately for the students, some middle school teachers, who were holding a meeting in a classroom that faced the park, noticed the students, rounded them up, and brought them back to the school. The school notified the parents, me being one of them, informing us of what happened and that the students would not be allowed to participate in any after-school activities for two weeks.

A few of the students were not actively involved in an activity at the time, but the rest of the students were involved in sports or cheerleading. Some parents of the athletes and cheerleaders protested the discipline, claiming it was unfair. Chris hoped we would jump on the bandwagon. Wrong! Joe and I explained to Chris that he made a choice to skip the class, and when you gamble you better be prepared to pay the price. Unfortunately for Chris this happened during soccer season, and he was captain of the team. He would not be able to play for the two weeks. He learned his pockets were full and he had more to lose than some of his friends.

Determining the right consequence to fit the situation can often be the hardest part of disciplining. Some situations are easy—the toy not picked up becomes my toy for the next day or two. Other situations take more thought and consideration—the boys bickering who sits where in the car led to assigned seats. Sometimes the discipline meant a privilege revoked, other times I assigned an additional chore or two. Time-out was effective, and still is, when situations warrant a child being removed from an activity or needing to calm down. Unfortunately, too many parents overuse time-out for every little offense, thus lessening its effectiveness. The same can hold true for other disciplinary actions. I remember the mom whose children did countless jumping jacks whenever they annoyed a sibling. The constant teasing continued in spite of the number doled out. The action did not change the behavior of the children—they actually thought it was funny. Ineffective discipline can be just as useless as no discipline.

I've learned over the years that many of us shy away from implementing consequences because we may have to pay a price in the form of inconvenience to ourselves. I learned from our first pediatrician, Dr. Richard Plessala, the father of six children, the importance of implementing a natural consequence in spite of the inconvenience it might cause me. When Tony and David were three and a half years old and two and a half years old they started urinating wherever they found it convenient at the moment in order to avoid interrupting their playtime. I was frustrated and asked Dr. Plessala what I should do. He turned the question back to me: "What do you think you should do?" "Put them back in diapers?" was my simple reply. He agreed. Yet, I didn't want or need two kids in diapers again with Chris due in another month. He assured me they wouldn't like wearing diapers and would quickly learn to "pee" only in the potty. He was right—it took only a day. I reassure you that more often than not the long-term benefits are well worth the temporary inconvenience.

I'll give another example. If the boys were late for curfew, they lost their driving privileges for a period of time. That meant they would not be able to drive the car to school or be driven by a friend. If one of the older boys wasn't driving, Joe or I needed to transport the boys to school, adding an additional forty minutes to the routine for one of us in the morning and in the afternoon. But by enforcing the restriction we sent a clear message that we would follow through with the consequence. We also learned that a high school senior really would prefer not having his mom dropping him off and picking him up from school—a great motivator for making curfew. I also remember the afternoon when Chris and Joe Pat were visibly annoyed that I was late picking them up from school. After reminding them that the bus was a viable alternative, they were more appreciative of my time and effort.

We also determined the discipline relevant to the infraction. In other words, we didn't tell our son he could *never* drive to school again for being thirty minutes late one night. If you're not ready to follow through with the consequence, don't impose it. You are setting yourself up for failure as well as worsening your ability to discipline in the future.

Temper tantrums are another source of dismay for parents, especially when they occur outside the home. The experience is embarrassing. Giving in to the child, essentially establishing peace at a high cost, conveys to the child that with enough whining and complaining to embarrass you, you will relent. Calmly standing your ground, completing the task at hand, and then returning home to deal with the misbehavior sends the message that the behavior will not be tolerated. I dealt with a few temper tantrums over the years. I know how unpleasant it is to have people criticize you with their eyes. I also know that when my son didn't garner the reaction he wanted from me or receive what he was demanding, he learned the whining and fussing was a useless effort on his part. If you give in, be assured the behavior will continue because he knows he will win the battle with enough yelling and screaming. At home, a son throwing a temper tantrum was either ignored or relegated to his room. If he wanted to fuss, he could do so by himself without an audience. I love hearing David and Rita softly remind our granddaughter,

Gabriela, when she whines: "Use words, please." The whining does not get her what she wants.

Recently a friend was visiting with her young daughter. Addison wanted some candy shortly before dinner. Her mom, Danielle, told her no. Addison looked at her mom and with a slight whine in her voice stated, "But, Mommy, I *want* the candy!" Danielle calmly responded, "I know you want it but it's too close to dinner." Addison knew her mom listened and then made a decision that a disappointed Addison knew she had to accept.

Our sons' acceptance of "No" or other consequences and disciplines didn't happen after one occurrence. It takes consistently following through with what you expect from your children. I wanted Garcia-Prats not Garcia-BRATS running around my house. The choice was mine—and took a lot of effort early on. But again, by investing the time and energy when the boys were young, less time was required disciplining later on.

Calmly standing your ground is another important lesson we can learn as parents. Our children **need** us to stay in control—verbally and physically. They need us to exemplify self-discipline in action. How often have we witnessed an out-of-control child in a grocery store followed by an out-of-control parent: The child yelling, "I want that candy!" and the parent yelling right back, "No! Be quiet. (or worse) You can't have it." Or another common scenario where one child is hitting his brother and the mother grabs the child and spanks him while telling him not to hit. I recently witnessed two pre-teen brothers pushing and shoving each other in a local store to the point where one finally got hurt. The parents ignored the fighting until there was "blood." The father then stepped in only to roughly push and shove the other son until he, too, was crying. A male customer asked him to stop only to be told that as his father he had the right to discipline his son in the manner he determined effective. Parental rights do not allow for abusive discipline as this father found out when security was called.

Joe and I learned that calmly addressing the boys, whether four or fourteen years old, with a quiet voice was much more effective than ranting and raving. Discipline is about changing behavior and choices. Firmly and lovingly stating the issue at hand and the consequence conveys respect but also demonstrates your own self-discipline in dealing with a child's misconduct.

Respectful discipline is imperative. Even though I may be upset and disappointed with one of the boys, I still have to avoid demeaning words and actions when disciplining. He **must** understand that, in spite of the infraction, I still love him. I do not advocate spanking or any type of corporal punishment—I consider that demeaning and ineffective. Utilizing methods that build up, teach, and motivate will guide a son to make better choices in the long term. I ultimately want the boys to make the right choice because it is the right choice, not out of fear of physical punishment or verbal abuse. I don't expect the boys to reach this level of moral development at three years of age but the process of learning and choosing right from wrong begins at three years of age.

My discipline style does not translate into being weak and permissive. On the contrary, Joe and I are firm but again loving. I remember the Saturday afternoon I asked fourteen-year-old Danny to mow the back yard, determining the front yard could wait another week. He looked at me and indignantly said, "I don't mow the back yard; Jamie mows the back yard. I mow the front." After I caught my breath, I looked out the window and told him that I thought the front yard needed to be mowed after all. He begrudgingly agreed to mow the front yard, still insisting though that Jamie mow the back. (Jamie was playing in a soccer tournament that weekend and not home to mow.) But that's not where the conversation ended. In very clear terms, I let him know that yes, he would mow the front yard—**and** the back. When he protested, I added edging and sweeping to the list. As he started to protest again, a wise eight-year-old Timmy chimed in, "I don't know about you, but I wouldn't say anything else." Danny proceeded to mow the front **and** back yards, edge, and sweep—and then went to his room where he banged on his drums, releasing the remnants of his anger and frustration.

Do I believe Danny learned from the experience? I do, and that is my hope for all the disciplinary actions Joe and I implement. We accept the fact that our sons are not perfect (neither are their parents) and will make mistakes and poor choices at times. I want them to learn from their mistakes, to learn that their actions affect other people, to learn to make different choices when confronted with a similar situation, to think before they act or speak, and to know that we love them unconditionally. More often than not, how Joe and I react and deal with a situation will determine whether it becomes a learning experience.

When Chris skipped the prep class and we supported the school's disciplinary action, he learned a few lessons: he disappointed his teachers and his parents, his mom and dad wouldn't rescue him from possible consequences, and his choice affected other people—in this case, his teammates. Our children need to learn that their choices and actions do have ramifications. Many adults have not learned this important lesson. Countless stories appear each day in the newspaper describing individuals involved in immoral, illegal, and unethical conduct from elected officials to prominent businessmen to teachers to athletes to law enforcement personnel and religious leaders. Their actions and decisions impacted others, most often their own families.

If a child is continually rescued from his mistakes and poor choices, he will begin to assume that he can do whatever he wants because mom or dad will take care of the problem. He is learning a powerful lesson, but not one I want my sons to learn. No mother wants her son to "suffer" or struggle, but letting your son face a consequence when he makes a mistake or a poor choice is a loving reaction. I know how hard it is to see a son do poorly on an exam, miss two weeks of soccer, or be restricted from being with friends. I know it's hard not running up to the school to deliver the forgotten lunch or homework assignment. I know it's hard requiring him to replace the lost book or jacket. He will not starve and, hopefully, after facing a consequence at school, he will remember next time to be organized and have the assignment in his backpack. He won't want to spend his money to replace the lost book or jacket, so maybe he will be more conscientious about his belongings in the future. Teaching this concept early and often is a gift to our sons, although they might not realize it at the moment. I have to continually remind myself to do what is best for my sons, not necessarily what is easy.

I still chuckle at the middle school principal's "rescue" story. She shared how parents had begun to fax forgotten homework to the school for their children. The student never received the fax because she wisely walked it from the fax machine over to the shredder.

When David was in second grade, he couldn't find his uniform vest one morning. He was responsible for having his uniform and backpack ready the night before. By the time David located his vest, the car pool had left. In addition to arriving late to school, he had to explain to the principal, a towering 6-foot figure, what happened. She listened patiently and then, suppressing a smile, proceeded to revoke his beloved recess time to complete missed class work. I could have helped David find the vest in time for the car pool, but he needed to learn to fulfill his responsibilities. I can't remember another instance when David didn't have his uniform and schoolwork ready in the morning.

Can you imagine the chaos in my home each morning if each of the boys was running around the house looking for his shoes, his math book, or a test that needed to be signed? It goes back to preventing problems and avoiding frustrations by teaching them to be organized and prepared from the beginning.

Empathy Matters

I found it helpful to put myself in my sons' place at times and in certain situations, remembering what it was like at his age under similar circumstances. When you empathize, you often react differently than you would otherwise. Can't each of us remember the power of peer pressure? Understanding doesn't mean we condone the behavior, but it may cause us an insight into where he's coming from.

When one of the boys came home from school with an "attitude," I came to realize that something happened during the day that had him uptight. While I won't let the boys treat me disrespectfully, I will let them blow off steam by sharing their day or encourage them to find an outlet. I have my bad days and my moods. So do my sons.

During the middle school years, being empathetic is a must. Our sons are going through major physical, emotional, intellectual, and social changes. A mom at a middle school presentation asked in frustration, "Cathy, I can't deal with my son's raging hormones. I'm having enough trouble dealing with my own. What am I suppose to do with him?" I suggested she should be rather understanding with her son since he had to deal with her emotional swings as well as his own. She laughed and admitted that she hadn't thought of it quite that way.

The middle school years are difficult years for our sons. I've always contended that if Joe and I could get a son through the middle school years intact, then the high school years would be easier sailing. And, for the most part, that has proven true. There are many new challenges our children face when they enter middle school. There are many pressures: finding acceptance from friends, achieving academically, and understanding the physical changes occurring in their bodies, which seems like a daily phenomenon. Not many of us would choose to relive those years.

In addition, with the advent of technology—computers, cell phones—new challenges arise in how to make them a positive in our son's life and not a source of conflict for himself and with us. While I appreciate that the boys can keep in touch with their brothers so easily and inexpensively versus when Tony and David were attending college, I also have to appreciate the downside of technology and how it is abused. Young people at this age don't always understand the implication of their actions and the effect on others. Bullying, either verbally or electronically, is hurtful and can be emotionally devastating to the recipient. Abusing the cell phone by copying a test and sending it to a friend is still cheating. Taking inappropriate pictures and sharing them on-line is not only wrong but also dangerous.

These are years not to throw in the towel but to stand firm and assure your son that you love him and are there for him. Remember, too, that laughter and humor can often diffuse difficult situations. How often did I do "roll call"—Tony, David, and Matt—when the name I **needed** was Mark? Chuckles ensued and the tension relieved. I still enjoy sharing the story of David and Jamie **and** the policeman. David's senior year in high school, he offered to pick up Chris from school following his exams. Jamie went along for the ride. They arrived home, ate lunch, and then went outside to shoot baskets. Later that afternoon, I left to pick up the younger boys from school. Jamie again came along for the ride. Driving to school, we saw a police car and I pointed it out to him. Jamie declared very matter-of-factly, "David talked to a policeman today." "What?" I said. "David talked to a policeman today," he repeated. Now why would David be talking to a policeman, I asked myself. The answer seemed obvious. When we returned home, David was still outside shooting baskets. I nonchalantly remarked, "David, I understand you had a nice conversation with a policeman this morning. Anything interesting?" David was rather amazed that I already knew he had received a speeding ticket. I teasingly reminded him he had a little brother in the car who, using Chris's terminology, "ratted," innocently I might add, on him.

While discipline matters, I have to make sure I keep the day-to-day mishaps in perspective. My friend, Mary, an experienced mother of eight, always asked herself, "In the scheme of life, how important is this?" I find it helpful to ask the same question. What may seem like a tsunami today may not be in a few days. Ultimately, you want to raise sons who are loving, caring, responsible, and self-disciplined—sons you enjoy!

Chapter 6

No Room for Complacency— Addressing Challenging Issues

In all your ways be mindful of him, And he will make straight your paths.
—Proverbs 3:6

Everyone can be serene when things run smoothly;
it is in difficult situations that fidelity and constancy are proven.
—St. Frances Xavier Cabrini

As I started writing this chapter, I kept hearing the words from one of Bob Dylan's songs: "And the times they are a-changin'." I have seen the times change right before my parenting eyes. Computers, internet, iPods, and cell phones were not a part of my older sons' lives during high school. The younger boys, though, do not know a world without computers and cell phones. Communicating today is more often achieved through texting than by phone. And, when a phone call is made, it is usually by cell phone rather than by a landline. With all the new and advanced technology come many benefits but also new challenges for parents to add to the list that already exists.

When I was pregnant with Timmy a mom commented to me that poor Timmy probably would have to go it alone being our tenth son. She determined that I would be tired of the parenting hassles by this time and most likely let him do whatever he wanted. So far, that hasn't happened—ask Timmy! I may have an even stronger determination to remain actively involved because I realize the many challenges our young men face and, in addition, I believe we reap what we sow. These times do not provide the luxury of sitting back and ignoring the issues our young men confront as they move through the middle school and high school years. Complacency is not advised—whether you have one son or ten.

Some of the issues our sons face and must learn to responsibly handle include alcohol, drugs—legal and illegal—dating and sex, driving, computers, media, cell phones, and the social pressures inherent in each of these at this age. Many of these are interconnected. Alcohol or drug use, for example, may lead to unplanned sexual behavior.

I found that dealing with each of these areas meant choosing to live and teach counterculturally. Although it's not easy to be different at any age, I found it brought a sense of peace knowing Joe and I were making these countercultural choices for the right reasons. Our sons need to know without a shadow of a doubt how we feel about each of these areas. At the same time, if we tell them one thing and live another, they see right through the hypocrisy. If we don't tell them where we stand and then set the example in our own choices, our sons will assume we agree with what society deems appropriate and moral.

I also found that I have to stay educated on the issues as best I can. That may happen through reading materials, programs provided through the schools, media stories, and the internet. I cannot assume that just because I attended one program five years ago that I am adequately educated. New challenges continually arise. "Raves" are one example. I had heard about raves in the Houston area, but not until I attended a parent education program at the boys' high school was I actually aware how dangerous raves truly are. I am going to share an excerpt from the National Drug Intelligence Center. "By the late 1990s, raves in the United States had become so commercialized that the events were little more than an exploitation of American youth. Today's raves are characterized by high entrance fees, extensive drug use, exorbitantly priced bottled water, very dark and often dangerously overcrowded dance floors, and "chill rooms," where teenage ravers go to cool down and often engage in open sexual activity. Moreover, many club owners and promoters appear to promote the use of drugs—especially MDMA (Ecstasy). They provide bottled water and sports drinks to manage hyperthermia and dehydration; pacifiers to prevent involuntary teeth clenching; and menthol nasal inhalers, chemical lights, and neon glow sticks to enhance the effects of MDMA." The high school program that evening included an expert on substance abuse and a video of a rave. The video was most disturbing. The school organized the evening so parents could attend the program and then proceed to parent-teacher conferences. Unfortunately, only a handful of parents took advantage of the program. Yet, when one mom and I were discussing the program and what we had just learned, another mom commented that she didn't attend because she didn't find it necessary. She admitted, though, when we asked her, that she had never heard of a rave or was aware of the proximity to the school of a drug paraphernalia store. A few weeks after the program, a teacher shared with me that flyers for a rave were distributed at a local middle school. Parents unbeknowingly took their children to the rave based on the information on the flyer that promoted it as a dance. Fortunately, their children realized that the event was not what they expected and called their parents to pick them up. Complacency, I reiterate, is not advised!

Materials are constantly being updated by concerned organizations. The internet is an excellent source of information, but it does us no good if we don't access it. Strake Jesuit College Preparatory provides parents with a very informative handbook *A Parent's Guide for the Prevention of Alcohol, Tobacco, and Other Drug Use* circulated by an organization called the Community of Concern. Again, it does me no good unless I take the time to read it and find the opportunity to share the information with my sons.

Does that mean by talking to your sons you will eliminate all problems down the road? No, but you have a better chance at success than if you don't. When dealing with our sons, I find it helpful to remember what it was like to be that age and the choices I confronted. I know I made my share of poor decisions along the way, not thinking through completely the possible consequences of what I was doing. Good people do make poor choices at times yet still must face the consequences of their actions. Our young people are no different. So when you ask your son, "Why did you do that?" and he answers, "I don't know," he really may not know why. And when he does find himself in a pickle, he needs to know his parents will stand by him and **together** get back on track. A strong family isn't one that never encounters difficulties but, rather, one who learns how to face the challenges placed before them in a constructive and healthy manner. The goal remains the same: guiding a son to reach his full potential.

I strongly advise getting to know your sons' friends and their parents. This may prove more challenging as they move into the middle school and high school years because students usually come from different feeder schools. Joe and I, though, want to know who our sons are socializing with and feel comfortable that they share similar values. Look for opportunities through school or extracurricular activities to get together. We found it beneficial to share with other parents our feelings on the acceptability of different activities. You'd be surprised how many parents share the same concerns as you do. If we stick together then we all benefit.

I am fortunate to have staff at the schools that don't hesitate to contact me when they have a concern about one of the boys. That is a blessing in and of itself. When they express a concern, I take it seriously—my antenna goes up even higher.

Driving

I was probably as excited about Tony obtaining his driver's license as he was. Jamie was a baby when Tony turned sixteen, and my days by then were filled with all the boys' activities. Having one more driver in the house would be a blessing, even if Tony only drove to and from school and his swimming practice. I still chuckle when I remember the dad of three children who insinuated his days were much more difficult than mine because I had an extra driver. I kindly reminded him that I had to wait sixteen years for the extra driver just like everyone else.

A driver's license brings with it not only new found freedom for our sons but also new levels of responsibility. The magic age of sixteen is not the sole determining factor required in the Garcia-Prats's household to obtain a license. Each of the boys had to first demonstrate that he was responsible in all areas of his life. In addition, Joe and I had to feel comfortable that he was ready to drive without adult supervision. A car powered by immature and irresponsible hands is a deadly weapon, as reflected in the number of teenage boys' traffic related deaths. Lives can change in a split second.

Driver education requirements differ in each state. In Texas a graduated program is now in place. With the implementation of the graduated program, the number of teenage traffic deaths has been significantly reduced. It makes sense. The program requires a minimum of six months driving before obtaining an unrestricted license. The days of completing a driver's education course one day and getting your license the next are gone. This requirement alone increases the level of experience of our young drivers. The graduated program also limits the number of non-siblings allowed in the car, reducing driver distractions, one cause of teenage accidents. In addition, there are designated hours when a sixteen year old is allowed to drive. In Houston we are also fortunate to have a midnight curfew for under eighteen year olds.

The experience factor cannot be underestimated. The difference in ability from week one to month one is dramatic, just as it is from the first month to the sixth month. Joe and I try to have our sons enroll in a sanctioned driver's education course as soon after their fifteenth birthday as possible. This provides our son with nearly a year of supervised driving. We start slowly, practicing in our neighborhood for weeks before heading on to a main street. Every afternoon for a half hour or so we go out, stopping, starting, turning left, and turning right. Highway driving is usually left to last—and I usually "allow" Joe to share in this hair-raising portion of a son's driver's education.

We clearly state the expectations we have once a son begins driving as well as the consequences that follow including revocation of the license if deemed appropriate. This is one area that consistency and follow through are essential. Driving under the influence of alcohol or drugs and street racing are never tolerated. Our sons know, in addition, that they are responsible for fines, required defensive driving courses, and the deductible in case of an accident. Since they are responsible for the passengers in the car, we expect them to remind their passengers to buckle up. The number of traffic related teen deaths could be reduced just by an increase in teenage seat belt use.

As an aside, Joe and I do not buy the boys a car on their sixteenth birthday or any birthday. We have a third car that the boys drive to school and to their activities. The boys purchase a used car upon graduation from college. (To date eight of the boys have survived without a car during the college years.) They do not expect us to buy them a car; they appreciate the financial commitment we make to their education.

Alcohol

When it comes to alcohol, too many parents, unfortunately, still hold to the belief that underage drinking is a right of passage or consider it less dangerous than drugs. Underage drinking is illegal and adults (meaning anyone 21 years of age or older in this context) who provide alcohol to a minor may be held legally responsible. Your son needs to know where you stand on alcohol. Your attitude and behavior influences his attitude and behavior. He needs to know as well how drinking affects his judgment and the decisions he makes while under the influence. He needs to appreciate the effects alcohol has on the body and how it may, for example, affect athletic performance. He needs to know if there is a history of alcoholism in the family because research indicates that alcohol dependency may be genetic, increasing his risk of alcoholism. In addition, he needs to fully understand there are consequences for underage drinking.

Underage drinking continues to be a problem in our high schools and colleges. I'm amazed at how many homes provide liquor to our young people under the guise of "chaperoning" their drinking. Even if the young person is not allowed to drive home, providing alcohol to a young person is wrong. I'm also amazed that students drink **then** have the nerve to show up at a school function knowing they might be asked to take a breathalyzer test. That decision alone is an indication of their lack of mature thinking.

The reasons young people drink are the same as when we were growing up: to put oneself at ease in social situations, to relieve anxiety or stressful situations, and to garner peer acceptance. Unfortunately, although they have heard the dangers of drinking, most students believe they will always be in control. The statistics don't bear that out. Every year there are over 5,000 alcohol related deaths in the under 21-year-old age group. Approximately 4,000 of the deaths are traffic related, and the remaining deaths are non-traffic related, such as alcohol poisoning (National Clearinghouse for Alcohol and Drug Information).

I was a resident assistant during my college years. I used to urge the girls on my floor to know, before a situation arose, where they stood on drinking, tobacco, drugs, and sex. When you know where you stand on these issues, you are less likely to make a spur of the moment decision you will later regret. When I was in college, the drinking age in New Orleans was eighteen, so it was important to know whether you were going to drink and, if so, how much. The difficulty arises, though, because young people don't usually know their limit so they can easily get high on what they consider barely drinking.

I will share with you a couple incidents that Joe and I encountered with our sons with regard to alcohol. One had to do with one son during high school who made a poor decision when he and a couple friends went to pick up another friend at a party. They had no intention of attending the party but were just picking up the friend and returning home. As they arrived, the police also arrived to raid the party. Although they had not entered the house or been drinking, the boys received an MIP (minor in possession). The son was furious that he had received the MIP when he had not consumed any alcohol, and we believed he had not. We also reminded him, though, that we had told him that one reason we discouraged attending parties was because, if alcohol is present on the property, you can receive an MIP even if you haven't consumed any. A hard lesson to learn but it is reality. He faced a $500 fine that he would be responsible to pay. In this case, the MIP was dropped.

With another son the experience was a little different. He was attending a fraternity party where alcohol was openly being served. The police raided the party, issuing MIP's to the underage students. The 21 year old and over students faced more serious charges. Our son faced a fine and community service. When we discussed the matter with him, his reaction was a little disconcerting. He felt, since he was paying the fine and performing the community service, we shouldn't be overly concerned. We let him know that if he had extra funds to be paying MIP fines, then we would expect him to carry more of the financial responsibility for his college expenses. Why should Joe and I sacrifice so he could continue to behave irresponsibly? If he received another MIP, he would be expected to increase the amount he contributed to his education.

There has been a recent push by many universities to lower the drinking age to 18 years of age. With the statistics on alcohol related deaths and injuries in the under 21-year-old age group (both college and non-college young people), I find it hard to believe that the universities really believe that lowering the drinking age is the answer to the problem, as if binge drinking will disappear with a lower drinking age. I would hope our universities could discern more creative and effective ways to address the problem. At one of the boy's colleges, the athletic and fitness center closes at 10 o'clock on weekend nights. Although it may not prevent all the students from going on drinking binges, I know my son has commented on how he and his friends wished they would change the ridiculous hours on the weekend. Universities and high schools need to offer positive alternatives to drinking, if they are determined to make a difference.

Drugs

The drug culture places many challenges before us as parents. Drugs have infiltrated our society at younger and younger ages with no segment of society immune. As with alcohol, our attitude and behavior regarding drug use, both legal and illegal, does influence our sons' attitude and behavior. They mimic us for good and for bad.

Drug abuse ranges from legal over-the-counter and prescription drugs such as painkillers, stimulants, and sedatives to illegal drugs such as marijuana, ecstasy, GHB, heroin, cocaine, and anabolic steroids. Striving to learn and understand the potential dangers of drugs is imperative. The street names of the drugs often change, increasing the learning curve. It takes a constant effort to keep up with these changes. That is another reason to take advantage of the programs the schools and community offer parents as well as to look for materials that help educate us, such as the booklet provided by the Community of Concern. They update their materials to keep us better informed.

As with parents who rationalize underage drinking, there are parents who are not that concerned with a son's use of marijuana. They may have smoked marijuana or, in some cases, still do, so they hesitate or feel hypocritical addressing smoking pot. They may also feel the concerns are over stated since they survived intact. Anyone who works with substance abuse will strongly disagree on this attitude and approach to dealing with the use of marijuana. The quality of marijuana and many other drugs are more potent than in years past, and remain just as illegal. We must always be concerned about a son putting **any** illegal substance into his body.

In addition to illegal drug use, we are faced with the growing problem of abuse of legal drugs. Research indicates that prescription drug abuse is on the rise among our youth, especially among our young men. According to an article by Lori Whitten (a National Institute on Drug Abuse staff writer, another informative website for parents), "Stimulant medication (Ritalin, Dexedrine and Adderall) was more prevalent among students who were white, members of fraternities or sororities and earning lower grades." She also pointed out that the more competitive academic programs reported higher rates of abuse. Although the research focused on drug abuse on college campuses, I believe, unfortunately, the research results would be similar if conducted in high schools. Maybe we should ask if the stresses our young people are experiencing due to unrealistic expectations are driving them to abuse drugs, legal and illegal, in order to cope with their stress-filled lives. Maybe we should also ask ourselves how do our children see us deal with the stresses in our own lives. Do we keep our goals realistic and our lives in perspective? Do they witness us resorting to drugs, legal or illegal, to relieve our anxieties?

I don't think any of us would argue that prevention rather than addiction is definitely the better route to follow. With that in mind, we need to focus on prevention, understanding that the reasons a son may experiment with drugs are the same reasons someone drinks. Times of transition in our sons' lives pose increased risk of drug and alcohol use, such as when entering a new school or moving to a new city with possibly new academic, athletic, or social challenges, heading off to college where they experience more independence and academic and social pressures, family upheavals such as divorce or illnesses, or maybe even training under a new coach or teacher with different expectations and demands. Staying connected with our sons during these times of transition is imperative. Although a young teen may not need us in the same ways he did at five or ten years of age, he still needs to know we are there for him and care about what he is doing, how he is doing, and with whom he is socializing. They know where our heart is by our commitment to them.

I know that eating dinner as a family provides Joe and me one very important opportunity to interact with the boys. It's a time not only to catch up on the events of our day but also to notice any nuances in their physical and/or emotional behavior. I know that middle school and high school aged boys tend to be moody anyway, so noticing additional changes in behavior can often be challenging. At the same time, if you are involved in their lives on a regular basis, you have a better chance—not a one hundred percent chance—but a better chance of picking up on little changes.

I say that because, even with all Joe and I have learned and our consistent involvement with the boys, one of the boys experimented with marijuana. Joe and I asked ourselves over and over again what did we miss. We had had reservations about a couple of his friends and made sure we were up when he got home after being with them. We noticed nothing. Dwelling on what we missed though was not going to make a difference at this point. We needed to tackle the situation head on and determine how best to help him make different choices and realize the consequences of continued use, even if he was just using occasionally with friends. We stuck firm to the consequences we had established—no driving and restricted activities to name a couple. Then we sought individual counseling, and also sent him to participate in some group sessions where he saw firsthand the struggles of long-term users. Both were effective. I will not deny it was a difficult time, a very difficult time. I found it hard not to blame myself for missing something or not providing him with enough self-respect and self-confidence to say no when he needed to. I will always be grateful to the counselor who worked with him and encouraged all of us as we healed. The counselor kept reminding Joe and me what a great kid he was, which we knew. We sincerely believe he learned from the experience. First and foremost he knew beyond a doubt that Joe and I loved him unconditionally and would continue to help him be the best he could be.

Every family will confront challenges along the way. How we deal with these challenges, whether major or minor, does make a difference. Ignoring a problem could have long-term effects—in this case, a serious drug addiction. Throwing in the towel and leaving him to fend for himself may have had the same result. Sometimes the situation may require a "tough love" approach. Whatever the challenge, I keep in mind the words of St. Francis de Sales: "Do not lose courage in considering your own imperfections but instantly start remedying them—in every day begin the task anew."

Media

I think it goes without saying that the media has an impact on our lives. Taking advantage of its benefits and minimizing its negative effects requires much diligence on my part. I thought about using the word "balance" with regards to television viewing time but decided against it because that would imply a semblance of equality. When it comes to television, videos, DVD's, CD's, and movies, the scale needs to weigh in on the side of minimal use and much discretion. The American Academy of Pediatrics actually discourages television viewing for children under the age of two. (I find that very hard to accomplish when you have older children in the home.) For all other children, the AAP recommends limiting viewing to one to two hours of television a day and monitoring the programs the children do watch. (A recommendation I can follow.) In addition, the AAP strongly recommends not having a television in a child's room.

A few years ago I cut out an article in the newspaper titled *Unplug It.* The recommendation was to unplug a television or computer that was in a child's room. Studies indicated there were negative affects on children who have free access to either. If you have allowed your son to have either or both in his room, I believe it wise to reconsider that decision. Of course, to "unplug" the television and computer after previously allowing them in his room may cause a confrontation. I would apologize for **my** mistake in allowing him to have a computer or television in his room and then remove them.

Another study published in the November 2008 issue of *Pediatrics* linked teen viewers of twenty-three television programs that contain sexual content to an increase in teen pregnancies and early sexual activity. Teens who regularly watched the shows *Sex and the City* and *Friends*, to name a couple, had twice the number of pregnancies or responsibility for a pregnancy than teens who rarely watched these shows. As I stated previously, we become desensitized to what's right when we're constantly bombarded by what's wrong. But in this case, we're dealing with young minds who are still learning and discerning what is right and wrong, moral and immoral, and appropriate and inappropriate. They need us, their parents, to monitor what they watch and discuss issues that arise during programs they do watch. I'm appalled at the sexual content and violence in promotional clips and commercials when I'm watching the news or the boys a sports event. That may be the reason I end up with TiVo, so I can choose to avoid inappropriate commercials.

Monitoring violent programming, especially in the younger years, is also prudent. I for one cannot comprehend why a mother would allow her son to watch violent television shows, videos, or movies where people are threatened, killed, blown up, mutilated, assaulted, or tortured. How will watching this fare make him a better person? I believe it desensitizes him to violent behavior, and certainly doesn't support the mission of love, respect, commitment, and faith.

How do Joe and I minimize the influence of television on the boys? We simply do not place a high priority on television viewing in our home. We didn't, and still don't, have cable and manage to survive with one television in our home. With those two choices we reduce many of the repercussions that are derived from watching violent, sexually provocative, and immoral programs on television. More often than not, our television is used to view soccer videos. The boys watch soccer videos over and over again to the extent that Robbie, one of the boy's friends, once commented when the boys were watching the video *500 Best Goals*, "It doesn't mean you have to watch it 500 times."

When the boys were little, Joe and I minimized the amount of television they watched. They watched *Sesame Street* and other programs on PBS as well as a few other select shows. During the day, the boys played outside. In the evenings, especially during the week and especially once the boys were in school, the television was not on. Joe and I were so busy getting everyone situated for the evening that television simply did not fit into our family's routine.

Parents tell me that they don't want their children to feel left out when the other kids are talking about a movie or television program. The boys survived not seeing all the programs and movies that everyone else was allowed to see, and they are no worse for it. In fact, I know it was in their best interest to **not** watch inappropriate movies, videos, and television programs.

I gave a presentation one evening right around the time of the last episode of *Seinfeld*. All the talk that week centered on saying good-bye to Seinfeld. I told the parents in attendance that night: "While most people are saying good-bye to Seinfeld, I never even said hello —and I'm okay."

The boys began to recognize on their own the appropriateness of a show. One evening we were watching America's Funniest Home Videos. One segment depicted a wedding reception. During the cutting of the cake, the groom took his piece and smeared it all over his bride's face. In retribution she took her piece and smeared it on his crotch. Five-year-old Timmy's simple comment: "Inappropriate!"

Being a discerning parent regarding the bombardment of the media into our lives is a parental responsibility. I use the movie rating system only as a guide. I've already mentioned how the boys did not watch PG-13 movies unless they were thirteen years old, but reaching the ripe age of thirteen did not give them carte blanche to attend any PG-13 movies. And, the same holds for R-rated movies. Adult situation television programming should be off limits for almost all ages. That may mean the adults in the home can't watch a program unless young eyes are in bed or doing something else.

Music also needs to be monitored. When the older boys first started listening to music on a regular basis, I got advice from young people I trusted on whether a group was acceptable. I remember tossing one CD because the cover was disgusting; I couldn't imagine the music and lyrics being much better. With the boys listening to music now from headsets, it is even harder to know what they are listening to. The new technologies create additional challenges for a parent.

Cell Phones

Cell phones are a way of life. How much a part of our lives and in which ways is the question we need to ask ourselves as mothers. As with media, we need to take advantage of a cell phone's benefits and minimize the negative effects. It is important to establish its acceptable use.

With a cell phone, Joe and I first determined at what age and for what reasons a son needed a cell phone. Just because everyone else may have one is not a legitimate reason to provide one to a son. Each family's circumstances will differ and with those differences come different timings. For example, we felt that the boys did not need a cell phone in the middle school years; they were dropped off and picked up each day. Once they were home, they had access to a phone. If they had walked to and from school, though, I probably would have had them carry a cell phone. Once they are in high school, the needs change, especially once they drive.

I recommend prudence when making the decision to provide a son with a cell phone. Consider, for example, the fact that cell phones are not just phones. They have multi uses that can create temptations and result in inappropriate choices. I know of situations when cell phones were used to take pictures of a test and then forwarded to a friend in a later class. Texting answers also occurred. Inappropriate photos were shared. Before a son receives a phone he needs to fully comprehend its proper use and the consequences when used inappropriately.

Establish a curfew for cell phone use just as you would for a landline. If the curfew is not kept, I would keep the phone during the restricted hours. If I were to determine inappropriate use of the phone, I would confiscate it for a determined period of time and/or eliminate certain features on the phone. If excessive minutes were tallied, I would require payment for the additional charges. Our young people need to learn that responsibility accompanies freedoms.

Cell phone use while driving is a hazard, especially texting. It is a major distraction to our young drivers who already lack experience. In this regard, do we set a good example and restrict cell phone use while driving?

I can't imagine a world without cell phones anymore. Joe and I stay more connected during the day but we also are able to stay in touch with all our sons wherever they may be living. The boys also stay in close contact with each other. The family has tried to stay with one company so we can call each other without additional minutes or charges—a true blessing. In addition, it provides a sense of security when one of us is driving late knowing we can call for help if needed, or in the case of any emergency, for that matter.

Cell phones, like all technology, will continue to become more and more sophisticated with more and more features. With these new benefits and new challenges, our continued responsibility as a parent is to reinforce responsible use.

Computers

I have a love-hate relationship with the computer. I often ask myself whether it has made my life easier or more complicated. But love or hate, computers are a reality in our lives.

Computers offer my sons many educational opportunities, as well as entertainment and communication. The challenges arise with the abundance of inappropriate material and sites also accessible to the boys. I resent that I have to add and pay for firewalls and protective software in order to block immoral and inappropriate material from my home. If someone wants to view these materials, they should be required to request and pay for access to it. Freedoms are being granted to the wrong constituency. Until our lawmakers have the courage to address the issue, parents have to strive to keep up with the ever-changing technology that entices our young people.

Our family has two computers in the home: one is located in the kitchen area accessible to everyone and easily monitored while the computer I use for my writing and other computer needs is located in an area off the kitchen. The boys use my computer when more than one has homework requiring a computer or internet access, which is happening more and more often as the schools integrate technology into the curriculum.

In our typical approach, Joe and I establish what is acceptable computer use and regulate how much time is spent on it. We trust the boys to use it appropriately or they know we will restrict its use or limit accessibility. In checking the history in the early years of having a computer, we discovered a pornographic site. We sat all the boys down and talked to them about the benefits of having a computer but also the negatives that bombard us on a daily basis through pop-ups, e-mails, etc. We made it quite clear what we would **not** tolerate and, as technology advances, that list continues to grow. I paraphrased the verse from Matthew 5:29: "If the computer is our trouble, throw it away! Better to not have a computer than to be cast into Gehenna." That is my belief for anything in our lives. If something is going to be a source of temptation, it is better to get rid of that something than continue to be tempted by it. Now, I most likely wouldn't throw the computer out but I would not hesitate to restrict its use as needed.

Our children need to appreciate the risks involved in computer use. In many ways I learned right along with the boys about the dangers the computer presents. Phishing is one example. I remember in my early computer days receiving an email from what appeared to be my bank. I fortunately called the bank because the email confused me. The bank assured me that the email was not from them. I quickly sent an email to the boys to ignore the email since they had accounts at the same institution. Obviously I didn't notify them fast enough because one very organized, efficient son had already "updated" his information and lost the entire balance in his account as a result. Fortunately, the bank covered the loss and we all learned a lesson.

Meeting "strangers" online is another danger that our children face. Just as we teach them not to talk to strangers in person, we need to talk to them about cyber-strangers. With numerous sites available to share their information, a son needs to learn what information is acceptable to post and what information **must** remain private. He should never share his full name, age, and address. Predators are capable of piecing the bits of information together and physically locating a child. They also are savvy in luring young people away. He needs to know that what he sees on the computer is not always reality. Educating our sons is for the sole purpose of keeping them safe. This is another reason for checking often the "who, what, and where" of your son's computer use.

A few years ago, the boys' middle school brought in an FBI agent to talk to the students about cyber-crime after a few issues had arisen regarding information and photos posted on students' sites. In the same time frame, a sting operation had occurred in Houston that had lured several professional men to a home where they thought they were meeting a female teen. The FBI agent made presentations to each grade level separately, informing them that one in five users are solicited. I was amazed how much more the eighth graders knew than the sixth graders. In two short years, the eighth graders were that much more sophisticated and also appeared unaffected by the presentation. Parents were encouraged to check their student's site for appropriateness. Unfortunately, few sites were altered after the presentation, even those with questionable photos.

The computer can easily absorb many hours of our sons' time, between games, communicating with friends, blogging, and schoolwork. How much time is appropriate is up to each of us to determine. If a significant amount of time is spent on the computer, less time is spent reading, socializing, or playing outside. I'm fortunate because the boys are often on the computer together watching an international soccer match or playing a game. The boys also had to learn to share computer time; they established and enforced their own rules. I didn't have to step in. And if I determine enough is enough, they find something else to occupy their time.

New technologies will continue to be a part of our lives. Striving to stay informed on the benefits and risks to our sons is the best we can ask of ourselves. And, when we know we need help, we have to seek it.

Bullying and Cyber-bullying

Bullying continues to be a problem for 25% of our children at all ages. Bullying is **not** a rite of passage, must be taken seriously, and cannot be tolerated. It is a form of physical and/or psychological abuse. If your son is being bullied, he needs your support and help in rectifying the bullying. If your son is the one bullying, he needs help as well.

Cyber-bullying is another issue of concern. Cyber-bullying is the use of technology (e-mails, instant messaging, websites, texting, cell phones, chat rooms, etc.) to send a hurtful, embarrassing, or derogatory communication to another. If you suspect a son is being cyber-bullied or is a part of sending hurtful communications, step in to put a stop to it immediately. Cyber-bullying has taken bullying to a whole new level of abuse with extremely serious results.

Self-esteem is fragile for our young people. We need to take every precaution to protect our children from those who maliciously tamper with it. School counselors and the authorities are aware of the problem and will help a family deal with the perpetrators. A complaint can be filed and may be necessary if the individual(s) does not alter his behavior. Most importantly, do **not** ignore the problem. (The Department of Health and Human Resources has a website *Stop Bullying Now* that is an excellent resource for additional information and references.)

Sex

We are all sexual beings. Our sexuality is an integral part of who we are. I've always wanted the boys from a very early age to understand and appreciate the gift of their sexuality, a gift given to each of us from God. It is a unique gift that deserves deep respect: respect of oneself, respect for others, and respect for God. Responsible sexuality encompasses all three. When all three are embraced in marriage, sexuality reaches the ultimate level of fulfillment—physically, emotionally, and spiritually.

My views on sexuality, like many other views shared in the book, are countercultural. My views are a reflection of my faith; that should not be a surprise since I strive to integrate my faith into all aspects of my life. If I compartmentalize the different facets of my life with different rules and values for each one, then I am no longer one integrated whole but contradicting pieces.

Each of us will approach sexuality with our sons from our own frame of reference and values—traditional or liberal, open or more reserved. I believe if I am comfortable with my own sexuality, a good starting point, then I am better able to convey a positive sexual attitude to my sons. Even more than what I say, my actions, life choices, and relationships will define my beliefs on sexuality to the boys. We cannot underestimate the influence and impact of what each of us says and does regarding sex, formally or informally, for good or for bad. I can explain, for example, in detail the facts of life and talk until I'm blue in the face about morality, but if I am not living a loving, respectful relationship with Joe, they are empty, futile words. Our loving gestures and kind expressions tell our sons that we are both friends **and** lovers. They witness reciprocal respect, commitment, and love.

I don't think many of us would deny that our sons need sex education. The sex education controversy arises from the issues involved: where sex education is taught, what content is taught, at what age, and by whom. If Joe and I want to be the primary source of sex education, then we must accept the responsibility of directing the conversation and making choices that foster our beliefs. I think it begins at an early age with teaching the proper terminology for body parts as well as teaching respect for one's body. It entails answering questions when the boys ask and tailoring the answers to their level of maturity and understanding. It encompasses fostering respectful relationships at home that lead to respectful relationships outside the home. It demands that we address the sexual issues and pressures that confront them in their world. We want them to understand that while society talks about "safe sex," our conversation revolves around "responsible sexuality." And they need to understand how we define "responsible sexuality" because that, too, may imply different meanings to different people.

Unfortunately, I feel society has reduced sex to a recreational sport— have sex whenever and with whomever, commitment and responsibility not required. I shared previously the results of a study on the relationship of sexually oriented television programming and increased sexual behavior. Sexual encounters in the media are portrayed independently of a long-term committed relationship. The sex act is relegated to physical self-gratification. Love and concern for the sexual partner, not to mention commitment, is of little consequence. Is that really what we want our sons to accept as responsible sexuality? Is that really what is best for them?

In addition, all media forms bombard us with sexually oriented commercials, advertisements, and articles. I've had to change the radio station while driving a son to soccer practice because of an inappropriate story or comment by a disc jockey. I cancelled *Sports Illustrated* when an article on a female athlete concentrated on her physical attributes rather than her athletic abilities. As a woman I found the article offensive.

Scantily clad females parade across the screens **and** in real life, providing visual stimulation to our sons. I laughed when the mother of a six-year-old daughter asked me to organize a "modest" fashion show for young girls; I reminded her I was the mother of ten sons. But the more I thought about the idea, the more I realized I should take a stand since what girls wear does impact my sons. The fashion show is on my "to-do list."

I also struggle with the assumption that our young men are incapable of self-control. It seems we expect high standards in other areas of their lives—no cheating, stealing, or lying—yet lower the expectations on sexual behavior. Too often, sex, like alcohol, is viewed as a right of passage or just a right. When I teach self-discipline, I do not compartmentalize the different facets of their lives or make self-discipline a cafeteria-style lesson—pick and choose to be self-disciplined and in control only when it suits your needs.

In addition, I want them to appreciate the "why" of our beliefs and the long-term benefits of holding them. The physical love expressed in a monogamous, committed relationship is truly one of God's greatest gifts and pleasures to us as husband and wife. I am a firm believer that "the truth will set you free." Just as I don't provide a "cheat-sheet" to my sons to have in case they choose to cheat on their next test, I do not hand out condoms to my sons to keep handy "just in case."

Homosexual orientation is of concern to many parents. My belief is that God intended marriage to be between a man and a woman and sex within the context of a marital relationship. Consistent with that view, I do not condone sex outside of marriage whether between heterosexuals or homosexuals. To become sexually active or remain chaste is a **choice** made independent of your orientation.

Throughout the book I have emphasized the importance I place on respect. Respect is essential to any relationship. I am often asked how I teach the boys to respect women when they live in an all male home. The boys learn respect of women from Joe. They witness how he treats me and talks to me on a daily basis as well as other women. In addition, I **expect** to be treated with respect by Joe and the boys. I reemphasize, if the boys learn respect at home, they are much more likely to be respectful to everyone outside the home. Respect is disregarded when one engages in sex for one's own self-pleasure, basically "using" the other person while ignoring the ramifications of the act.

That leads to pornography. Pornography is disrespect for a woman, treating her as a sex object. Unfortunately, pornographic material is readily available, especially via the internet. My sons know where Joe and I stand on inappropriate sites as well as the consequences, even if it means restricting access to the internet or removal of the computer. I reiterate, "garbage in, garbage out." At a mini-conference on sexual addiction that I attended a few years ago, one of the speakers, a convicted sex offender, told the attendees that the Internet is "sexual cocaine" to a sex addict and warned those of us with children to realize the negative influence of pornographic material on young minds.

Another issue to be addressed with our sons is "date rape." They need to understand what defines "date rape" and the serious consequences of the accusation. The scenario reverts to his word against her word. Was the sex consensual or not? As evidenced in the Duke University lacrosse players' case, the male is assumed guilty. In more instances than not, alcohol is involved in date rape cases as well as the majority of casual sexual encounters. Even when of legal age, drinking responsibly makes a difference in other behaviors. My family knew a young man who was charged with rape. Although he acknowledged he had sex with the girl, he asserted the sex was consensual. His life changed. He had planned on attending college out of state but he lost that privilege. And until the young woman retracted her story, he was looking at possible jail time. Our sons need to understand there are legal implications of casual sex.

Recent news events also highlight the issue of entrapment where a young lady wants to get pregnant and entices a young man into having sex with her. If a child is fathered, he is held legally responsible for supporting the baby. And that is the case whenever a child is fathered. Our sons **must** understand this responsibility, and it goes beyond the financial responsibilities and needs of the child. The birth of a child is always life changing, but when the child is born out of wedlock, the changes can be dramatic.

Our sons also need to appreciate the health risks involved in sexual behavior. Sexually transmitted diseases are epidemic from genital herpes to HIV. It only takes having sex once with an infected person to contract one of the diseases. Joe and I share with the boys that neither of us worries about contracting one of these diseases because we live in a committed, monogamous relationship, and from the beginning of our relationship we did not have to confess to the other that we harbored a sexually transmitted disease. Being free from an STD is a gift you give your spouse.

Oral sex is another issue that must be confronted. Oral sex is sex contrary to the belief of many young people. Many parents don't like to face these issues but they are reality. A friend of mine who teaches in a middle school shared with me her disbelief when she chanced upon two middle school students engaged in oral sex under one of the school's stairwells during school hours. She was more upset by the encounter than they were. The local news carried a story of middle school aged students engaging in oral sex in movie theaters. A news story broke a few years ago when a middle school girl went to her school counselor because she had attended a party where oral sex was openly taking place. While this topic did not come up with my older sons, it has become an issue to address today.

I feel fortunate that the school our sons attended from first through eighth grade provided a strong family life program. The program provided parents an opportunity to teach sexuality in the confines of the home with guided lessons geared to the developmental stage of the boys. Topics that might be difficult to approach were easier to address, especially if you had worked with the program from first grade on and created an environment conducive for discussion. In addition, Joe participated with some of the boys in a church sponsored sexuality program offered through the archdiocesan family life ministry office. Again, it provided an environment that made it easier to discuss sexuality.

Dating

The whole dating scene has not proven to be a big issue for us. Most of the boys went around in groups rather than one-on-one. (I'm referring to dating in the high school years; I would not encourage dating prior to high school.) I think the group scenario provides a healthier way to start developing relationships. This is a time to get to meet different girls and to begin to discern what is important in a relationship. One speaker at a "Sex, God & Me" program, a human sexuality course for teenagers and parents, told the teens that dating and dumping go hand-in-hand during this phase of their lives, a good piece of advice to remember. The high school years are not a good time to get too serious about one person.

When the boys go out on a date, we ask all the same "w" questions we ask whenever they go out: Who are you going with? Where are you going? When will you be home? What will you be doing? The boundaries are set and expectations established from the beginning. If, for example, any part of the plan changes, Joe and I expect them to call and let us know.

I find one challenge as the mother of a boy is meeting the girl, if she is not someone I've met before. Since the boy usually picks the girl up, we are at a disadvantage in that department. If she is someone he intends to date more frequently, he will take the bold step of bringing her to the house to meet all of us. The question then becomes: "Will she come back again?"

Homecoming freshman year is usually one of the first dating experiences. Growing up without a sister, the boys are clueless as to what is entailed as far as "the mum" for the game and the corsage for the dance are concerned. They can't understand why I'm asking what color her dress is or whether she needs a wrist corsage or regular corsage. It's all a learning process, and I thoroughly enjoy watching each one mature year by year.

The dating process must have worked because I am now blessed with five wonderful daughters-in-law. They add a whole new dimension to my life—and I must admit that it is nice to talk about something besides sports once in a while.

So while the times they are a'changin', I'm a'changing too—no room for complacency. I've learned to face the challenges with a commitment to making decisions that, hopefully, guide my sons to make good choices.

Chapter 7

Not a One Woman Show—
Fathers, Mentors, and Brothers Needed!

When a man walks in integrity and justice,
happy are his sons after him.
—Proverbs 20:7

Sometimes being a brother is even better than being a superhero.
—Marc Brown

Our greatest need is to feel that we have value,
are worthy, and can do beautiful things.
—Jean Vanier

People often wonder how I do what I do—raise ten sons. I remind them that I don't raise my sons alone. Although I may be an essential provider of their needs, I also humbly acknowledge and recognize that I am not the sole source of the boys' upbringing. Raising a son is not a one-person responsibility—how limiting for the development of the child. Rather, raising a son encompasses the relationships and influences of other people of both family and non-family origins. The impact on my sons' lives and mine through the love, guidance, and support of their father, their grandparents, aunts and uncles, mentors, and each other has helped shape them into the individuals they are today. They all add a dimension to my sons' growth that I may not. I think it would be rather haughty, naïve, and unrealistic on my part to think that I alone, their mom, can provide each of the boys, as unique as they are, all that they need.

Each mother's situation may differ regarding a support system, but what doesn't differ is our **need** for a support system in bringing up our sons. As part of that support system, our sons need a strong, **positive** male influence and role model to balance out our maternal approach. Even in my upbringing I saw how my mom and dad addressed issues from a different perspective, allowing me to gain insights I might not have acquired otherwise. Surrounding your son with strong, positive role models, male and female, is a gift you give your son.

A Father

"Don't misunderstand me, both (mothering and fathering) are needed —but an emphasis on fathering is necessary because of the enormity of its absence." The words of William P. Young reverberate through our society. The role of a father is too often unappreciated and misunderstood by himself as well as society—unappreciated for the importance and impact a father has on the development, self-assurance, and well-being of his son. A son **needs** and **wants** a father, not just a physical father figure but, even more importantly, a father who emotionally invests of himself in his son. A father who shares with his son his love, time, and attention. A simple concept, yet not an easy one to fulfill.

When Joe and I married 35 years ago, we shared similar values and goals, one of them being to raise a family. No one, though, could have prepared either of us for what was eventually to be a family of ten sons. While our family grew in size, Joe and I evolved as father and mother —we grew to understand the needs of our sons, we grew to respect the uniqueness of each one of them, and we grew to appreciate the time, energy, and commitment raising children entailed. We weren't given a how-to-book on raising sons other than the general parenting books that were available at the time. We depended on what we knew from our own experiences growing up, by observing other parents, and asking many questions of our pediatrician.

Joe and I gradually realized, in ways we hadn't prior to having children, that the upbringing in our families of origin had been significantly different. How my parents parented and how Joe's parents parented were not the same. That is not to say that one style was necessarily better than the other, but they were different. We brought these differences to our individual parenting, thus requiring us to work through some of the differences. Additionally, Joe brought a male approach to his parenting style while I brought my feminine touch. Our sons needed both.

Joe is a neonatologist, a pediatrician who specializes in the care of the critically ill newborn. He works with newborns every day. When Tony was born, Joe was much more comfortable holding him than I was, and he knew much more than I did about caring for his basic needs. As I took on the day-to-day caring of Tony and spent considerably more time with him due to Joe's residency schedule, recognizing Tony's needs and wants became easier for me than Joe. Thus he began to take cues from me, not uncomfortable doing so. Joe also came to appreciate from hands-on experience that developmental milestones taught in medical school were only guidelines and that each child develops uniquely. This concept was reinforced with each of our sons as no two sons reached milestones at the exact same time or in the exact same manner, from sleeping through the night, to walking, to talking, to teething, or to potty-training to name a few.

Although Joe had a good understanding of the role of a father and desired to be a good father, appreciating and accepting the time commitment, the physical and emotional demands, and the changes in one's daily life took a little longer, just as it did for me. He had to make choices about what he would do with his "free" time (time not at the hospital) and where his son, and gradually sons, fit into that discretionary time. Fortunately for the boys, he became an active part of their lives, although as he admits, more out of pure necessity in the early years of his parenting as our family quickly grew.

Joe shares a story with other parents about the morning his heart caught up with his head in regards to why he was doing what he was doing—committing so much of his time and energy—for his sons and me. He had woken up early on a Saturday morning with our first five sons, all under the age of nine at the time. He was letting me sleep in; I was pregnant—a common occurrence at that point in our lives. He changed more than a few diapers, fed the boys breakfast, and then started cleaning the breakfast dishes, feeling sorry for himself the whole time. He was convinced that he was probably the only physician in the city of Houston, if not the world, up on a Saturday morning changing diapers and cleaning dishes. "Why am I doing this?" he commiserated. As he asked the question, a cool breeze came through the kitchen window (I tease him that the breeze was probably the Holy Spirit) awakening in him the answer to his own question: **"I am doing this because I love Cathy and the boys."** His heart caught up with his head and his parenting was never the same again.

Joe's love, time, and attention have made a significant difference in the lives of the boys. Turning off *Monday Night Football* and reading to the boys, while a little difficult those first years as a father, became a no-brainer. He found it emotionally rewarding to have Tony leaning against him on one side and David leaning against him on the other as he read story after story. On weekends you were more likely to see Joe throwing a football or a baseball with the boys than watching a game on television. Attending the boys' activities and sports events not only demonstrated his support of them, his demeanor made it obvious that he enjoyed being there and being an active part of their lives. Even mundane bath time became a fun time for him and the boys, reinforcing the belief that quality time is any time you are together. Joe's bath time routine may have unfolded very differently from mine, but the boys enjoyed the change and came out just as clean.

Joe reinforced through his actions the concept that roles and responsibilities are not gender specific. The boys witnessed both of us taking on non-traditional roles and responsibilities, more often than not out of necessity. I acquired new skills due to Joe's long and demanding hours in our early years of marriage and parenting. If a faucet was dripping, I better figure out how to fix it or decide who to call to repair it. Likewise, Joe's culinary skills improved, and he willingly accepted household chores as needed. The boys grew to appreciate that each individual in the family needed to help fulfill the myriad responsibilities that are part and parcel in a home with ten sons. Mom and dad couldn't and shouldn't have to do everything. The boys learned from Joe and me that responsibilities were often filled by whomever had the time, the desire, or the ability to complete the task. The expectation as well was that, even though the chore was not to your liking, the responsibility was to be fulfilled with a good attitude. Joe and I reminded the boys often, as well as modeled, that Jesus loves a joyful giver.

Each one of the boys **knows** and **feels** Joe's love. They appreciate that their dad accepts and celebrates their God-given gifts and that he doesn't expect them to be carbon copies of each other or of himself. Joe didn't express his love only to the most intellectual, the most athletic, or the most socially gifted son. He identified and, I emphasize again, celebrated what was and continues to be unique in each one. His expectations emphasized being the best they could be not necessarily **the** best. Having their father accept and love them **unconditionally** for who they are with their unique physical, intellectual, emotional, and spiritual gifts instills a priceless sense of self-assurance and self-acceptance. I am convinced that all sons **need** the acceptance of their father. When they have their father's love and acceptance, they thrive, and when they don't they struggle with self-confidence and self-acceptance, often feeling they are inadequate in their father's eyes, or for that matter, in other people's eyes as well. In addition, they need to feel confident that they are respected and accepted by their father whether or not they choose to follow in his footsteps or his dreams for them.

I highly recommend an excellent movie that came out a few years ago, *October Sky*, based on the life of Homer Hickman, a young man who grew up in a mining town. The story focuses on the accomplishments of Homer while also sharing the struggle this young man encountered when his father did not accept him. After *Sputnik* was launched, Homer developed a strong interest in rocketry, supported by his science teacher but profoundly discouraged by his father. His father considered anything beyond working in the mines as a waste of time. He also found his son's newfound interest an embarrassment to him in a town that recognized physical work to be manlier than intellectual pursuits. Homer wrestled with his father's lack of acceptance and his desire to pursue the study of rocket science and to work in the evolving space program.

I've seen this scenario replayed over and over again when parents have expectations of their son that encompass their dreams and not the dreams of their son or the expectations they have of their sons are simply unrealistic. I met a young man a few years ago who shared with me that he had received a degree in engineering. Upon graduating, he handed the degree to his parents explaining that he had fulfilled **their** dream for him; now he would pursue **his** dream of being a photographer. A friend of one of the boys felt called to teaching but when he shared his career goal with his parents they were not pleased. They told him they would not pay for his education if all he wanted to be was a teacher. He pursued a different major. What a sad commentary on two fronts: first, that the young man was not supported in his endeavors and his dream, and second, that the teaching profession was held in such low esteem. Unfortunately, I too frequently witness parents who expect their son to attend a specific university, even when it may be an academic, athletic, or social stretch or misfit. The choice becomes more about meeting a parent's need than the needs of the son. A young man will struggle with his self-worth when he cannot meet his father's unrealistic expectations. Our sons have attended eight different universities because each son had different academic abilities, athletic abilities, and interests. Would it have been easier for

Joe and I if all the boys attended the same university? Possibly, but I doubt any one university would have been a good fit for all the boys with their individual strengths and weaknesses. The college choice each son made revolved around what was best for him, not what was easiest for mom and dad.

My sons realize the "sacrifices" that their father has made in order to provide them with the best education possible and involvement in extracurriculars, especially sports—and he does so without a complaint or a sense of regret. They know how hard he works, committing to extra call nights during the many years when simultaneous high school and college financial demands deemed it necessary—and he does so out of love. They rightfully believe, too, that he would do it all over again if given the choice.

Joe, thankfully, balances out my motherly, emotional, and protective approach to parenting. He grants his sons the freedom to be all boy, playing physically and aggressively with them and allowing them to do things I may consider too risky. I learned to step back and let Joe make those decisions, trusting and believing that he, too, has their best interest at heart. I came to realize fairly early on in my parenting of sons that they have a wild side and are a risky bunch by nature. Joe gives them permission to be comfortable in their wildness and risk taking. Is it hard for me? At times, darn hard! I still shiver at times when Joe tells them "yes" --and then I say a few extra prayers.

While addressing the wild dimension of the boys, Joe also cultivates the boys' sensitivity. Society often identifies sensitivity with weakness. As Joe often emphasizes, and unknowingly models, compassion and sensitivity are human traits, and a male who possesses them is strong and confident. Joe didn't want the boys to develop into crybabies, but he did want them to mature into sensitive young men—not the same thing. I'm grateful to Joe because the boys are aware of and sensitive to the needs of others, both at home and outside the home. They feel comfortable tapping into the emotions surrounding both joyful and sorrowful experiences. In addition, that sensitivity instills in them a sense of justice, leading them to strive to make the world a better place.

As the boys aged, I grew to appreciate and accept how the boys' relationship with Joe and me changed. Because Joe is male and experienced many similar situations and concerns growing up, he brings an understanding and appreciation to these situations and concerns that I may not. I assume if I had daughters the same would hold true. I've grown as a mother from listening to Joe's perspective on discipline, friendships, relationships, sports, and the other countless areas of my sons' lives, even if I don't fully understand it all. I find it satisfying to see the relationship between Joe and each of the boys develop. He enjoys being with them and vice versa. They share, for example, a common interest in sports, especially soccer, and talk about games, teams, and players in depth. Although I enjoy sports, my level of interest is at a different level of appreciation and understanding. Even when one of the boys is playing, I don't remember all the details of how each goal was scored or defended. Joe and the boys do. In addition, they enjoy similar movies, games, and physical outlets. These connections with their father enrich the lives of my sons.

The level of respect the boys have for each other, their wives, friends, colleagues, **and** me is a reflection of the respect Joe demonstrates. After a presentation I gave one evening, a mother shared with me a concern that her son was not treating her with respect. As we talked it became evident that her husband, likewise, did not talk to her or treat her respectfully. Her son was mirroring the behavior of his father, unfortunately for the mother, in a negative way. In a previous chapter, I discussed the importance of respect in our homes. Each individual— mother, father, and child—has a right to feel loved and secure in his or her own home. When disrespect is a part of the home environment, love and security is minimized or absent. Remembering that "good sons don't just happen," a father's modeling of respect is imperative for a young man to learn and live respectfully in present as well as future relationships.

Joe's daily example of love, respect, commitment, **and** faith was and continues to be the greatest gift he has given his sons. The boys witness firsthand his faith and integrity through the choices and the decisions he makes. To paraphrase the words of Clarence Budington Kelland: **Joe didn't tell his sons how to live; he lived, and let them watch him do it.** All the preaching in the world would not have made a difference if Joe didn't live out the words.

How grateful and blessed I am that Joe is the father of our sons. A poster in our home reads: "The person you marry will determine 90% of your happiness or 90% of your sorrow in life. Choose well." I chose well. Not only am I blessed with a wonderful husband, my sons are blessed with Joe as their father—and they know it. His direct, loving involvement in their upbringing, in spite of his demanding hours at the hospital, enriched my parenting experience and fostered the secure, loving environment that exists in our home today. "When a man walks in integrity and justice, happy are his sons after him" (Proverbs 20:7).

Brothers

Parenting has brought many surprises over the years. I could never have imagined, for example, the value of the gift the boys would be to each other. Knowing that my sons treasure each other as much as I treasure them is one of my greatest rewards. Likewise, I did not foresee the impact the boys would have on each other's lives; fortunately for me, the influence has been positive. Beginning with Tony and David, the boys have been playmates, partners in mischief, role models, leaders, teachers, coaches, teammates, babysitters, cheerleaders, sympathizers, and most importantly, best friends—and still are. I really shouldn't be that surprised because my sisters and I were no different. My older sisters, Linda and Patty, and my younger sisters, Paula and Michele, had a role in the person I am today.

Tony was 360 days old when David arrived on the scene. I felt fortunate that the jealousy and sibling rivalry often described in parenting books **never** happened. Tony's gentle, jovial nature lent itself to being a good big brother. The compassionate and quiet concern that is part of Tony today was evident at that young age. They were inseparable, so much like twins. At David's wedding, Tony's toast included the words: "I have never known life without David." They were each other's best friend. They set the standards in many ways for their younger brothers, in large part because Joe and I expected them to lead the way. We wanted Tony and David, and eventually all the boys, to appreciate that God would hold them accountable for the example they set for their brothers, what they did and said or didn't do and say day-in and day-out. Their younger brothers looked up to them and wanted to emulate them.

Tony and David's "big" brother role continues, but the other brothers stepped up as well. Joe and I found it fascinating that, as the oldest brother at home headed to college, the next brother in line took on the leadership role, accepting the responsibilities that that role entailed. Tony and David had set the standard. The oldest at home garnered a "little" privilege with his new leadership role because the younger brothers understood that "seniority" ruled in the GP home. David was "subtly" reminded of the seniority rule one summer when he inadvertently forgot the pecking order with Tony home from college.

The values Joe and I were teaching the boys were being reinforced in their relationships with each other. They accepted each other for the person each is with their individual abilities, talents, and personalities. That in and of itself is a tremendous gift they shared with each other. Each of us wants to be loved and accepted by those closest to us. When an older or younger brother loves and accepts you for who you are, especially when you look up to that brother, you garner an appreciation for your uniqueness and for your ability to accomplish in your own right. Although the boys may emulate the qualities, attitudes, work ethic, and values of a brother, they didn't feel compelled to be a carbon copy of each other. For example, a brother might emulate Chris's work ethic when it came to soccer, appreciating, though, that he might not attain his level of expertise. Or one of the boys might emulate Tony's study habits, realizing that even with good study habits he may not achieve the same level of academic success but will be able to do his best.

Their support and teaching of each other unfolds in different ways. One simple example revolves around building with Legos. Over the years, as I've shared before, the Garcia-Prats boys have accumulated bins of Legos. When they were younger and one of them received a new set of Legos that might have been more complicated to assemble than usual, they worked **together** to construct it. The same scenario was evident with the Playmobile sets that they enjoyed immensely. The older brother would teach the younger brother how to follow the directions so he could piece the set together by himself the next time. When a new set arrived, Legos or Playmobile, the bins were brought out so everyone could join in the play with the new and the old sets.

They followed a similar procedure when they played outside. The older brothers discovered it was more fun if everyone played, so they spent the time to teach their brothers how to kick the soccer ball, hit the baseball off the tee, dribble and shoot the basketball, and learn to swim. They are still teaching each other new games or adaptations of others whether it is Take Two, Butts Up, or the Taiwanese Jumping Game. I'm convinced the game names are often made up as well.

As their mom, I enjoy watching them in action. I remember David teaching four-year-old Timmy chess. Timmy caught on quickly and loved playing with David, absorbing the strategies and thought processes chess entails. David realized he had a competitor to face when one afternoon he offered Timmy some possible moves to make only to have Timmy negate them. He was able to discern what would happen two moves down the line if he followed David's advice. Mission accomplished—a brother to play a competitive game of chess with.

The boys enjoy playing board games and realize it's much more fun when more of the brothers are able to play. Mexican train is a favorite family game, lending itself to a big crowd. When the older brothers had friends come to Houston for spring breaks, the table included the college kids as well as all the brothers at home. The laughter and the fun that surrounded the table was a joy to behold. The college friends were inclusive of the younger GPs realizing, from the example of the older GP brothers, exclusivity was not an accepted practice in our home.

The boys were each other's cheerleaders as well. They were proud of each other's accomplishments and talents. Jamie's soccer skills developed early. He has a natural left-foot and eight older brothers who taught him how to use it effectively. When Jamie started playing in our neighborhood league, the brothers who were still home would attend early Saturday morning games to cheer for him, often video taping the games so the brothers away at college could eventually watch them. Jamie, then Timmy, had their own pep squad on the sidelines just as the older boys had had their younger brothers cheering for them. Danny and Jamie spent many an afternoon after arriving home from kindergarten and preschool making banners to bring to David's high school soccer games. They would run up and down the sidelines waving the banners.

When Chris played soccer for Trinity University, the GP pep squad drove the 400 mile round trip as often as possible to cheer him on. Even today the GP pep squad follows Chris's games as head men's soccer coach at Luther College. Although they may not be able to physically attend the game, live streaming allows them to share in the action and talk about the ups and downs of the game later.

Support and commitment to each other is witnessed in non-sports activities as well. Tony is presently working in Lesotho, Africa, with the Baylor Pediatric International AIDS Initiative. One of the tragic outcomes of the AIDS pandemic is the number of children orphaned. In response to their needs, the school Matty taught at in the Los Angeles area, St. Raymond, raised funds to assist a woman who had taken in 15 to 20 orphans. The funds raised reduced the stress she faced in meeting the day-to-day needs of the children. St. Francis de Sales school, the school all the boys attended, also raised funds for the orphans. Their efforts were another example of appreciating and supporting the work of one of their brothers.

Joe and I often refer to our sons as the "older" boys and the "younger" boys—a natural division with a three-year gap, large by our standards, between Matty, our fifth son, and Mark, our sixth. The younger brothers' experience growing up was enriched by having their older brothers not only jostle and tumble them about—being all boy—but also by their example of loving concern displayed in random acts of kindness. Each of them knew that their brothers were there for him.

Brother Casey, SJ, still recounts Joe Pat's instant response to Timmy's needs when warming up at an afternoon soccer game on a weekend Joe and I had another commitment. Obviously hurt, Joe Pat ran over and scooped up a crying Timmy to console him. Although the incident occurred during warm-ups, I have no doubt that Joe Pat's reaction would have been the same even if he had fallen during the game itself.

When our family was a guest on *The Gayle King Show*, Gayle asked the boys whether they felt responsible for each other. Chris quickly responded: "Yes, we do feel responsible for our younger brothers" and then added, with a smile as he looked in David's direction, "and our **older** brothers, too."

Knowing the boys watched out for each other made my days easier whether they were just playing together or babysitting. I was confident leaving the younger boys in the care of their older brothers. Once Tony and David were old enough to watch their brothers for short periods of time, I was able to run errands without all the boys accompanying me. Think of the time I saved coming and going if just from the perspective of the seat-belting routine. I'm convinced the boys were more excited about this new freedom than I was. Grocery shopping, post office runs, and doctor appointments were not exactly high on their list of fun activities. Danny, Jamie, and Timmy were blessed with built-in babysitters from that point on.

They often exceeded my expectations. One fond memory was the night of "follow your son's schedule" at Strake Jesuit the September Jamie was born. I was hesitant leaving Tony and David home with six younger brothers and two-week-old Jamie. Tony and David, fourteen and fifteen years old at the time, insisted they could handle the routine. Joe and I went to the school, reachable by Joe's pager if needed. Two hours later we returned home to a quiet home. The six younger boys were in bed. David was completing homework at the kitchen table. And Tony? Tony was studying in the den with baby Jamie nestled in the cup of his rocking, crossed legs—peacefully sleeping.

Five years later, Joe and I trusted Tony and David, now nineteen and twenty years old, with the care of their brothers when we had the opportunity to attend a medical meeting in Italy. Recently David teasingly questioned our wisdom in leaving Jamie and Timmy in the care of Mark and Tommy, twenty-two and twenty-three years old, when Joe and I traveled to Lesotho, Africa, to visit Tony and Heather. I submitted that the time to have questioned our wisdom was when we left Tony and him in charge of eight younger brothers ranging in age from two to sixteen years old.

I am reminded of the many ways the older boys helped Joe and I in raising their brothers as I watch with pride when Danny, Jamie, and Timmy willingly help out with their nieces and nephews—changing a diaper, reading a story, following one of them up and down the stairs, kicking a soccer ball, or simply holding them. They laugh and enjoy their many antics, just as their brothers did with them. I still recall Tony's comment when one of his brothers started crawling: "They're great, Mom, 'til they crawl." He realized that Legos and Playmobile pieces needed extra care until the crawler was on board with the program. Danny, Jamie, and Timmy have grasped that fact, too—a mobile niece or nephew requires more energy and attention than a stationary one. I am grateful that the younger boys have the opportunity to be actively involved in their nieces' and nephews' lives and to learn the importance of setting a good example and being good role models as their brothers were for them.

While helping with the physical needs of their brothers, the older boys also helped their brothers discern right from wrong, good from bad, and appropriate from inappropriate. As parents we often assume our children innately know the difference between right and wrong, but that's not always the case. There are levels of moral development that our children move through. They need to be taught and shown correctness. A non-parent, sometimes a brother or two, may teach these lessons. That's what transpired one afternoon when the boys were organizing their baseball cards. There was a period of time when the older boys were baseball card aficionados. They bought, sold, and traded the cards, keeping track of their monetary value from week to week. This particular afternoon, Chris, 5 years old at the time, appeared in the bedroom with a bunch of gum and new baseball cards. "Where did you get those?" Tony and David excitedly asked. "In Daddy's closet," Chris innocently answered. "Uh, oh!" Tony and David knew right away that the cards were not theirs to keep and that Chris should not have been in their dad's closet or opened the packs of cards. (Joe kept a box of baseball cards in the closet so he could dole them out to the boys at special times, knowing how much they enjoyed collecting them.) Tony and David wisely gathered the gum and cards, set them aside, and advised Chris to return them to Joe when he got home. Chris timidly did so to an understanding father, explaining that Tony and David had told him what he had done was wrong. Joe rewarded Chris's and his brothers' honesty and integrity with a couple packs of baseball cards each.

The older boys took their responsibility to be good role models seriously, sharing their feelings on its importance in a chapter they wrote in our first book, *Good Families Don't Just Happen*.

The chapter excerpt was titled: **Being Role Models for Each Other**
Being the older two of the bunch, we realize that we are being looked up to on a daily basis. Like it or not, we are role models for our younger brothers. Everything we do, whether at home, school, or on the soccer field, is watched and frequently imitated by them. When our brothers see us studying hard for a test, they realize that it's okay to study, and they can do the same. Likewise, if they see us disobeying our parents, they think that it's okay. We can't remember how many times our parents have reprimanded us for something our little brothers have done because they saw us do it first. One afternoon, one of our younger brothers told our parents that he was "going to take a piss." Mom and Dad sat our brother down to explain that what he said was inappropriate; they also sat us down to remind us that our brother did not learn the language from them and that we needed to clean up our act.

There are other aspects of being a good role model besides having good study habits, and appropriate language and behavior. Our brothers observe how we treat each other and our parents. If they see us show respect to the family, our friends, and others around us, they begin to develop that same sense of respect.

We also try to pass down our sense of good sportsmanship to our younger brothers. We're all extremely competitive. But there is more to sports and life than just winning. When we were younger, two-on-two basketball games became so competitive that they usually ended up with one player not talking to the other, because of a bad call or a hard foul. As we've grown older, we've learned that when playing sports, especially with our brothers, our goal isn't winning or losing, but having a good time. Now in our friendly soccer games at the neighborhood field, we have an unwritten rule: We never keep score. The games are still competitive, but they always remain fun because it doesn't matter whether or not the last goal counts or who wins or loses.

Since we're all close in age, sometimes our younger brothers have to compete against each other in soccer or race each other in a swim meet. After the meet or game, they always congratulate each other, no matter who won. They are genuinely happy for the other.

We've also noticed times when Danny, our eight-year-old budding artist, will be drawing with one of his younger brothers and they will show him some indecipherable scribbles and ask, "Danny, how do you like my dinosaur?" Without hesitating for a second, he always compliments the work. The younger one proudly returns to his art with a smile on his face. It's amazing to see the results that can be produced by a positive compliment from a sibling.

We are supportive of each other and free from sibling rivalry because of the way our parents treat us. It's almost impossible to feel genuinely happy for someone when you feel that your skills and abilities are inadequate. Our parents never compare us with each other; rather, they celebrate our differences. They've never announced someone's straight-A report card or ridiculed another son's less stellar grades. We each excel at different things, and we know we're loved because of who we are and not because of what we accomplish. Our parents accept us as individuals and encourage us to develop our own talents. They help us to build self-esteem and confidence in our abilities. As older brothers, we try to imitate our parents in how we treat our younger siblings. It's easy to be supportive of each other when we are secure with ourselves. We're sad to see other people be jealous of their siblings' accomplishments. We feel sad because we know that the person has little confidence in himself or herself, but also because often our proudest moments have not been about our own accomplishments but about our brothers' successes.

As the boys have gotten older and the age differences have become less obvious, the modeling is balanced among all the boys—older to younger and younger to older. They turn to each other in good times and in bad, sharing their love, acceptance, admiration, and support. I am comforted knowing they have each other to talk to about their day-to-day experiences because they can appreciate each other's experiences in ways I can't. After a high school soccer game, going all the way back to David, the player would call his brother or brothers away at college to rehash the game. Or the college-aged brother would call home to talk to his brothers. Joe and I would talk to him, too, but we knew he really needed the time with his brothers.

While the older boys played an incredible role in their brothers' upbringing, Joe and I never wanted them to feel burdened by their brothers or to give them the impression that we expected them to take over our parental roles and responsibilities. I had heard too often older siblings complain that they had already raised enough kids and, as a result, didn't want children of their own. When Tony and David both chose careers that involved working with children, Joe and I sighed, "Thank goodness, we didn't burn them out on children."

I am convinced, too, that they believe the words of Marc Brown: "Sometimes being a brother is even better than being a superhero."

Mentors

Although my parents and sisters had the most influence on my development, I was blessed with mentors and friends who contributed greatly to my values and life choices. I hoped and prayed that my sons would also be blessed with wise and trusting individuals who would augment their development in a positive way.

Mentors are important in building character and values in a son whatever the composition of your family. The mentor(s) can be another parent, a teacher, a coach, a counselor, a priest, rabbi, or minister, or a friend. I wanted the boys to feel comfortable with a responsible adult, someone they could rely on to ask questions or share ideas, knowing that individual cared about them.

Fortunately, my sons had mentors at the different stages of their lives and in different areas of their lives. The mentors may have been a coach and a teacher or two who inspired and motivated them to reach higher goals while maintaining strong character. Although the list of the boys' mentors is extensive, I am going to share the mentorship of one individual in particular for two reasons: one, she was exceptionally gifted with the ability to relate to young people, appreciate their individual talents, and share her zest and joy for life with them; second, to some degree she mentored **all** my sons.

Marilyn Smith Ebling was the Extended Day Program (EDP) Director for the after-school program at our parish school, St. Francis de Sales. Along with adults, Marilyn hired high school and college students as counselors to work with the kindergarten through eighth grade students. Before Marilyn Smith directed the program, most students, especially the middle school students, dreaded EDP. Marilyn Smith changed all that. Parents who needed the program due to work commitments were grateful for her realistic approach to the time their children spent in the after-school hours. They had time to complete homework but were also allowed to be children in an unstructured structured environment. By that I mean that the children had boundaries and expectations but each student was provided some freedom and choice in how they spent their time. All the extended day students were not required to do everything at the same time in the same way. If they wanted to play outside on the playground, there were counselors stationed outside to watch them. If they wanted to play a board game with some friends, a room with a counselor was provided. If they wanted to sit and read, piece together a puzzle, or talk with friends, they had the freedom to do so. In many ways, the experience was not that different from my sons' experience at home where they were in a structured but unstructured environment. Parents stopped hearing complaints about having to attend EDP. In fact, many students were disappointed when a parent picked them up early because they enjoyed the after-school hours.

The Garcia-Prats boys were counselors at EDP. Marilyn used to tell people she was the Garcia-Prats family's biggest employer. She was right, although our neighborhood pool ran a close second. The older boys began working during high school when they were not committed to a sport. They would help out after school for three hours a few days a week. On those days, even after a long day at school, they returned home laughing and sharing the antics of EDP. A couple summers, Marilyn ran a summer program as well, and David, Chris, Joe Pat, and Matt worked at the camps. What drew the boys to EDP was Marilyn Smith. She respected the counselors, guided them, taught them how to work with young children, recognized and took advantage of their varied talents and interests, and made the time fun for them just as she did for the children. From her words, actions, and laughter, each of the boys knew she cared about them.

After David graduated from Creighton University and before he returned to school to attain an advanced degree in education, he was the assistant director of EDP. During those few years, Marilyn mentored David, encouraging and motivating him in his quest to find his niche in life. She offered the non-parent perspective; young people need this perspective, whether it's always in agreement with the parent or not. She supported each of the boys in their endeavors, enjoying and celebrating the different personalities and styles of each of them. They truly grew to love her, and her love for them was obvious. Rarely did they miss an opportunity to visit her whenever they were in town. They would pick up right where they left off, laughing and enjoying being in each other's company.

"The amazing thing about Marilyn Smith was that she made each of us feel so great about what we did at EDP," shared Chris. "She was able to use our personalities and talents to enhance EDP. She made it **not** feel like work. We enjoyed every minute that we were with Marilyn because she made us laugh and made us feel special. The last time we all went over to see her, I think all of us were nervous about how the experience would unfold because she was so sick. For a few of us, it had been some time since we had seen her. We were with her for a couple of hours and all we did the entire time was laugh and share stories just like we had when we worked for her. Her sense of humor fit in so well with our family and she will **always** have a special place in all of our hearts."

Jean Vanier states: "Our greatest need is to feel that we have value, are worthy, and can do beautiful things." Marilyn enriched my sons' lives, filling the need that each of our sons has to be loved, valued, respected, and accepted by someone other than mom and dad. I am eternally grateful to Marilyn for joyfully mentoring them. Unfortunately, Marilyn passed away a year ago, but the impact she had on my sons will continue as they emulate the joy-filled life she led and shared, believing they, too, can do beautiful things.

Chapter 8

Laughter—Music in a Loving Home

There is an appointed time for everything . . .
a time to laugh.
—Ecclesiastes 3:1,4

Lord, give me a sense of humor,
and I will find happiness in life enough to share with others.
—St. Thomas More

This is the day that the Lord has made;
let us be glad and rejoice in it.
—Psalm 118:24

A loving home is a home filled with laughter and peace, providing an unspoken sense of security that each of us needs and wants. An atmosphere that encompasses laughter, happiness, and peace doesn't just happen, though. It requires an attitude and approach to living that embraces love, respect, commitment, and faith with a huge dose of humor thrown in—starting with me. While I often espouse teaching children through the gift of their five senses—touch, taste, sight, hearing, and smell—I also emphasize the importance of that other significant sense—a sense of humor. I've learned that a home without laughter and the sharing of good times soon becomes drudgery. A home without laugher is a home filled with the rigor of rules and responsibilities without the enjoyment of what those rules and responsibilities can bring. Rules and responsibilities balance freedom and privileges, enabling us to enjoy each other.

The daily interactions are what create the joy in the Garcia-Prats household. When I think of my family, it's the everyday laughter that sparks our overall sense of happiness. The healthy teasing and joking, the lively dinner conversations, the shared tales of our daily experiences, the three-, four-, or five-way hugs, the tumbling and wrestling on the floor, and the singing and dancing lighten our spirits and bring joy to our hearts. We face enough stress and frustrations out in the world; I want my home to be a haven where the boys, Joe, and I can relax and enjoy each other.

When family members rarely interact, experiencing happiness and building fond memories is difficult. I can't truly enjoy the boys or get to know them if I don't spend time with them or do anything with them. There are countless ways to interact with them on a daily basis, as I've continually emphasized throughout the book. When the boys were little, we baked brownies and cookies, played in the back yard, made Play-Doh, read stories, played board games, worked on puzzles, rode bikes, went for walks, swam at the neighborhood pool, played soccer or tee-ball, visited museums and the zoo, and went on picnics. I don't peel a potato today when I don't think of little Danny sitting across the counter relating every detail of his school day. I think of Jamie whenever a game of Sequence is played; we played Sequence countless afternoons during his preschool years while Timmy napped. Tommy loved pouring over puzzles, and the more pieces the better. All these activities allowed us to relate as individuals as well as created a closeness that is measured by the comfort each of us felt being around the other. In addition, the activities created memories that we treasure.

As the boys got older, different activities took the place of Play-Doh and tee-ball. Dinner was and is the primary way we interact on a daily basis. With all the boys in school or working, dinner proves to be the time that we usually come together. A festive atmosphere almost always encompasses the dinner table, whether it is just another Wednesday evening dinner or a birthday celebration. If it's a quiet, peaceful dinner you are looking for, then the Garcia-Prats home is not the place. The conversation may revolve around recent sports competitions, school activities, national and local news, upcoming events, or all of these. In more recent years, many "stories" from the past are revisited when we are all together; sometimes the escapades are a retelling for the brothers but a first for Joe and me. Even dinner prayers may add humor. On Timmy's first day of preschool, he solemnly asked us to pray for all his new girlfriends; the solemnity went out of our prayer time.

The boys' sports activities provide countless opportunities to interact and have fun. Many of the soccer fields and natatoriums are located a distance from our home. The long drives back and forth create opportunities to talk or laugh, aided on many Saturday mornings by listening to Click and Clack on *Car Talk*. Over the years, we planned picnics around soccer games or swim meets when they were played at a suitable location. We organized mini-vacations around out-of-town tournaments. Countless Garcia-Prats memories were made during these trips, as well as when attending college graduations and weddings.

Most of the trips were made by car. The boys found ways to entertain themselves and each other. They kept a journal on the long jaunt to El Paso for Joe's mother's funeral. Creative and funny is the only way to describe the journal. On other trips, the boys video taped the car experience, creating laughter at the time of the video taping as well as later when we watched the tape. I worry that families are losing these unique opportunities today because many parents provide DVD players in the car to entertain their children, even on quick trips to school or the store. I understand the value of the DVD player and hand-held video games on a long trip but not in lieu of spending some time interacting, whether it's reading stories, playing word games, or listening to children's music. I previously wrote about the mental math and spelling games I played with the boys. If they had been watching a movie or playing individual games whenever they rode in the car, we would have missed some precious and fun moments in our lives.

Too often in today's world, we let the stresses and demands of everyday living rob us of opportunities to enjoy life. I remember Richard Carlson's book *Don't Sweat the Small Stuff—and it's all small stuff*. What great advice! If I keep the day-to-day demands in perspective, joyfully fulfill my responsibilities, not waste a lot of energy chasing the wrong dreams—power, money, fame—in pursuit of happiness, hopefully, my sons will learn from my example. Joe often shares a simple reminder in his presentations: "The best things in life aren't things."

Children tend to sense our moods, and their moods often reflect ours. If I want the temperament of my home to be joy-filled, then I must make the choice each day to approach life with a happy heart—in good times and in bad, in sickness and in health, during an exciting event or when completing a mundane chore, on calm days and on totally chaotic days. The alternative is not a worthwhile option. Nine years ago on Cinco de Mayo, our family had one of those days when we were bombarded with emotional challenges. The day started out as usual, filled with an extra touch of excitement because Joe Pat was returning home that morning from Regis University. Around eleven o'clock, Joe called from work to inform me that he wasn't feeling well and that a colleague was walking him over to the emergency room. My first reaction, of course, was to head to the hospital to be with him. Joe knew, though, that I needed to pick up Joe Pat and so advised me to wait until he knew if there was a definite medical concern. Shortly after Joe's phone call, his brother called, trying to get in touch with him because their father had passed away that morning. Vic couldn't reach Joe on his pager because, unbeknownst to him, he was in the emergency room. Until I knew Joe's condition, I didn't want Vic to know that Joe was in the hospital. At the same time, I didn't want Joe to learn about his father's death until I knew his condition. I quickly called Tony, a medical student at the time, and David at work; they both immediately came home to be with me. Joe Pat finally arrived home, Tony and I went to the hospital to be with Joe and tell him about his father, and David held down the home front with the younger boys. When Tony and I returned from the hospital later that afternoon, we gathered the family together to explain the day's happenings. At the end of the explanation, Timmy looked at me and said, "Mommy, is this what they call a **bad** day?" In a typical childlike, unknowing manner, Timmy added that little touch of humor on a "bad" day.

Humor and laughter often diffuse difficult or uncomfortable situations. I can't even count the number of times I have gone through the litany of the saints, my sons' names, before I landed, or didn't land, on the appropriate son's name who needed disciplining. To have an innocent little face look at you and declare, "Mommy, I'm not David—I'm Chris," lessens the tension of the moment. I still have a scribbled multi-folded note found on my bed one afternoon after school. It reminded me of an origami fortune teller: pick a number and then a color to discover your fortune. On one outside fold it read: To the Parents of Me. On another fold it read: "I'm stupid and sorry. I just wanted to fit in." And on another flap were the words "more inside." Amused and definitely curious at that point, I opened the note to read: "Just ground me (the word ground highlighted in yellow) from everything and I don't want to talk about it. I have learned my lesson."

If I didn't laugh at our many joys and mishaps, I'd be spending a lot of wasted time crying and fretting. I may not always laugh at the moment but often can shortly after. Take the afternoon I was the designated passenger for one of the boys on his first driving outing. As he rounded a sharp curve near our home, he did not turn the steering wheel enough and went over the curb and nearly hit a telephone pole. I calmly asked him to put the car in park so I could go around and return the car to the street. As I stepped out of the car, a postal carrier was standing there in total disbelief. He was concerned that everything was all right. I explained that it was my son's first time behind the wheel. A huge smile broke out on his face as he burst into laughter, his shoulders moving up and down as he turned to continue his route.

I will never forget the afternoon I looked out the window, pregnant with Matty (my ten-pounder), to witness Tony, David, Chris, and Joe Pat romping merrily in a pool of mud. They were having the time of their lives. Their ability to create their own fun was evident as Tony had turned the hose on and proceeded to add water to a corner of the yard where grass refused to grow. The boys were unidentifiable by name due to the amount of mud covering their bodies. Bathing four mud-soaked boys, especially when I could barely reach the tub due to the size of my belly, was the last thing I needed or wanted at that point in my day. It wasn't like we were at the beach covered with sand and all they had to do was run into the water to rinse off. I stripped each one of them outside, paraded them into the bathroom, and slowly rediscovered who was who. At the moment, it was not funny. When I related the experience to Joe later that evening, the expressions on the boys' faces came to mind, both while they were playing and once they were discovered, and I realized it wasn't really all that bad. I was provided another quick reminder that boys are boys.

Some of the boys' choices lead to humorous situations. Joe Pat's club soccer team won state one year and qualified to attend the national tournament in North Carolina. Upon arriving home, he walked up to our neighborhood pool where I was overseeing a swim team practice. On our walk home, he mentioned that the players as a group had done "something" before the games to identify themselves. I immediately started looking for tattoos, earrings—anything out of the ordinary—only to have him remove his baseball cap to reveal an orange, bright orange, crop of hair. "What do you think?" he nervously asked, explaining the team was trying to bleach each player's hair blonde. "Well, I think God's color choice was more appealing, but the hair will grow out the natural color," I replied as I tried desperately to keep from giggling. We arrived home to the rest of the family sitting in the den waiting for us to say evening prayers. Of course, it is unacceptable to wear a hat during prayers, so Joe Pat removed his cap. As the boys are often reminded, when you make a choice you must realize there are consequences, good or bad, depending on the choice. The consequence in this circumstance was a room full of brothers' laughter as well as hearing Chris and Matt reflect on the difficulty they were going to have sleeping with a glow-in-the-dark brother; the three of them shared a room. Joe Pat joined in the laughter determined, though, to buzz his hair at the earliest possible opportunity. I've seen long hair, bushy hair, and close-cropped hair since, but no one else has attempted the glow-in-the-dark look.

Some of the boys' artwork brings a smile to my face, especially those I've framed and, thus, see often. There's usually a story behind specific pieces that add to the work's significance. At the preschool the boys attended, the end of the year program highlighted the drawings the children created of their parents. Joe and I have a collection of these masterpieces, framed and hanging in our hallway. Timmy's drawing of Joe needed some clarification because, while he drew me with bright blue eyes, Joe had simple lines depicting his eyes. When I asked Timmy why he had drawn straight lines for his daddy's eyes, his answer made incredible sense: "Mommy, Daddy's always tired!"

Tommy drew a classic picture of our family when he was in first grade; it also hangs in the hallway. The picture is classic for two reasons: one, the story behind the picture, and second, the picture itself. Tommy's art teacher asked the class to draw a picture of their family. When Tommy hadn't made much progress on his picture, the teacher assumed that Tommy was overwhelmed with the prospect of drawing so many family members. She told him he didn't have to draw everyone if he didn't want to. A little while later, she noticed Tommy seemed upset, with his drawing still not completed. She asked if everything was okay. His simple response: "Who **don't** I draw?" She immediately notified his classroom teacher that he would be delayed, and then encouraged him to finish drawing the entire family. What also brings a smile to my face each time I see the picture is Tommy's perspective at six years of age of each family member. The final picture depicts all of us in a line happily waving, with Joe and I at each end and with the boys in the middle. While Joe and I are in relative proportion to the younger boys, Tony, David, and Chris are giants in comparison, obviously loving giants in Tommy's eyes.

A happy home environment is a gift we give our children. Laughter and humor obviously make a difference in a home, whether it's from the stories shared at dinner, or during the celebration of a family milestone, or me crazily mopping the floor dancing along to the songs from *West Side Story*, or the boys bopping to their music choices as they clean the kitchen or mow the yard. If you need a touch of humor to start off your day, I highly recommend reading the comic strips *Baby Blues, For Better or Worse* and/or *Zits*. They beat a cup of coffee for starting off the day. I usually identify with one of the storylines each day. If you don't receive a newspaper, you can actually access the strips on-line and, in some cases, have them sent daily to your computer. I guarantee you'll smile—and maybe even realize, appreciate, and laugh at the normality of your life.

When David was twelve years old, he wrote an essay titled *A Happy Family*. I share it with you.

A happy family is but an early heaven. This means a lot to me for many reasons but the most important reason being my special family.

Heaven is a place where happiness prevails. My family stays together like a horse and carriage, and that's why it is an early heaven. Why should I wait until I die to reach heaven when I can have it now? Each member of this elite group makes it possible for each other to obtain joy here on earth. In my family, it is apparent that we work together to strive for an even happier household.

We care for the family and we care for others. This makes the house an easier environment to live in. Each person is like an angel helping and caring for each other. God plays an important role in our family and my parents emphasize religion. Therefore, heaven isn't just a farfetched reward somebody imagined. It's on earth right here and now.

Is your family an early heaven? If not, try and make it one. Hopefully, someday I'll be resting on clouds, but why wait for someday?

Treasure the time you spend with each other. As we often hear, the years fly by—some days may not fly by so quickly, but the years do fly by. Choose to make the most of the time God grants us together. Create and foster traditions and memories that build your family's identity and bind you together through seasons and generations. And, of course, celebrate laughter every day of every year—it is music in a loving home.

Chapter 9

The Never-Ending Story

Be the change you wish to see in the world.
—Mahatma Gandhi

The stress the average mother deals with would bring
most executives to their knees.
—20-year-old advertisement clipping on my refrigerator, company unknown

I can do all things through Him who strengthens me.
—Philippians 4:13

The Garcia-Prats family story is constantly changing and is, what I've come to realize, a never-ending story. My brother-in-law Steve used to tease me that our family Christmas picture was usually outdated soon after arrival. I do remember, though, there were a few years when the number of family members remained constant. That wasn't to last long. As the boys transitioned to college and began new phases in their lives, graduations followed—and then weddings! We celebrated three weddings in one year in three different cities: Joe Pat and Megan in Chicago, Tony and Heather in Madison, and David and Rita in Houston. It was a year to be extremely grateful for sons. Chris and Steph married three years later, and Matt and Mary the next year. Talk about outdated Christmas pictures! The grandchildren followed: Logan, Lucas, Gabriela, and Matías. Three additional granddaughters—Mosa, Palesa, and Olivia—have blessed our family during the last months of writing this book. Richard Nevle, the principal at Strake Jesuit College Preparatory, once referred to me as the richest woman he knew. If I was considered rich then, I am enriched even more by the addition of five loving daughters-in-law and seven grandchildren into our family—with Chris and Steph expecting our eighth grandchild.

Along with the blessings I received over the months bringing the book to fruition, I also faced challenges. Hurricane Ike stormed through Galveston and Houston with a vengeance, redesigning our beach house and what was my stimulating writing environment. I shifted back to Houston and adapted, trying to refocus and meet deadlines, more often than not, unsuccessfully. Then a few months after Hurricane Ike, a thirty-two year old retina condition resurfaced, requiring multiple eye surgeries over the next five months. With the vision in the left eye significantly compromised, I've had to adapt to a new normal. Friends ask, "Are you back to normal since your surgeries?" I realize that my normal today is not the normal I had five months ago. But then, when I think about it, my "normal" has continually changed over the years, whether due to the birth of each of the boys, to health issues, to job changes, or to the boys moving into another phase of their lives. As I've emphasized throughout the book, it is how we, moms and sons, accept and handle the changes in our lives—the blessings and the challenges, the successes and the failures—that define us in many ways.

When we—meaning all of us as mothers—are in the throes of parenting, it is easy to lose perspective on where we are, where we're going, and even where we've been. We often may feel overwhelmed with the every day demands, constancy, and challenges, whether we are raising one son, two, three, or ten. We want our sons to be strong, successful, and spirited young boys who become strong, successful, and spirited men. We want to be good moms who help our sons reach their full potential. When we feel we have been less than the adequate mom, we lavish guilt upon ourselves. Aren't we moms good at that? If our sons make a mistake or inappropriate choice, which they will, whether at five, fifteen, or twenty-five years of age, we tend to blame ourselves and to question our ability to parent. And when our sons become adults, we should refrain from the urge to parent, even though we are still our son's parent/mother. It is also important to appreciate that each of our sons has a free will to make choices. While my responsibility is to give each son roots, it is also my responsibility to give him wings and not hover over him the rest of his life telling him what to do and what not to do, even when the choices he makes may be counter to what I believe and what he was taught.

I assure you, all the fretting will not make us better moms. What I find important to remember is that I am not perfect. Instead of worrying about being the perfect mom, I need to concentrate on being the best mom I can be. At the same time, I need to strive each day for the perfection I seek, pausing and reflecting on the words of St. Francis de Sales: "What a great pity that the desire for perfection is not itself sufficient for having it, but it must be acquired by the sweat of our brow and hard work."

People will tell me, "Cathy, you are so lucky," insinuating that the love and joy we experience in our family is due to luck. The only luck I can attest to is the luck Timmy described when he was nine years old. One afternoon out of the blue, like so many comments our children make, he enthusiastically shared with me that when he got married he wanted five children. Curious to know how he settled on the number five, I asked him. His answer took my breath away: "Mommy, you and Daddy are so lucky. Most people only get a couple kids. They don't get ten like you. I just hope God lets me have five." While I do feel blessed in life, I assure you luck is not the glue that keeps my marriage together. Luck is not the driving force behind the love, respect, commitment, and faith that prevail in our home. Luck did not teach our sons to be responsible and respectful. Luck is not the source of the laughter and joy that permeates our walls. The love and happiness we share as a family is the result of hard work and trusting that God will provide.

I have never denied, and will never deny, that raising sons is hard work—constant, demanding, and challenging work, albeit extremely rewarding work when done well and with love. There is the interrupted sleep, the days without rest, the worries, the decisions, the fears, and the tears coupled with the warmth of love, hugs, kisses, laughter, successes, pride, and joy. "A mother of a son works from son up to son down," the magnet on my refrigerator reads. How true, but knowing I will reap what I sow provides me daily encouragement. I agree with the words of Jacqueline Kennedy Onassis: "If you bungle raising your children, I don't think whatever else you do well matters very much."

I have no doubt that striving to be a loving, caring, compassionate, forgiving, responsible, respectful, well-educated, and faith-filled mother makes a difference in the lives of my sons. I have no doubt that living and reinforcing with my sons the belief that it is who we are, what we do with the gifts God has bestowed on us, and how we live our lives makes a difference. I have no doubt that teaching them to appreciate the importance of love, respect, commitment, and faith in all their relationships and daily interactions makes a difference. I have no doubt that sharing my love, time, and attention with my sons makes a difference.

I am reminded, usually by my sons, that it is often the simple gifts and experiences that prove the most valuable and memorable. When Danny was in elementary school, he gave me a Mother's Day card with an essay enclosed titled *Mother's Memory*. I share it with you here.

Do you have a favorite memory with your mother? My favorite memory with my mom is when my mom and I took a long walk together. It was a sunny morning and it was just me and my mom, so we went on a walk to the bayou. We walked along the bayou talking about anything we wanted to. My mom and I both laughed loudly, told old jokes, and told funny stories. We saw some ducks swimming, some birds flying, and even saw a few small fish in the bayou. We then decided to walk back home. When my mom and I got home, we talked about how much fun the walk was. Then we relaxed for the rest of the day. I had the greatest time I had ever had with my mom. That was my greatest memory with my mom. Tell me yours some time.

The afternoon with Danny was special, especially because **he** considered it special. But am I able to give each one of my sons the gift of one-on-one time **every** day? No. I learned, though, not to put too much emphasis on one-on-one time but, instead, to focus on being there for all the boys and interacting with them over the course of the day. Sometimes that involves one-on-one time, and sometimes it doesn't. At a presentation at a preschool, a concerned, guilt-ridden young mother asked me how I provided one-on-one time with each son every day; a psychologist the previous month had admonished the young moms for not spending one-on-one time with **each** of their children **every** day. When this mom explained to the psychologist that she had five young children, the psychologist recommended she hire a babysitter. My response to that answer: "GET REAL!" Number one, my sons would not have been pleased with that arrangement at all. If I took one of the boys to the park or the zoo by himself, he would have been miserable without his brothers. When Timmy was in preschool, the two of us visited my parents in Virginia. One morning, he sighed, looked at me, and bemoaned, "Next time, could I **please** bring a brother?" And secondly, following that formula would have made my day too structured with little room for spontaneity, not to mention the expense of a daily babysitter. When opportunities arise to spend one-on-one time with one of the boys, I take advantage of it and relish it: reading a story, working on homework, playing a game, driving to a soccer game or swim meet, listening to a son's retelling of his day's events, taking a walk, visiting colleges, or talking to them as I tuck them in each night. Otherwise, I let the day flow accordingly, enjoying each moment as it comes.

Am I tired at the end of the day? Of course, I am; "tired" is a parent's middle name. Both Joe and I are exhausted after our nonstop days. When we finally sit down to watch the ten o'clock news or read, whatever energy we have left drains right out of our bodies; inevitably, we begin to doze off. Most nights we don't stay awake through the entire broadcast or one page in a book. Now the older boys are sending **us** to bed: "Mom and Dad, you can go to bed now." During the summer Olympics a few years back, Joe and I sat down to watch the news, and right on cue we started nodding off. I was awake enough, though, to hear Matt tell Joe Pat, "Look, Joe Pat, synchronized sleeping."

As I bring another chapter to the never-ending story to a close, I recommend *carpe diem*! Seize the day! Although many days don't seem to go quickly enough, the years do fly by. And because research, based on the Sami tribe over 200 years from the 1600s to the 1800s, indicates that bearing and raising boys shortens a mother's life span—**34 weeks per son**—we mothers of boys do not have one hour of one day to waste in loving and enjoying our sons. With ten sons, I'm looking at minus 6.54 years!

Another word of advice is to deem, if at all possible, one bathroom off limits to your sons. I figure I gain at least one year back on my life span following this practice. I will walk all the way across the house to use the master bedroom bathroom versus dealing with toilet seats up and other myriad concerns. I often threatened the boys with target practice to improve their aim and to remind them to pay attention to what they were doing. Their minds, more often than not, were not focused on the task at hand but, rather, on quickly returning to more important activities. When we constructed an addition to our home over twenty years ago, the plumber, when hearing we already had six sons, seriously recommended encasing the new bathroom upstairs in stainless steel with a drain in the floor so I could hose down the bathroom as needed. There have been many days when I think I should have followed his words of wisdom and experience—he shared that he lived in a men's dorm with communal bathrooms at Texas A&M University.

As mothers of boys, we also need to bring a little femininity into our homes to counter all the testosterone. While you may not see any pink in the GP house, I do keep a vase of cut flowers, a plant, or a seasonal decoration on the kitchen table as well as around the house. The boys have soccer posters decorating their walls; I have art pieces and family photos scattered throughout our home. When one of the bedrooms became empty with the older boys moving on, I painted it yellow and bought a floral bed cover. With young ladies beginning to visit, I thought a conversion was appropriate. The first time Chris came home from Trinity University after the room change, he came out to me upon seeing the bedroom and exclaimed, "What were you thinking?" I told him I thought it was time for a pretty room; the room is now referred to as the "pretty" room.

Many changes have occurred in the Garcia-Prats family over my thirty-two years of parenting, besides the décor in a bedroom or two. While the normal day-to-day changes continually take place, I have remained focused on what my sons need in order to reach their full emotional, physical, intellectual, and spiritual potential, reminding myself often that **"good sons don't just happen."** I appreciate and accept the awesome responsibility that God has entrusted to me in raising sons. I count my blessings each and every day.

Our sons are gifts in our lives. Treasure them for the gifts they are. Celebrate their uniqueness. Laugh with them—often. Provide them with the love, respect, commitment, and faith they need to become strong, successful, and spirited men. I truly believe mothers of sons have the ability to change our world—one son at a time.

Enjoy the adventure! *Carpe diem!* And, may God's love and guidance be with you.

Praying the Jesuit Examination of Conscience

1. Thanksgiving

Lord, I realize that all, even myself, is a gift from you.
- *Today, for what things am I most grateful?*

2. Intention

Lord, open my eyes and ears to be more honest with myself.
- *Today, what do I really want for myself?*

3. Examination

Lord, show me what has been happening to me and in me this day.
- *Today, in what ways have I experienced your love?*

4. Contrition

Lord, I am still learning to grow in your love.
- *Today, what choices have been inadequate responses to your love?*

5. Hope

Lord, let me look with longing toward the future.
- *Today, how will I let you lead me to a brighter tomorrow?*

Adapted from *Through All the Days of Life*, a collection of prayers compiled by Fr. Nick Schiro, S.J.

A Reflection

Pedro Arrupe, S.J.

Nothing is more practical than

Finding God, that is, than

Falling in love.

In a quite, absolute, final way,

What you are in love with,

What seizes your imagination,

Will affect everything.

It will decide

What will get you out of bed in the morning,

What you do with your evenings,

How you spend your weekends,

What you read,

Who you know,

What breaks your heart,

And what amazes you with

Joy and gratitude.

Fall in love, stay in love,

And it will decide everything.

Age Appropriate Responsibilities

2 and 3 year olds
put pajamas under pillow
put shoes away
put dirty clothes in hamper
help put toys away
help select clothes to wear
learn to dress themselves
get newspaper
put silverware away (great sorting activity)
sort laundry by colors
help carry dirty clothes to washer
carry small grocery items into the house
pick up pine cones when ready to mow
wash hands before eating
brush teeth with assistance

4 and 5 year olds
set the table: napkins, placemats, silverware
help clear the table
make bed
put clothes in drawers after washed
keep room straightened up
put toys away
carry recycling items to bin
turn on/off outside lights
dust
help pick up leaves/grass in yard
sweep with push broom
feed/water pet
empty small trash cans
have clothes ready for the morning

Age Appropriate Responsibilities

6, 7 and 8 year olds
keep room clean
have clothes, school items ready for school
make sure homework papers etc. are signed
put school paraphernalia away
dry dishes and put away
rake/sweep outside

9, 10 and 11 year olds
put dishes in dishwasher or wash dishes
vacuum
put trash cans/recycling bins away
complete homework with minimal parent involvement
take care of school, home, sports paraphernalia
take garbage out

12, 13 and 14 year olds
wash, dry and fold clothes
mow and edge yard
clean kitchen after dinner
babysit younger siblings
wash car
keep track of sports (extracurricular) uniforms, schedules, practice times
clean room
complete homework and necessary assignments
help prepare simple dinner

High school years
get themselves up in the morning on time
balance commitments: home, school, church, sports, community
financial: checking account, savings account (determine what financial
    responsibilities they will assume)
driving: where they're going, with whom; keep curfew; assist with family
    carpools; pay partial car insurance, gas, fines
prepare a meal

Favorite Books of the Garcia-Prats Boys

Early Years

Amos and Boris, by William Steig

Brown Bear, Brown Bear, by Eric Carle

The Busy Spider, by Eric Carle

Caps for Sale, by Esphyr Slobodkina

Cloudy with a Chance of Meatballs, by Judi Barrett

Corduroy, by Don Freeman

Curious George, by H. A. Rey

Drummer Hoff, by Barbara Emberley

Dr. Seuss Books, by Dr. Seuss

Goodnight Moon, by Margaret Wise Brown

The Hungry Caterpillar, by Eric Carle

The Little Engine that Could, by Watty Piper

*The Little Mouse, the Red Ripe Strawberry,
        and the Big Hungry Bear*, by Audrey Woods

Make Way for Ducklings, by Robert McCloskey

Mike Mulligan and His Steam Shovel, by Virginia Lee Burton

Quick as a Cricket, by Audrey Woods

Richard Scarry Books, by Richard Scarry

The Napping House, by Audrey Woods

The Snowy Day, by Ezra Jack Keats

The Story of Ping, by Marjorie Flack

The Story of Ferdinand, by Munro Leaf

Tikki Tikki Tembo, by Arlene Mosel

We're Going on a Bear Hunt, by Michael Rosen

Where the Wild Things Are, by Maurice Senda

Favorite Books of the Garcia-Prats Boys

Elementary School Years
Al Capone Does My Shirts, by Gennifer Choldenko
Bridge to Terabithia, by Katherine Paterson
Castle in the Attic, by Elizabeth Winthrop
The Cay, by Theodore Taylor
Charlotte's Web, by E. B. White
The Clown of God, by Tomie de Paola
Freckle Juice, by Judy Blume
Frindle, by Andrew Clements
The Girl Who Loved Wild Horses, by Paul Goble
Harry and Mudge Series, by Cynthia Rylant
Hatchet, by Gary Paulsen
Haunted Island, by Joan Lowery Nixon
Hardy Boys Series, by Franklin W. Dixon
The Indian in the Cupboard, by Lynne Reid Banks
James and the Giant Peach, by Roald Dahl
Knute Rockne, from the Childhood of Famous Americans Series
The Lion, the Witch and the Wardrobe and The Narnia Series by C.S. Lewis
The Magic Treehouse Series, by Mary Pope Osborne
Mr. Popper's Penguins, by Richard and Florence Atwater
Mrs. Frisby and the Rats of NIMH, by Robert C. O'Brien
Nate the Great Series, by Marjorie Weinman Sharmat
Number the Stars, by Lois Lowry
Series of Unfortunate Events, by Lemony Snicket
Sounder, by William H. Armstrong
Sylvester and the Magic Pebble, by William Steig
Strega Nona and other books, by Tomie De Paola
The Story of Babar, by Jean de Brunhoff
Wayside School is Falling Down and other books, by Louis Sachar
Weasel, by Cynthia DeFelice

Favorite Books of the Garcia-Prats Boys

Middle School Years

Alas Babylon, by Pat Frank

Animal Farm, by George Orwell

Anne Frank: The Diary of a Young Girl, by Anne Frank

Artemis Fowl, by Eoin Colter

Bridge on the River Kwai, by Pierre Boulle

Bud, Not Buddy, by Christopher Paul Curtis

Call of the Wild, by Jack London

Daniel's Story, by Carol Matas

Dark is Rising Sequence, by Susan Cooper

Dr. Jekyl & Mr. Hyde, by Robert Louis Stevenson

Eragon, by Christopher Paolini

Flowers for Algernon, by Daniel Keyes

Harry Potter, by J.K. Rowling

Holes, by Jerry Spinelli

The Hobbit, by J.R.R. Tolkien

House of the Scorpion, by Nancy Farmer

The Hunt for Red October, by Tom Clancy

Johnny Tremain, by Esther Forbes

Jurassic Park, by Michael Crichton

The Lord of the Rings Trilogy, by J.R.R. Tolkien

Maniac Magee, by Jerry Spinelli

Milkweed, by Jerry Spinelli

The Outsiders, by S.E. Hinton

The Well: David's Story, by Mildred D. Taylor

The Westing Game, by Ellen Raskin

Where the Red Fern Grows, by Wilson Rawls

Whispers from the Dead and other books, by Joan Lowery Nixon

Z for Zachariah, by Robert C. O'Brien

Favorite Books of the Garcia-Prats Boys

High School Years
1984, by George Orwell
The Alchemist, by Paulo Coelho
All Quiet on the Western Front, by Erich Maria Remarque
The Autobiography of Malcom X, by Malcom X
The Autobiography of Martin Luther King, Jr., by Martin Luther King, Jr.
Black Like Me, by John Howard Griffin
Brave New World, by Alsous Huxley
Catch 22, by Joseph Heller
Cry; the Beloved Country, by Alan Paton
Ender's Game, by Orson Scott Card
Farwell to Arms, by Ernest Hemingway
Fight Club, by Chuch Palahnuik
For Whom the Bell Tolls, by Ernest Hemingway
Gandhi An Autobiography, by Mahatma Gandhi
Kite Runner, by Khalid Hosseini
Life of Pi, by Yann Martel
Lord of the Flies, by William Golding
Lords of Discipline, by Pat Conroy
Night, by Elie Wiesel
A Night to Remember, by Walter Lord
Of Mice and Men, by John Steinbeck
The Perfect Storm, by Sebastian Junger
The Power of One, by Bryce Courtenay
Profiles in Courage, by John F. Kennedy
Shogun, by James Clavell
Things Fall Apart, by Chinua Achebe
To Kill a Mockingbird, by Lee Harper

The Garcia-Prats
Play Dough Recipe

Two cups of flour

One cup of salt

Four teaspoons of cream of tartar

Two cups of water

Two tablespoons of salad oil

Food coloring

Mix all the ingredients together. Cook over medium heat until a small ball forms. Knead until smooth. Store in Ziploc bag.

Mama Musco's
Spaghetti Sauce Recipe
or
Cathy's Most Requested Recipe

Sauce:

6lbs+ can whole tomatoes
2 6oz cans tomato paste
1 finely chopped medium onion
3-4 cloves of minced garlic
2 packages pepperoni (Hormel stick 5oz) cut in 1/2 inch pieces
2 Tbsp Italian seasoning (adjust to taste)
1/2 cup olive oil

Sauté the onion, garlic and pepperoni chunks in the olive oil. Blend whole tomatoes. Add to sautéed onion, etc. Add tomato paste. Mix in well. Add Italian seasoning.

Cook over low heat (crock pot works) several hours.
(I usually start the sauce around 10 a.m. for 6 p.m. dinner.)

Meatballs:

To each pound of ground beef add:
1 egg
1/2 cup Italian bread crumbs
1/2 cup Parmesan cheese

Mix well. Form into whatever size meatballs you want. Coat frying pan or griddle with small amount of olive oil. Brown slowly. Add to sauce.

Recipe can be easily halved. Serves a big crowd. Freezes well.

By Catherine Musco Garcia-Prats
& Joseph A. Garcia-Prats, M.D.

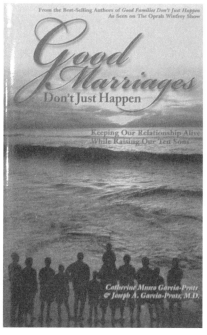

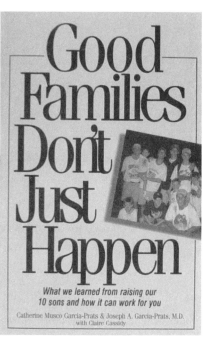

ISBN # 978-0-9763294-2-8

ISBN # 978-0-9763294-0-4

The Boys as of the Summer of 2009

Tony and Heather, after serving in Maseru, Lesotho, for two and half years, presently work in Mbeya, Tanzania. Tony accepted the medical director position at the Baylor College of Medicine Children's Clinical Center of Excellence in Mbeya. Their twin daughters, Mosa and Palesa, are 15 months old. Tony is the recipient of the 2009 Chapman University Albert Schweitzer Award of Excellence, presented to an individual who exemplifies Schweitzer's ethics of reverence for life and his dedication to a life of service.

David is the Dean of Students at the new Cristo Rey Jesuit College Preparatory, Houston, Texas. His wife, Rita, is teaching with the Spanish Over Coffee language program. Their daughter, Gabriela, is 2 1⁄2 years old and their son, Matías, is 16 months old.

Chris continues as the men's Head Soccer Coach at Luther College, in Decorah Iowa. He and his wife, Stephanie, a social worker, are expecting their first child in December.

Joe Pat enjoys his work in the Chicago area cell phone industry. He and Megan reside in Waucanda, Illinois, along with their children Logan 4 years old, Lucas 2 1⁄2 years old, and Olivia 3 months old.

Matthew is the Dean of Students at Our Lady of Guadalupe Catholic School, Houston, Texas. Mary is a first grade teacher at St. Laurence Catholic School, Sugar Land, Texas.

Mark, after his adventure in Africa, is residing and writing in Houston.

Tommy graduated from Providence College. He is discerning what he will do for the next phase of his life.

Danny continues his engineering studies at Santa Clara University. He is studying abroad first semester of his junior year in Brisbane, Australia at the University of Queensland.

Jamie enters his senior year at Strake Jesuit College Preparatory.

Timmy begins his sophomore year at Strake Jesuit College Preparatory.

 Catherine (Cathy) Musco Garcia-Prats is a wife and mother, a former first grade teacher, a writer, and motivational speaker. She received her Bachelor of Science degree from Loyola University New Orleans. She and her husband Joseph, a practicing neonatologist at Baylor College of Medicine, have been married 35 years and are the proud parents of ten sons ranging in age from 32 to 14—from a pediatrician to a freshman in high school.

Cathy and Joseph are the authors of the bestseller *Good Families Don't Just Happen* and *Good Marriages Don't Just Happen*. They lecture nationally and internationally, individually and as a couple, on parenting, family, marriage, and relationships. The Garcia-Prats family has appeared on many television programs including *The Oprah Winfrey Show*, the *Gayle King Show, American Journal* and *Primer Impacto*. They also have been featured in many major newspapers and magazines throughout the United States. In 1998, Family Services of Greater Houston honored the Garcia-Prats family as "Houston Family of the Year." Cathy and Joseph are the 2009 recipients of the "Standard of Christ Award" presented by the Jesuit Volunteer Corps South.

Outside of her writing and motivational speaking, Cathy volunteers with her church, her sons' school and sports activities, and in the community. She presently serves on the board of Family Services of Greater Houston and the founding board of Cristo Rey Jesuit College Preparatory School of Houston. Cathy and Joseph have been sponsor couples for their parish marriage preparation ministry for 27 years.

Visit Cathy and her family at www.garcia-prats.com

Front Cover: (back row) Tony, Jamie, David, Chris, Joe Pat, and Matt
(front row) Danny, Mom, Timmy, Mark, and Tommy

Back Cover: (left to right) David, Chris, Jamie, Tommy, Matt, Timmy,
Tony, Danny, Mark, and Joe Pat

Cover design: Solitaire Creative Services
Back cover photo: Erin Bushey
Author photo: Alexander's